Leaders of the Civil Wars
1642-1648

LEADERS
of the
CIVIL WARS
1642-1648

GEOFFREY RIDSDILL SMITH

and

Doctor MARGARET TOYNBEE

General Editor
Brigadier PETER YOUNG

Kineton: The Roundwood Press 1977

Margaret Toynbee has also written

S. LOUIS OF TOULOUSE AND THE PROCESS OF CANONISATION IN THE FOURTEENTH
    CENTURY
THE PAPERS OF CAPTAIN HENRY STEVENS WAGGON-MASTER-GENERAL TO
    KING CHARLES I (ed.)
KING CHARLES I
CROPREDY BRIDGE 1644 *(with Peter Young)*

Geoffrey Ridsdill Smith has also written

WITHOUT TOUCH OF DISHONOUR

First published in 1977 by The Roundwood Press (Publishers) Ltd.

ISBN 0 900093 56 0

Set in Monotype Caslon series 128 and printed by
Gordon Norwood at the Roundwood Press, Kineton, in the County of Warwick
Made and printed in England

Contents

v

Illustrations

Acknowledgements

The Publishers, Authors and Editor acknowledge with gratitude the assistance they have received from the following:

Wilf Emberton for his help with the text
Steven Beck for the tailpieces
Neil Gordon for the chronology and map
The Staff of the National Portrait Gallery and the Ashmolean Museum, Oxford for their invaluable help in locating engravings and portraits.
The Courtauld Institute of Art, The Department of the Environment, J. F. Bell Esq., John Wright, H. H. Wills Esq. and the Royal Martyr Church Union for photographs.

The pictures are reproduced by courtesy of:

The National Portrait Gallery
The Ashmolean Museum, Oxford
The Trustees of the British Museum
The Iveagh Bequest, Kenwood House
The National Maritime Museum, London
The Administrative Trustees of the Chequers Trust
The Royal Commission on Historic Monuments (England)
The National Portrait Gallery of Scotland
Nationalmuseum, Stockholm
York Art Gallery
The Society of Antiquaries of London
The Bodleian Library, Oxford
The Tate Gallery, London
H.M. Treasury and The National Trust, Egremont Collection
The Victoria and Albert Museum
Dunedin Public Art Gallery Society Inc., New Zealand
The National Gallery of Canada
The Cromwell Museum, Huntingdon
Newark Corporation
Radio Times Hulton Picture Library
The Pitti Gallery, Florence
Stadtische Galerie in Landesmuseum, Hanover
The Dean and Chapter of Westminster
The Duke of Portland
The Countess of Sutherland
The Earl of Pembroke

The Earl of Dartmouth
Earl Fitzwilliam
Lord Brooke and Warwick Castle
Viscount Harcourt K.C.M.G.
Marguerite Lady Hastings
Lord Saye & Sele
Lord Hotham
Lord Manton
The Hon. Robin Neville
The Trustees of the late Lord Berkeley
The Governors of Kimbolton School
Lt. Col. J. L. B. Leicester Warren
Mrs Burnett Brown
Robert Innes-Smith Esq.
Alfred N. Little Esq.

Chronology

	29 October	Charles occupies Oxford.
	12 November	Rupert storms Brentford.
	13 November	Charles checked by the London Trained Bands at Turnham Green.
	29 November	Charles returns to Oxford.
	5 December	Wilmot (R) takes Marlborough.
	7 December	Action at Tadcaster. Town occupied by Newcastle (R).
1643	2-13 January	Unsuccessful negotiations for peace.
	19 January	Hopton (R) routs Ruthin (P) at Braddock Down.
	2 February	Rupert storms Cirencester.
	22 February	Henrietta Maria lands at Bridlington with arms for the Royalists.
	28 February	Parliamentarians fail to take Newark.
	19 March	The victorious Earl of Northampton killed at the Battle of Hopton Heath.
	24 March	Parliamentarians under Waller defeat the Welsh at Highnam, near Gloucester.
	30 March	Goring defeats Fairfax (P) at Seacroft Moor.
	3 April	Rupert storms Birmingham.
	13 April	Prince Maurice (R) defeats Waller at Ripple Field.
	21 April	Rupert takes Lichfield.
1643	27 April	Reading falls to Parliament.
	13 May	Charles receives arms convoy at Woodstock. Parliamentarian success in skirmish at Grantham.
	16 May	Hopton victorious at Battle of Stratton.
	21 May	Fairfax storms Wakefield.
	18 June	Rupert's victory in the action at Chalgrove Field. Hampden (P) mortally wounded.
	30 June	Fairfax defeated by Newcastle (R) at the Battle of Adwalton Moor.
	5 July	Hopton wins the Battle of Lansdown.
	13 July	Waller's Army destroyed by Wilmot and Maurice at the Battle of Roundway Down.
	14 July	The King and Queen enter Oxford after meeting near Edgehill on 13th.
	26 July	Rupert storms Bristol.
	28 July	Action at Gainsborough. Cromwell victorious.
	10 August– 5 September	Siege of Gloucester.
	17 August	The Scottish *Solemn League and Covenant* proposed.
	4 September	Maurice takes Exeter.
	20 September	First Battle of Newbury. Charles withdraws overnight leaving the field to Essex.
	25 September	The *Solemn League and Covenant* signed.

	3 October	Reading occupied by Royalists.
	6 October	Dartmouth (and 40 merchant ships) taken by Maurice.
	11 October	Royalists defeated by Fairfax and Manchester at Winceby.
	11 October	Newcastle breaks up Siege of Hull.
	23 October	First regiments land from Ireland to join the Royalists.
1644	19 January	Leven's Scottish Army enters England.
	22 January	Oxford Parliament meets.
	25 January	Fairfax defeats Byron (R) at the Battle of Nantwich.
	21 March	Rupert relieves Newark. Meldrum (P) surrenders.
	29 March	Hopton and Brentford defeated by Waller at the Battle of Cheriton.
	11 April	Fairfax captures Selby.
	16 April	Prorogation of the Oxford Parliament.
	18 April	Newcastle enters York and prepares against a siege by Fairfax and Leven.
	6 May	Manchester storms Lincoln.
	29 June	Waller defeated by Charles at the Battle of Cropredy Bridge.
	2 July	The Parliamentarian and Scottish Armies defeat Rupert at the Battle of Marston Moor.
	16 July	Surrender of York to Parliamentarians.
	1 September	Essex leaves his army at Lostwithiel which surrenders the next day.
	September	Montrose's successful First Campaign in Scotland (including Tippermuir [1st] and Aberdeen [13th]).
	20 October	The Scots take Newcastle.
	27 October	The Second Battle of Newbury. Indecisive. The King's Army, outnumbered, withdraws by night.
	24 November	Milton's *Areopagitica* published.
	19 December	The *Self Denying Ordinance* passed in the Commons.
1645	10 January	Archbishop Laud executed.
	9 or 11 January	The *New Model Ordinance* accepted by the Commons.
	21 January	Fairfax given command of the New Model Army.
	2 February	Montrose routs Covenanters at Inverlochy. Royalists lose Shrewsbury.
	3 April	The House of Lords passes the *Self Denying Ordinance* forbidding all peers and M.P's. to hold commissions.
	9 May	Montrose defeats Covenanters under Urry at Auldearn.
	31 May	Rupert storms Leicester.
	10 June	Cromwell appointed Lieutenant General of the New Model Army.
	14 June	The New Model Army defeats the King's Army at the Battle of Naseby.
	18 June	Leicester surrenders to Parliament.

	2 July	Montrose destroys Baillie's Covenant Army at the Battle of Alford.
	10 July	New Model Army defeats Goring at the Battle of Langport.
	15 August	Montrose defeats Baillie's second Covenant Army at the Battle of Kilsyth.
	10 September	Rupert surrenders Bristol.
	13 September	Montrose's Army destroyed by Leslie at Philiphaugh.
	24 September	Langdale's Royalist cavalry defeated at Rowton Heath.
	14 October	The storming of Basing House.
1646	January and February	Fairfax's Western Campaign.
	16 February	Hopton defeated at the Battle of Torrington.
	20 March	The Royalist field army in the West disbanded.
	21 March	Sir Jacob Astley's Royalist force defeated at Stow-on-the-Wold.
	27 April	Charles leaves Oxford in disguise.
	5 May	Charles gives himself up to the Scots at Southwell.
	31 May	Montrose ordered by Charles to lay down his arms. Leaves Scotland on 3 September.
	24 June	Surrender of Oxford. The Royalist army is disbanded.
	July	Parliament offers terms to the King.
	October	Episcopy abolished – temporarily!
1647	30 January	Scots hand Charles over to the English Parliament.
	3 June	Charles abducted by Cornet Joyce at Holdenby House.
	6 August	Army marches into London and forces the withdrawal of the Presbyterian leaders from the Commons.
	28 October	Start of the Army Debates at St. Mary's, Putney.
	9 November	The *Agreement of the People* rejected by Parliament.
	11 November	Charles escapes from Hampton Court.
	14 November	Charles arrives at Carisbrooke Castle.
	15 November	Mutiny of the Army radicals suppressed.
	26 December	Charles signs agreement with the Scottish Commissioners while still negotiating with Parliament until 3 January 1648.
1648	March and April	Parliamentarian troops in Pembrokeshire declare for the King. Royalist risings widespread.
	March	Rising in South Wales.
	May	Revolt breaks out in Kent.
	27 May	The Fleet mutinies.
	1 June	Fairfax defeats Royalists at Maidstone.
	4 June	Royalist rising in Essex.
	13 June	Siege of Colchester begins.
	8 July	The Scottish Royalist Army (The Engagers) under Hamilton invades England.

	11 July	Pembroke Castle falls to Cromwell.
	17 August	Hamilton defeated by Cromwell at Preston.
	25 August	Hamilton captured by Lambert at Battle of Uttoxeter.
	28 August	Colchester capitulates. Lucas and Lisle shot.
	18 September	Commisioners from both Houses negotiate with Charles. Negotiations end 24 November.
	November	Fairfax marches on London 'for the public interest.'
	1 December	Charles moved to Hurst Castle.
	6 December	Pride's Purge of the House of Commons.
	23 December	Charles arrives at Windsor.
1649	1 January	The Commons accuse Charles of treason.
	20 January	The Trial of King Charles opens.
	30 January	Charles beheaded.
	5 February	Prince Charles proclaimed King in Scotland.
	7 February	Monarchy abolished.
	May	Leveller mutinies.
	13 August	Cromwell sails for Ireland, lands on 15th.
1650	23 March	Montrose lands in the Orkneys to organize an army.
	27 April	Montrose captured. Executed in May.
	26 May	Cromwell leaves Ireland.
	24 June	Prince Charles arrives in Scotland.
	3 September	Leslie's Scottish Army routed by Cromwell at the Battle of Dunbar.
1651	1 January	Prince Charles crowned at Scone.
	August–September	Scottish risings suppressed by Monck.
	3 September	Charles II defeated at the Battle of Worcester.
	13 October	Charles flees England.
1655	March	Penruddock's rising.

FOREWORD

THIS BOOK IS about the generation that fought the English Civil Wars, the men and women who laid down the political foundations of modern England.

In choosing only 100 leaders the authors have run the risk of omitting people of real importance, men who made their mark in their times, some in the Parliament House, others in the tented field. Yet those who do figure in these pages certainly include all the greatest leaders, both Royalist and Parliamentarian.

It has been said that by the age of fifty every man has the face he deserves. It is not, perhaps, a very helpful comment, if only because so many historical characters never attained their fiftieth year : and surely character develops much earlier. The Cavaliers who sat to Dobson at Oxford in the period 1642-1646 were men in their thirties and forties, but already their nature may be seen in their countenances : in the dogged, rather stupid Byron ; Willys, with a mask to hide his selfishness and deceit ; Lucas fierce and proud as a falcon.

When we were younger these were faces of the Olden Days, with their flowing manes and their Van Dyck beards. To men of the 'short back and sides' period they simply seemed to be dressing up. But now, for the first time in 330 years we live in an age of beards. Helmet faces may be seen today on every side : faces that would look right under a pott or a morion. Suddenly the men of Charles I's day seem to be people such as ourselves, and that must help us a little when we try to understand them. It is perhaps not so of their rather doll-like women. They oddly enough show little physical resemblance to the young women of today, though in fact they had much of their vigour, boldness and independence.

Curiously enough we are in important respects closer to the men of 1640 than those of 1776 ot 1876. They had no empire to speak of and ours is shrunk to almost as small a compass, and like them we seem to live in a period of continual and insoluble crises !

Sir Arthur Bryant has told us :
  "The key to a nation's future is in her past.
  A nation that loses it has no future."

It may be that the key to our future lies in the generation that saw the Long Parliaments, the struggle between Cavalier and Roundhead, the Protectorate and the Restoration.

In this book you may read of the men and women that moulded a formative period in the story of this country, and who, each as his conscience dictated, hazarded his person for King or Parliament – sometimes for Both !

It would be a grand thing, if with a population ten times as great, our Country today could show a hundred people to equal them.

RIPPLE 1976   PETER YOUNG

Leaders of the
Civil Wars
1642-1648

GEORGE MONCK, 1st DUKE OF ALBEMARLE
(1606-1670)

That honest general . . . who is a simple-hearted man.

OLIVER CROMWELL

GEORGE MONCK was the second son of Sir Thomas Monck of Potheridge, Devon, and Elizabeth, daughter of Sir George Smith of Mayford in Heavitree, Devonshire. He served in the Cadiz expedition of 1625 and in 1627 was promoted ensign in Sir John Borough's Regiment, and was at the famous Siege of Breda in 1637.

The outbreak of the Scottish War gave him a chance of service in his own country. He was Lt-Colonel to the Earl of Newport's Regiment of Foot, and at Newburn (28 August 1640), where he won distinction, helped to save the guns. Sent to Ireland early in 1642, he commanded a regiment, and was in the Battle of Kilrush. Later in the year he took Castlenock, and the castles of Rathroffy and Clongoweswood (June), relieved the Siege of Ballinakill, and defeated an Irish expedition to prevent his return to Dublin at Tymachoe in December.

Monck returned to England in September 1643 and for various reasons was suspected of Parliamentarian sympathies. After an interview with Charles I, in which he cleared his name, he rejoined the army just before Byron's defeat at Nantwich (25 January 1644) where he was taken prisoner. On 8 July he was brought to the bar of the House of Commons charged with high treason and committed to the Tower where he stayed for two years, during which time he wrote his book *Observations on Political and Military Affairs.*

On 12 November 1646 Monck accepted Parliament's offer to fight in Ireland. In February 1647 he set out for that country, taking up the appointment of Adjutant-General. In July 1650 Cromwell recalled him to England for the invasion of Scotland. The regiment now known as the Coldstream Guards was formed for him. At Dunbar (3 September) Monck led a brigade of foot, and when Cromwell went south in pursuit of Charles II he was left behind as Commander-in-Chief in Scotland, and completed the work of conquest.

Leaving Scotland in 1652, Monck was made a general at sea.

With virtually no previous naval experience, he fought in a three-day battle against the Dutch admiral Marten van Tromp off Portland (18 February 1653); and on 2-3 June was in sole command when Richard Deane was killed and his other colleague, Robert Blake, did not arrive until late on the first day. The decisive sea battle on 27 July resulted in the death of Tromp and the loss of twenty-six Dutch warships.

In 1654 Monck was again in command in Scotland where, by a vigorous campaign, he once more brought that country under control. He had been on cordial terms with Oliver Cromwell, and upon the succession of Richard he promised to support him. But the Royalists had him in their sights as a suitable instrument to bring about a Restoration. By careful manipulation, during which Monck proved not quite so simple as they thought, the Royalists eventually had him invade England at the head of an army of 5000 foot and 2000 horse (6 January 1660). On 19 March he opened the secret negotiations with Charles II which resulted in the restoration of the monarchy. On 25 May the King landed at Dover and was greeted by Monck, who next day was made Master of the Horse and a Knight of the Garter. Further honours followed: on 7 July he was created Duke of Albemarle, Earl of Torrington, and Baron Monck of Potheridge, Beauchamp, and Teyes.

For a period Monck had held the destiny of his country in the palm of his hand. Had he been cast in a different mould, with loftier ambitions, he might well have sat in Oliver's place and exercised a Protector's powers. Fortunately he was content to be the head of his own profession. He remained Captain-General from 1660 to the end of his life. He died 3 January 1670 and was buried in Westminster Abbey.

Monck was a very able soldier and an excellent administrator. Brave and efficient, he was a popular commander. His *Observations on Political and Military Affairs*, which were published posthumously in 1671, are evidence of his wisdom and experience.

JACOB, LORD ASTLEY
(1579-1652)

JACOB'S FATHER, ISAAC ASTLEY, was a Norfolk man of Melton Constable. From the age of 18 Astley served in the Netherlands and was present at the Battle of Newport and the Siege of Ostend. He became a friend of the Queen of Bohemia, who once called him 'her monkey', and for a time he was Rupert's tutor. In 1638 he was appointed Governor of Plymouth, and next year was Sergeant-Major at Newcastle where he had difficulty in persuading the trained bands to leave their town to repel the Scots. From his Dutch service he knew all about fortifications and said that he preferred a dry ditch and strong rampart to a moat, provided the town was well garrisoned, because in a dry ditch they could 'change and turne the workes att pleasure.'[1] He was ordered by King Charles to report on the fortifications of Hull, Newcastle, and Berwick, and asked for artillery, to be drawn by Durham pit-ponies, and muskets to replace the bows and arrows. As if to refute him, at the Siege of Gloucester four years later (1643) he nearly met his end when 'a bearded arrow struck into the ground betwixt his legs. He plucked it out with both hands and cried "You rogues, you mist your aim".'[2]

In 1642 Astley joined the King at Nottingham and was made Sergeant-Major-General of the Foot, ' a command he was very equal to and had exercised before, and executed with great appro-bation.'[3] He took over command of the foot at Edgehill after Lindsey's quarrel with Rupert (whom he knew how to handle) over drawing up the army according to the Swedish Brigade in-stead of the Dutch fashion, in which both Astley and Lindsey had been trained. After a brief prayer – "O Lord, thou knowest how busy I must be this day. If I forget thee, do not thou forget me" – he led the foot forward crying "March on, Boys!", and was wounded in the fight. At the Siege of Gloucester in August 1643 he commanded the foot and, after First Newbury, occupied Read-ing. In the Lostwithiel campaign (1644) he cut off Essex from the sea by securing the posts which Essex had abandoned on the east of Fowey harbour. Against Manchester's attacks at Second New-bury in October he gallantly defended Shaw House, and next month was created Baron Astley of Reading. At Naseby he com-

3

manded the infantry in the centre who pushed their opponents up and over the hill till, attacked on three sides, they were forced to surrender. When, after the battle, the King went to South Wales, he placed Astley in command of the Welsh levies instead of the unpopular General Gerard. Charles then planned to join Montrose in Scotland, relieving Chester on the way. But this scheme failed when Poyntz defeated the small Royalist force at Rowton Heath, outside Chester, in which Astley commanded the foot. He now returned to Worcester, where he was Governor and where Rupert came, glad of his old tutor's friendship after the King had banished him for surrendering Bristol.

Early next year (1646) the King ordered Astley to fight his way through to Oxford. He reached Stow-on-the-Wold, where Brereton attacked him, his Welsh levies put up little fight, the horse fled and, unhorsed himself, he was captured. A soldier brought him a drum to sit on, and to the men round him he said 'You have done your work, boys, you may go play, unless you fall out among yourselves.'[4] When Oxford surrendered he was released from Warwick Castle and retired to Kent, giving his parole not to serve against Parliament again. It was deemed prudent however to shut him up in the Fleet when Charles II was advancing south in 1651. After the Battle of Worcester he was allowed to return to Kent on £1000 bail and here, in the old palace of Maidstone, he died 27 February 1652. He was survived by his wife, Agnes Imple, a German lady who bore him several children of whom there survived one daughter and two sons, Isaac and Bernard; they both fought for the King, Bernard being mortally wounded at the Siege of Bristol in 1645.

An attractive picture of Astley emerges from R. W. Ketton-Cremer's *Three Generations*.[5] Clarendon calls him 'honest, brave, plain . . . prompt in giving orders . . . cheerful . . . in any action' and a man of few words who 'rather collected the ends of debates, and what he was himself to do, than enlarged them by his own discourses.'[6] The perfect councillor!

NOTES

[1] 'Diary of the Earl of Rutland', April 1639: H.M.C. Rutland, Vol. I, p. 506.
[2] John Gwyn, *Military Memoirs* (1967), p. 52.
[3] *Edgehill*, p. 16.
[4] Rushworth, Vol. VI, p. 140.
[5] Privately printed (1958).
[6] Clarendon, Bk. VIII, § 32.

P.S.

SIR ARTHUR ASTON

(c. 1593-1649)

ARTHUR ASTON, 'a testy, froward, imperious and tirannical person, hated in Oxon and elsewhere by God and man',[1] as Wood described him, was the younger son of Sir Arthur Aston of Fulham, Middlesex. In 1613 he went to Russia with letters of recommendation from James I to the young Tsar Michael Romanoff and served him against the Poles until 1618, when he joined Sigismund III, King of Poland, and fought for him against the Turks and later the Swedes. His meritorious services were extolled in testimonials by Sigismund who, in 1625, granted him a pension of 700 florins per annum. He returned to England as Lt-Colonel, raised a company and, in 1631, joined his old opponent, Gustavus Adolphus, in the Lützen campaign. In 1639 he returned to England accompanied by a number of experienced soldiers. He was appointed Sergeant-Major-General of the regiments under Conway in the Second Scots War and fought at Newburn. Discharged as a Roman Catholic on 11 December 1640, he was knighted on

5

15 February 1641 and in 1642 offered his services to Charles I who refused them because of his Catholicism. Fairfax, however, accepted him, whereupon Rupert commissioned him Colonel-General of Dragoons, 'of whose soldiery there was then very great esteem,' and encouraged other Catholics to join his forces.

At Edgehill (October 1642) Aston's dragoons on the Royalist left wing beat off Parliamentarian dragoons 'with great courage and dexterity',[2] clearing the way for Wilmot's charge. In November he was made Governor of Reading, where the severity of his discipline during the siege the following spring was said to have been more suited 'to ordering a loose Army in the Field than in aweing a regular Garrison in a Town.'[3] He repelled three of Essex's assaults but, having gone out of doors to read a letter, was struck on the head by a falling tile and apparently rendered speechless. When Reading surrendered in April 1643 he led the march out to Oxford in a horse-litter. On his recovery he became Rupert's Major-General of Horse and commanded the right wing of cavalry at the storming of Bristol in July, supporting Belasyse in his attack on Frome Gate.

On the death of Sir William Pennyman (22 August) he succeeded him as Governor of Oxford, to the satisfaction of the Queen – if of nobody else – for she felt safer with a Catholic in command. Although the University honoured him with a degree, Clarendon stresses his rough rule, his inordinate love of money, and the unscrupulous methods he used to gain it. He was reported, on 2 February 1644, to have been confined to his chamber 'for beating the Maior of the Towne'.[4] In September he was thrown, while "kerveting on horseback" before some ladies, and broke his leg which went gangrenous and had to be amputated in December. The Puritans called this a retributory act of God for his having allegedly ordered a soldier's right hand to be sawn off because, it was rumoured, he bore him a grudge. He was replaced as Governor by Sir Henry Gage, his Deputy, but in January 1645 Gage was mortally wounded at Culham Bridge in an attempt to take Abingdon. Aston, who declared he 'was able to do cervice with one legge as ever he had been',[5] was furious when the King refused his request to be reinstated and appointed instead William Legge. In 1645 Aston went to Ireland where Ormonde made him Governor

6

of Drogheda. When Cromwell besieged it in 1649 Aston beat off three assaults and refused to surrender. In the general massacre that followed its capture he was hacked to pieces and had his brains knocked out with his wooden leg (10 September).

It was said that the King had no officer of greater reputation and of whom the enemy had a greater dread. Like Montrose, he had 'in extremity some operative Phrases wherewith he could bespeak his souldiers to do wonders.'[6] Though he brought to the more chivalrous conduct of the English Civil War some of the ruthlessness of the northern European Wars, he was the possessor of an indomitable spirit which burned in him to the very end.

NOTES

1 Anthony Wood, *Life and Times*, ed. A. Clark, Vol. I (1891), p. 110.
2 *Edgehill*, p. 110.
3 Lloyd, p. 644.
4 *Journal of Sir Samuel Luke*, ed. I. G. Philip: Oxon. Record Society, Vol. XXXIII (1953), p. 243.
5 Slingsby, p. 139.
6 Lloyd, p. 644.

MARY, LADY BANKES
(d. 1661)

LADY BANKES, one of the heroines of the Civil War, was the only daughter of Ralph Hawtrey of Ruislip, and in 1618 she married Sir John Bankes (1589-1644), Chief Justice of Common Pleas in the latter years of Charles I's reign.

When war broke out she retired with her children to her husband's newly purchased residence of Corfe Castle in the Isle of Purbeck, one of the strongest castles in England and needed by the Roundheads to complete their hold on the coast. Following a local May Day custom, when great crowds collected there to watch the gentry invited to hunt the stag, troops of horse were sent from Dorchester on 1 May 1643 'to hunt other Game'[1] – i.e. to surprise the gentry and seize the castle. But Lady Bankes, warned of their intention, shut herself up in the castle. When the commissioners of Poole then sent out 40 seamen to demand her four small cannon (the largest of which was but a 3-pounder) she refused to hand them over and, although there were only five men and her children and maid-servants in the castle, ordered one of the guns to be loaded and fired. This frightened the sailors off. But, being short of supplies, she subsequently agreed to surrender the guns and in the meantime stocked up with powder and match, and persuaded Prince Maurice to let her have 80 men under a Captain Lawrence. In June Sir Walter Erle invested the castle with 500 or 600 men, a demicannon, a culverin, and two sakers. Though threatened with no quarter, she refused his summons and inspired the garrison to repel all attacks. When the besiegers moved up a wooden 'Sow' lined with wool 'to dead the shot' the musketeers on the battlements shot at their exposed legs so that 'she lost 9 of all of her Farrow' and the companion 'Boar' durst not advance'.[2] After a bullet had pierced Erle's coat, he donned a bear's skin and, it is said, was observed crawling on all fours round the hillside, well out of range. As a last resort, he divided his forces, by now pot-valiant, and sent the main body against the middle ward defended by Captain Lawrence, and the remainder against the upper ward held only by Lady Bankes, her daughters, and maid-servants, who heaved stones and hot embers from warming-pans on to the heads of the enemy attempting to scale the walls. After losing 100 men, killed and wounded, and hearing that a Royalist force was approaching, Erle abandoned the siege at the end of six weeks, leaving behind his artillery, ammunition, and 100 horses.

For the next two years Corfe Castle was left alone and Lady Bankes lived part of the time near London and part in Oxford, where her husband died in December 1644. Next summer Corfe was attacked several times, and early in 1646 was again closely invested. After a siege lasting 48 weeks, it was betrayed by one of Lady Bankes's officers who, 'weary of the King's service', introduced fifty of the enemy, allegedly as reinforcements. The castle was slighted, but Lady Bankes was allowed to leave with her children, abandoning all her household effects. She appealed to the sequestrators to allow her her jointure, but it was not until Cromwell came into power that, after paying a heavy fine, the sequestration was removed. She died in 1661 and her son and heir, Sir Ralph Bankes, erected a monument in Ruislip church with an inscription which proclaimed that 'Having had the honour to have borne with a constancy and courage above her sex a noble proportion of the late calamities, and the happiness to have outlived them so far as to have seen the restitution of the government', she 'with great peace of mind laid down her most desired life 11 April 1661 ' She had borne four sons and six daughters.[3]

NOTES

[1] *Mercurius Rusticus*, No. XI, pp. 113-123.

[2] *Ibid.*

[3] *C.C.C.*, 15 October 1645, says 5 sons and 5 daughters: *D.N.B.* 4 sons and 6 daughters: Lloyd 9 children. So presumably one died, but whether a boy or a girl is unknown.

SIR JOHN GRENVILE, EARL OF BATH
(1628-1701)

JOHN GRENVILE, eldest surviving son of Colonel Sir Bevill Grenvile (q.v.) and Grace, daughter of Sir George Smith, successively
served four Kings[1] and plotted against the Protector. When only
fifteen, he was present at the Battle of Lansdown Hill where his
father was killed. Sir Bevill's henchman wrote a touching report to
Lady Grenvile : 'When I mounted Master John upon his father's
horse he rode him into the war like a young prince . . . and our men
followed with their swords drawn and with tears in their eyes.'[2] He
was knighted after the Siege of Bristol, took part in the Lostwithiel
campaign, and was desperately wounded at Second Newbury
where he was found lying unconscious among the dead. In 1646 he
went with the Prince of Wales to Scilly and Jersey whence he
returned in February 1649 to assume the Governorship of the
Scilly Isles. His stubborn defence caused Parliament so much
anxiety that Desborough was ordered in March 1651 to imprison
his relatives in Cornwall until he had freed the merchants captured
and held in Scilly. But in the meantime he had arranged with Blake
to deliver up the Islands in June. He was thereafter allowed to visit
Charles in exile, and then return to England with leave to pass up
and down the country. His activities were ostensibly peaceful, but
he was arrested in 1655 and imprisoned in Exeter as one of the
leaders of the Western Rising who had planned to seize Pendennis
Castle and Plymouth. By 1659 he had joined the Great Trust,
successor to the Sealed Knot. Since 1658 he had been author
ized by Charles II to negotiate secretly with Monck, who
was his first cousin, and had appointed to the fat living of
Kilkhampton Monck's brother Nicholas. In August 1659 he sent
Nicholas up to Monck in Scotland with a verbal message from
Charles. But Monck kept quiet till next year when he reached
London with his army and realized the strength of the Royalist
reaction. Sir John waited till he could get a private interview with
Monck at St. James's, and then handed him the letter from Charles
which Nicholas had refused to carry. Monck, after reading it, made
Sir John memorize his reply and dispatched him that night to
Charles, who sent him back with the Declaration of Breda. This
was read by the Speaker to Parliament and he was rewarded with

£300 by the City and £500 by Parliament, and returned to Charles with a gift of £50,000, which was rapturously received.[3] At the Restoration the King created him Earl of Bath, Groom of the Stole, Governor of Plymouth and St. Nicholas Island, with a grant of £2000 p.a. and a ten-years lease of duties on the pre-emption and coinage of tin in Cornwall.

Bath's last Royal service, shared with the Earl of Feversham, was to be present when Father Huddleston administered to the dying King the last Sacraments of the Roman Church. James II dismissed him, as a Protestant, from the office of Groom of the Stole, and in 1687-8 sent him into the West to see how the gentry were affected by the penal laws and tests. They roundly asserted that Protestantism was dearer to them than life or property. Although commanding at Plymouth when William of Orange landed, Bath did not declare his intentions until the Prince had reached Exeter; in December he summoned the gentry of Cornwall and Devon to Saltash to read the Prince's declaration. In 1689 he was made a Privy Councillor but spent the next seven years in proving successfully, but at great cost, his title to the Albemarle estates. From 1694 onwards he handed over various offices which he was holding, hoping to be made Duke of Albemarle, a hope that was dashed when Keppel was created an earl with the same title. He died 21 August 1701, survived by his wife, Jane, daughter of Sir Peter Wych. Fourteen days later his eldest son, Charles, suffering from melancholia, shot himself. Father and son were buried at Kilkhampton on 22 September. The title passed to Charles's son William Henry. In the days before the funeral it was remarked that 'there were three Earls of Bath above the ground at the same time.'[4]

NOTES
1 Charles I and II, James II William III.
2 Roger Granville, *History of the Granville Family* (privately printed, 1895), p. 268.
3 Pepys, *Diary*, 16 May 1660. 'And how overjoyed the King was when Sir J. Greenville brought him some money ;so joyful that he called the Princess Royal and the Duke of York to look upon it as it lay in the portmanteau before it was taken out.'
4 Roger Granville, *op. cit.*

JOHN, LORD BELASYSE
(1614-1689)

JOHN BELASYSE, second son of Thomas, 1st Viscount Fauconberg of Newburgh, and Barbara, daughter of Sir Henry Cholmley of Roxby, was born on St. John Baptist's Day, 24 June, and was educated at Peterhouse, Cambridge, and in France. During the last of his many confinements in the Tower he dictated a brief account of his life[1] to Joshua Moone, his secretary, in which he described, among other things, the gaieties at the French Court which he attended as a young man, and how he once ran a race for a ring of diamonds which he won, but was challenged by a jealous loser, and responded. He married in 1636 a young Hertfordshire heiress, Jane, daughter of Sir Robert Boteler of Watton Woodhall. In the Short and Long Parliaments he sat for Thirsk, and in 1642 was one of the first to join Charles I at Nottingham with the regiment of foot which he had raised. At Edgehill and Brentford he commanded a brigade of foot, and in 1643 took part in the defence of Reading and the capture of Bristol where he was wounded in a most curious fashion. A bullet struck his sword and, bending it like a bow, drove the point into his forehead, but did not draw blood, though a piece of the bullet remained in his head.

When Newcastle marched north against the invading Scots in February 1644 Belasyse was left as Governor of York and Commander-in-Chief in Yorkshire. But he was defeated, wounded, and captured when his cousins, the Fairfaxes, stormed Selby in April, and spent the next ten months in the Tower. Exchanged in January 1645, he joined the King at Oxford and was created Baron Belasyse of Worlaby, his Lincolnshire home.[2] He fought as a volunteer at Naseby (14 June 1645) and in October succeeded Sir Richard Willys, dismissed by the King, as Governor of Newark where he so organized the defences that it held out for six months against forces four times the size of the garrison. In May 1646 he received a Royal command 'wrapped up in lead'[3] and in the messenger's belly, in which the King disclosed 'the secret imparted by this Extraordinary way of Conveyance'[4] which was almost as extraordinary as its way of conveyance. For Charles disclosed that he had planned to ride in disguise from Oxford and surrender to the Scottish army besieging Newark, and ordered Belasyse to make the best terms of surrender he could. This he did but, finding Worlaby ransacked, he went to France and served under Condé at the Siege of Mardyke. After the King was beheaded he returned to England and became one of the six members of the Sealed Knot, and the only Roman Catholic.

In 1659 he married again, this time a wealthy widow, Anne, daughter of Sir William Armyne. Next year he was made Governor of Hull and Lord Lieutenant of the East Riding, and in 1664 Governor of Tangier. In the meantime his 12 years-old step-daughter, Susanna, had married his son, Sir Henry, but was widowed five years later when he was killed duelling. She later went to Court where the Duke of York, himself now a widower, fell violently in love with her and 'gave her a promise under his hand to marry her'. Had Belasyse not intervened she might have become the second Duchess of York and later Queen of England,[5] with unpredictable results on Anglo-Irish history (for she was a most zealous Protestant) and on Belasyse himself who was soon to be caught up in the 'Popish Plot'. He was accused by Bedloe, Titus Oates's villainous accomplice, of having planned the murder of Godfrey, a London magistrate who was investigating the plot, of being privy (with the Catholic Duchess of York and others) to a plot to murder the King, and of being named General of the Popish Army to invade England. He was committed to the Tower, with four other Catholic peers, but was never tried, for Bedloe died. James II on his accession made him a Privy Councillor and, in 1686, First Lord of the Treasury. Three years later he died, 10 September 1689, survived by his third wife, Lady Anne Paulet, daughter of the 5th Marquess of Winchester, and was buried in St. Giles-in-the-Fields where a monumental brass was set up by two of his daughters. A more practical memorial however are the almshouses for four poor widows which he had built at Worlaby as a thank-offering for his safe return from the War.

NOTES
[1] H.M.C. *Ormonde*, New Series, Vol. II, pp. 381-90.
[2] Pevsner, *Lincolnshire*, p. 431, describes it as 'a bizarre brick house', with 'decorative details of the weirdest.' The present Worlaby Hall he dates c. 1799.
[3] Pepys, *Diary*, 4 February 1665.
[4] H.M.C. *Ormonde*, New Series Vol. II, pp. 392-3.
[5] Margaret Toynbee, *Notes and Queries*, 10 March 1945, p. 93.

JOHN, 1st LORD BERKELEY OF STRATTON
(1606?-1678)

AN ABLE OFFICER but fit only for a subordinate post, was Clarendon's assessment of Sir John, youngest son of Sir Maurice Berkeley of Bruton, Somerset, and Elizabeth Killigrew of Hanworth, Middlesex. But behind this disparagement lay a mutual dislike which originated in Paris in 1652 when Clarendon (or Hyde as he then was) advised Princess Henrietta's governess, Lady Dalkeith, to refuse Berkeley's proposal of marriage. In 1637 Charles I sent Berkeley as ambassador to Christina, Queen of Sweden, to suggest joint help for the Elector Palatine, and in 1639 knighted him at Berwick. He was M.P. for Heytesbury in 1640 but became involved in the first Army Plot and was imprisoned in the Tower. In 1642 he was sent into Cornwall as Commissary-General to Hopton, and distinguished himself at Stratton where he threw back a counter-attack. As Commander-in-Chief of forces in Devonshire, he blockaded Exeter till the Earl of Stamford surrendered in 1643, and as Governor in 1644 attended the baptism of Princess Henrietta in Exeter Cathedral. After unsuccessfully investing Taunton next year, he superseded the rapacious Sir Richard Grenvile who was blockading Plymouth. But April 1646 saw his surrender of Exeter to Fairfax on honourable terms, after which he joined his kinsman Jermyn in Paris.

In July 1647 Berkeley was invited by Cromwell to mediate between the King and the Army. He found the King distrustful of the Army, and when *Heads of the Proposals* were officially presented at Woburn, remonstrated with him on the high-handed way in which he received them. And when the King turned down another attempt to reach agreement at Hampton Court, Berkeley and John Ashburnham were ordered to leave him. The King, now fearing for his life, determined to escape and Berkeley, Will Legge, and Ashburnham met for dinner at Thames Ditton to discuss where he should go. Ashburnham optimistically pressed for London, but Berkeley for the Continent. On 11 November they assisted the King's escape and rode through the night to Titchfield, where the King sent Berkeley and Ashburnham on to the Isle of Wight to sound the Governor, Colonel Robert Hammond, saying that he would make for France if they did not return. But they took

the fatal step, for which Berkeley blamed Ashburnham, of bringing Hammond back with them. The King, shocked at their indis-
cretion, had now no option but to cross to the Island. From Carisbrooke he sent Berkeley to urge the Army to oppose Parliament.
But he was rebuffed, and Cromwell said he would no longer try
to re-establish the King on the throne. In April Berkeley and Legge
bore a final offer from the Army which may have hinted at the
King's deposition in favour of the Duke of York, whose escape to
Holland was hurriedly arranged. Berkeley now retired to Paris
and later became the Duke's governor.

From 1652 to 1655 Berkeley served under Turenne in the
Netherlands where, in 1658, he was created Baron Berkeley of
Stratton (the Royalist commander at the Battle of Stratton being
by this time dead). At the Restoration he was made President of
Connaught (1661), a Privy Councillor (1663), and a member of the
Admiralty staff. He also became one of the Masters of Ordnance
(1663), was appointed to the Committee of Tangier (1665), and
made Lord Lieutenant of Ireland (1670). From 1676 to 1677 he
was one of the ambassadors extraordinary to the Congress of
Nimeguen which finally brought peace between France, Holland,
Spain, and the Emperor. He died 28 August 1678 and was buried
in Twickenham church. His wife, Christian, daughter of Sir
Andrew Riccard, a wealthy London merchant, had borne him
three sons (each of whom succeeded in turn to the title) and one
daughter. His career was viewed with mingled envy and amaze-
ment, and its success ascribed to Jermyn's influence. In his *Memoirs*
(1699), which are of great historical interest, he magnifies the part
that he himself played as mediator.

15

COLONEL and GENERAL AT SEA ROBERT BLAKE
(1599-1657)

ROBERT BLAKE was the eldest of the twelve sons of Humphrey Blake, of Bridgwater, and Sarah, daughter of Humphrey Williams of Plainsfield, Somerset. He was educated at Bridgwater Grammar School, St. Alban Hall, and Wadham College, Oxford, where he spent ten years. He failed to gain a Fellowship at Merton College largely, it was said, because of his short, squat, ungainly figure which offended the artistic sense of the Warden. The soldiers and sailors whom he later led to victory were less discriminating. At first he carried on the family business as a merchant and probably made voyages, as most pushing merchants did. He was M.P. for Bridgwater in 1640 and 1645. In 1642 he had joined Sir John Horner's forces and next year, when Rupert captured Bristol, he held his post there for 24 hours after the Governor, Fiennes, had surrendered. As Lt-Colonel of Popham's Regiment he took part in an unsuccessful attempt to capture Bridgwater, and then occupied Lyme where he held out, his supplies replenished from the sea by Warwick's squadron, for eight precious weeks in 1644 against all Prince Maurice's attempts to storm the town. After the Prince had withdrawn, he occupied Taunton. Essex's surrender in September left him with little hope of relief but, short of provisions, he scorned all summonses to surrender, saying he would eat his boots first. He held out for nearly a year and, after being relieved, in May 1645, spent the following winter helping the inhabitants to restore order.

In February 1649 Blake was appointed Admiral and General at Sea to blockade Rupert in Kinsale. But Rupert escaped in a gale and, with Maurice, made for Portugal. Blake pursued and blockaded them in the Tagus, where he also seized nine merchantmen and converted them into men-of-war. When the Princes sailed out into the Mediterranean, Blake caught up with part of their fleet and destroyed all but three of their ships in Malaga harbour. Returning to England, he reduced the Scilly Isles, a nest of Royalist privateers, and Jersey. Next year, 1652, he defeated Van Tromp in the Downs, but was beaten by him off Dungeness in November. For this he blamed himself, but the Council refused to supersede him though they appointed Deane and Monck to share the command. In February 1653 he attacked the Dutch off Port-

16

PLATE I   George Monck, 1st Duke of Albemarle   *Studio of Lely*

PLATE 2   Jacob, Lord Astley   *Sir Anthony van Dyck*

PLATE 3   Sir Arthur Aston

PLATE 4   Sir John Grenvile, Earl of Bath

PLATE 5   John, Lord Belasyse

OHN *the first* Lord BERKELEY *of*
TRATTON, *youngest Son of Sir*
MAURICE

PLATE 6   John, 1st Lord Berkeley of Stratton

PLATE 7   Col. and Gen. at Sea Sir Robert Blake   *Samuel Cooper*

PLATE 8   George Digby, 2nd Earl of Bristol *(right)*
and William Russell, Earl of Bedford   *Sir Anthony van Dyck*

land, with his squadron unsupported, and was severely wounded and saved only by the timely reinforcements of Monck and Penn. He was still weak when he sailed out to reinforce Deane and Monck, hard pressed in the battle of 3 June which ended in victory. Being ordered, in September 1654, to show the flag in the Mediterranean, he determined also to free the crews of English ships captured by the Barbary pirates. In February 1655 he sailed into Porto Farina in Tunis and, when the Bey refused to release his prisoners, fired the nine ships in the harbour. When war broke out between England and Spain, the news of a treasure fleet in April 1656 in Santa Cruz, Teneriffe, sent him south with all speed. He found the fleet that August close inshore, covered by the guns of the castle and forts. Nevertheless, he attacked, and burnt or blew up every ship. For this gallant action Cromwell sent him a small jewelled portrait and ordered him home. But on the voyage, in 1657, he contracted scorbutic fever, and died, 7 August, as his ships were entering Plymouth Sound. After lying in state at Greenwich, he was buried in Henry VII's Chapel, Westminster Abbey. At the Restoration his body was exhumed. But soon after the Second World War a handsome monumental inscription was placed there to his memory; and a good statue of him has stood in Bridgwater since 1900. Clarendon remembers him as one who 'despised those rules which had been long in practice, to keep his ship and his men out of danger.'[1] And Nelson, when planning his attack on the treasure fleet in Santa Cruz in 1797, said 'I do not reckon myself equal to Blake.'[2]

NOTES
[1] Clarendon, Bk. XV, § 57.
[2] Robert Southey, *Life of Nelson* (1813), p. 107.

GEORGE DIGBY, 2nd EARL OF BRISTOL
(1612-1677)

GEORGE DIGBY, who grew up to be one of the smoothest intriguers of his age, was born in Madrid where his father, John Digby, created Earl of Bristol in 1622, was ambassador. He went up to Magdalen College, Oxford, in 1626. As M.P. for Dorset in the Long Parliament, he supported Pym over the impeachment of Strafford. But his bold speech opposing the Act of Attainder, and his equivocal attitude towards the King's attempted arrest of the Five Members, increased his unpopularity in Parliament. When, in 1642, he was accused of advising the King to use force against Parliament, he fled to Holland and was impeached for high treason. Returning in disguise, he visited the King at York, but was captured in the Humber on his way back and brought to Hull where he tried to persuade Sir John Hotham to betray the port to the King. Hotham sent him back to York, indicating that he would do so if the King came in sufficient force. Digby was wounded at Powick Bridge (September 1642), commanded the reserve of horse on the left at Edgehill, stormed Marlborough with Wilmot, and was wounded again at Lichfield and Aldbourne Chase. He succeeded Falkland, killed at First Newbury in September 1643, as Secretary of State, and thereafter had the King's ear, with fatal results for, quite apart from his lack of judgement, he was determined to ruin Rupert. It was on his advice, and against Rupert's, that the King faced Fairfax and Cromwell at Naseby. Even more damaging to the Royal cause than the defeat was the capture of the King's cabinet for which Digby, as Secretary of State, should have been responsible. Rupert's surrender of Bristol in August 1645 gave him the chance to discredit the Prince and his friends in the eyes of the King. To keep the two from meeting, he advised Charles to move to Newark instead of Worcester.[1] In October, commanding the Northern Horse, he and Langdale went north to join Montrose. But at Sherburn-in-Elmet his destruction of Poyntz's foot was turned to defeat when his horse mistook foes for friends in flight, and joined them! Digby reached Dumfries but had to retreat and flee to the Isle of Man, and thence to Dublin, where the Protestant Ormonde was working for a treaty with the confederate Irish Catholics.

In June 1646 Digby sailed to Jersey to bring Prince Charles to Ireland. When this was prevented by the Prince's councillors, he went on to the Queen in Paris, and back again to Jersey with a message that the Prince be sent to her. He returned to Dublin without the Prince, but with a promise of French help when the Ormonde treaty was signed. No sooner was it signed than religious intrigues wrecked it and Digby returned to France where he became a Lt-General in the French Army and, in 1653, 2nd Earl of Bristol on his father's death. Charles II reappointed him Secretary of State in 1657, but on his conversion to Catholicism, he had to surrender the seals, and at the Restoration could not hold any high office of state. In 1663, in the interest of Spain, he charged Clarendon with high treason for negotiating a marriage between Charles II and the Infanta of Portugal. The King threatened to arrest him if he persisted, and he had to spend the next four years in hiding, reappearing on Clarendon's fall in 1667. He died at Chelsea 20 March 1677, leaving one son and four daughters by his wife, Lady Anne Russell, daughter of the 4th Earl of Bedford.

Handsome, charming, and witty, but thoroughly unreliable, a shifty intriguer who in his jealousy would have broken Rupert if he could, a man whose life was one contradiction and whose trust in the success of incongruous projects proved disastrous to the Royalist cause – these are some of the things which historians have said about him. Yet he never gave up hope, and, in Clarendon's words, was 'the least appalled upon danger that I have ever known.'

NOTES

1 Clarendon, Bk. IX, § 121.

MAJOR GENERAL SIR RICHARD BROWNE, BART.
(d. 1669)

THE ROYALISTS called him 'faggot-monger Browne', and our earliest information about him is that his name appears as a wood-monger on the list of adventurers for the reconquest of Ireland to which he subscribed £600. He obtained a command in the Trained Bands and in September 1642 disarmed the Royalist gentry of Kent. In December his regiment was first into the breach when Waller took Winchester; and in March 1644, commanding the two London regiments, the White and the Yellow, he was with him at the victory of Cheriton. In June they were assembling forces to subdue Oxford, but when the King reached Buckingham, Browne was ordered to prevent a Royalist advance on London and summoned the Hertfordshire and Essex Trained Bands to meet him at Dunstable. He rejoined Waller after Cropredy Bridge (29 June), when both their armies were in a mutinous state and Browne's men actually attacked him, wounding him in the face. However he captured Greenland House (11 July), a Royalist garrison near Henley, and then occupied Abingdon where he was 'a continuall thorn in the eyes and goad in the sides of Oxford and the adjacent Royalist garrisons.'[1] But, short of supplies, with his men unpaid, plundering and deserting, he was known to be dis-contented, and Digby secretly tried to persuade him to surrender Abingdon. Browne feigned interest, while strengthening his defences, and then repudiated Digby's advances. In January 1645 Rupert launched a surprise night attack on the town over Culham Bridge, but was counter-attacked by Browne's men wading the icy river, and driven back with heavy casualties, among whom was Sir Henry Gage, the Governor of Oxford. In accordance with a Parliamentary Ordinance for dealing with Irish prisoners, Browne hanged, in Abingdon market-place, five soldiers who had served in Ireland. In May he joined Fairfax for the first Siege of Oxford, and again a year later when it surrendered after the King had escaped. As recruiter M.P. for Wycombe he was one of the Parliamentary commissioners who received the King from the Scots, and remained with him at Holdenby where he is said to have been converted by Charles's discourses.

In 1648 Browne was elected Alderman and Sheriff of London,

and appointed to command the Trained Bands in the City, where, according to Clarendon, he had 'a great name and interest . . . with all the Presbyterian party.'[2] The Army's suspicions of intrigues with the King and the Scots led, after Pride's Purge (December 1648), to his arrest and that of four other Presbyterian commanders. They were kept in prison, untried, for several years and, as Browne wrote, treated worse than Cavaliers or Newgate felons – 'my wife and children could not come under roof to see me in prison and my letters could not pass.'[3] No wonder he sympathized with the Royalist risings of 1655 and, from time to time, was approached by the Sealed Knot. Although freed by 1656, he was excluded from Parliament, but did sit in Richard Cromwell's Parliament where the 1648 vote disabling him was annulled, and he was lucky enough to be given £9016 owed him by the State. Suspect again at the time of Booth's Rising in 1659, he hid in Stationers Hall. In December he resumed command of the apprentices in an unsuccessful attempt by Parliament to seize the Tower. He continued to urge the recall of Charles II and, when this occurred, led the Royal procession into London at the head of a troop of gentlemen in cloth of silver doublets. Charles knighted him and his eldest son, and he was elected Lord Mayor. For suppressing Venner's rising of Fifth Monarchists in 1661, he was rewarded with a baronetcy and pension of £500. He also became commissioner of appeals in the Excise and President of Bethlehem and Bridewell Hospitals. He died 24 September 1669 in a house near Saffron Walden. It is a slur on his memory that, at Adrian Scroope's trial as a regicide, he repeated some casual remarks which Scroope had made justifying the King's execution, which cost Scroope his life. But he had, from the 1650s, become more and more convinced that the best hope of stability lay in a Restoration.

NOTES
[1] John Vicars, *England's Worthies* (1647), p. 101.
[2] Clarendon, Bk. X, § 70.
[3] Thomas Burton, *Diary*, ed. J. T. Rutt (1828), Vol. IV, p. 263.

JOHN, 1st LORD BYRON
(c. 1603-1652)

A person of a very ancient family, an honourable extraction, good fortune, and as unblemished a reputation as any gentleman of England.

CLARENDON

NO FAMILY, not even the Comptons, served the King more heartily than the Byrons. Seven brothers and an uncle, all field officers or above, is no mean record. Amongst this loyal band John was pre-eminent. Yet brave and resolute though he was it could be argued that no Royalist officer did more to lose the First Civil War than John Byron : his tactical blunders at Edgehill, Nantwich, Marston Moor, Ormskirk, and Montgomery Castle were scarcely offset by his success at Roundway Down, his valour at First Newbury, and his dogged defence of Chester. Proud, ambitious, and heavy-handed he certainly was : it may be that he was stupid as well. He was the eldest son of Sir John Byron, K.B., of Newstead Abbey, Nottinghamshire, and his wife, Anne, daughter of Sir Richard Molineux of Sefton, Lancashire.

Byron sat in the last Parliament of James I and the first of Charles I, and was High Sheriff of Nottinghamshire in 1634. It seems that he spent some years soldiering in the Low Countries and he also served in the Scots War of 1640. He was one of the first to join the King at York, and his Regiment of Horse was the first raised. He fought at Powick Bridge, and at Edgehill where the second line of the right wing under Rupert consisted of his Regiment. The first line disposed of all the cavalry of the Parliamentarian left, and had Byron been acuter he might have kept his men in hand as a reserve, or led them against the Roundhead foot. Instead he simply followed the chase.

In 1643 he was instrumental in the important Royalist victory at Roundway Down, and played a leading part in the First Battle of Newbury. He was created Baron Byron of Rochdale, 24 October 1643, and early in November became Field-Marshal-General of all his Majesty's forces in Worcestershire, Shropshire, Cheshire, Lancashire, and the six counties of North Wales after ousting his worthier predecessor, Lord Capel. At the same time he took care to retain his appointment of Governor to the Duke of York. On 26 December Byron summoned the Parliamentarian garrison of

Barthomley Church. They refused to surrender and he stormed the place. 'I put them all to the sword', he wrote, 'which I find to be the best way to proceed with these kind of people, for mercy to them is cruelty.' He had acted in strict accordance with the usages of war, but the massacre was, if not a crime, at least a blunder.

Byron's command was reinforced by troops released from Ireland by the cessation of arms. These he led to besiege Nantwich, where he managed to lose 1500 prisoners and all his guns when Sir Thomas Fairfax soundly defeated him on 18 January 1644. At Marston Moor he commanded Prince Rupert's right wing of horse and led his men out to meet Cromwell's charge. This may have been a good idea, but it was not what Rupert intended and, since he was routed, he inevitably bears much of the blame for the disaster that followed. He suffered a minor defeat at Ormskirk in August – 'my Lord Byron engaged the enemy when he needed not', wrote honest Will. Legge – and in September he attempted to recapture Montgomery Castle, but was defeated by Sir William Brereton with serious losses. In the last stages of the First Civil War he hung on to Chester with commendable tenacity. Urged to surrender, he invited the chief magistrates to dinner and offered them his own diet of boiled wheat and spring water. When eventually compelled to surrender, he got good terms from the enemy, and thereafter held out in Caernarvon Castle until 4 June 1646. In 1648 he attempted to raise North Wales for the King, but in vain, and spent the rest of his life in exile, being one of those who could expect no pardon from the Parliament. He died, childless, in August 1652, though he had been married twice : first to Cecilia, widow of Sir Francis Bindloss, and secondly to Eleanor, daughter of Viscount Kilmorey and, according to Pepys, 'the King's seventeenth mistress abroad.'

Byron was a man with many soldierlike qualities, but if he had the optimism to surmount Disaster, he lacked the tactical skill to command Triumph.

PJ·W·B.

ARTHUR, LORD CAPEL
(1604-1649)

HE WAS THE only son of Sir Arthur Capel of Raines Hall, Essex, and Theodosia, daughter of Sir Edward Montagu of Boughton, Northamptonshire. Up at Queens' College, Cambridge, in 1619 he met two Yorkshiremen, Harry Slingsby, who became his friend (and was to suffer the same fate as himself after the War), and Philip Stapylton, who was to fight against them in that War. In 1627 he married Elizabeth, daughter of Sir Charles Morrison of Cashiobury, Hertfordshire. They had five sons and four daughters. Capel was M.P. for Hertfordshire in the Short and Long Parliaments and presented a petition from the county freeholders against Ship Money. But, shocked by the virulence of the King's Parliamentary opponents, he desisted. On 6 August 1641 he was created Lord Capel of Hadham Parva, and next year fought at Edgehill as one of the King's Lifeguard. In 1643 certain jealous members of the Council persuaded the King to send him away to Shrewsbury as Lieutenant-General of Worcestershire, Shropshire, Cheshire, and North Wales. With great gallantry he stormed Wem (which blocked the way to Chester) after luring part of its garrison out to repel a feint attack on Nantwich. Ousted from his command by Lord Byron's machinations, he was appointed to attend the Prince of Wales in the West, and ordered, in 1645, to raise a regiment of horse and another of foot. With Hopton he fought Fairfax at Torrington. In April 1646 he joined the Prince in Scilly and accompanied him to Jersey whence he was sent to Paris in order to oppose the Queen's plan for the Prince to join her there. He returned to Jersey and refused to go with the Prince to France.

When the Queen proposed to cede the Channel Isles to France in return for French aid, Capel was sent to express the Royalists' strong disapproval, and no more was heard of the plan. With the Prince's leave he now compounded and returned to Little Hadham where he found many of his estates in Essex's hands.

In June 1648 he joined forces with Norwich and Lucas at Chelmsford and together they marched to Colchester where Fairfax besieged them. During that 76-day siege Capel at times went on guard himself, and once led a counter-attack, pike in hand. When his 16-years-old son, kidnapped from Hadham Hall, was paraded round the walls of the city he proclaimed that even if his wife and all their children were held hostages he would not surrender. But starvation finally forced the Royalists to accept Fairfax's terms. Capel was sent to the Tower, but escaped by rope, wading the moat with the water up to his chin. He hid for some days in the Temple, but the waterman who rowed him to a safer place of hiding betrayed him. He was tried, with Holland, Norwich, and Sir John Owen, by a special tribunal of sixty. The President, Bradshaw, sentenced them, subject to ratification by Parliament, to be hanged, drawn, and quartered. But a thinly attended House voted, by a majority of one, that Holland and Capel should be beheaded in Old Palace Yard. Owen and Norwich, by the casting vote of the Speaker, were spared. On 9 March Capel and Holland, joined by Hamilton, were carried in sedan-chairs through St James's Park to a house next to Westminster Hall, where they sat waiting their turn. Capel, who was last to go, smoked his pipe. From the scaffold he raised his hat to the crowd.[1] His body was buried by the altar in Little Hadham church, but his wish for his heart to be buried with Charles I proved impossible at the time. Enclosed in a silver casket, it was given to Charles II who restored it to the family when his father's grave could not be found. In a farewell letter to his wife Capel had written 'God will be unto thee better than a Husband, and to my children better than a Father.' For his eldest son he sent a text from the Psalms and a message ' "Lord, lead me in a plain path" for, Boy, I would have you a plain honest man and hate dissimulation.'[2] This son, Arthur, was created Earl of Essex in 1661, a title made vacant by the death in 1646 of Robert Devereux, Earl of Essex, and so, by a stroke of poetic justice, succeeded to the honours of the man who had dispossessed his father.

NOTES

[1] For a full account of his death see H.M.C. XIIth Report, Appendix IX, pp. 34-8.
[2] Lloyd, p. 485.

25

ROBERT DORMER, EARL OF CARNARVON
(c. 1607-1643)

ROBERT DORMER, eldest son of Sir William Dormer and Alice, daughter of Sir Richard Molyneux of Sefton, Lancashire, was left a Royal ward when his father died in 1616 : James I assigned this lucrative wardship to his favourite, Philip Herbert, 4th Earl of Pembroke and Montgomery. He was brought up a Catholic and in 1625 married Anne Sophia, Pembroke's daughter. Three years later he was created Viscount Ascot and Earl of Carnarvon, and filled the office of chief avenor and master of the hawks. He was Captain of the Lt-General's troop in the first Scots War and commanded his own regiment in the second, fighting valiantly at Newburn. He did his utmost to save Strafford and, in 1641, as Lord Lieutenant of Buckinghamshire, countered Hampden's recruiting activities by raising forces for the King whom he joined at York in 1642. He is said to have raised a regiment of horse, for which he was excluded from pardon in Parliament's instructions to Essex, and with Northampton commanded the Royalist forces at Southam. At Edgehill Carnarvon's Regiment was in reserve on the left under Wilmot. In February 1643 he was with Rupert at the storming of Cirencester where his merciful treatment of the prisoners was long remembered. As Hertford's Lt-General of Horse he attacked Waller's rearguard at Chewton Mendip in June and carried the pursuit dangerously far for, as Clarendon remarks, 'he always charged home'.[1] After Lansdown (5 July), where, according to the *Parliament Scout*, he was wounded, his regiment and Hertford's Lifeguards swept the Roundheads back, but the Royalist foot were shut up in Devizes.

Carnarvon retired with Hertford and the cavalry to Oxford but soon returned with the relief force under Wilmot and fought as a volunteer in Byron's Brigade at Roundway Down (13 July). Here, 'by charging near and drawing his men up to advantage, not above six in a File that they might all engage,'[2] Carnarvon turned the fortune of the day. He is also credited by Clarendon with having advised Wilmot to go first for Heselrige's Lobsters, 'that impenetrable regiment', who were finally driven off the field. After this victory he was sent into Dorset and captured Dorchester, Weymouth, and Portland. But, being a strict disciplinarian himself and a man of his word, he left the army of the West in disgust when Prince Maurice's plundering troops violated the articles of capitulation which he had made with these towns, and joined the King before Gloucester. He stayed with the Royal Army on its march to cut off Essex's retreat to London, but in the ensuing Battle of First Newbury was mortally wounded. Manley[3] says that, after repelling a charge by Stapylton's Regiment, he pursued the enemy too far and was shot at the head of his men. But Clarendon and Money[4] say he was killed with a sword by an enemy trooper as he rode carelessly back from the charge. As he lay on the heath he was asked if he had any suit to the King and replied that he would not die with a suit in his mouth save only for the King of Heaven.[5] Defoe relates that the King came to see him in an inn in Newbury and would not leave him till all hope of life had gone. 'The debonairness of his parts when disposed to be merry . . . and the vastness of his parts when disposed to be serious'[6] made his death a grievous personal blow to the King. There is an elegy on his death in Sir Francis Wortley's *Characters and Elegies* (1646) and in 1878 a monument was erected to him, Falkland, and Sunderland not far from the site of the battle. His body was taken to Oxford, where his wife had died of smallpox the previous June, and buried in Jesus College chapel; but in 1650 it was moved to the family vault at Wing. The earldom became extinct with the death of his eldest son, Charles, in 1709.

NOTES

[1] Clarendon, Bk. VII, § 101.

[2] Lloyd, p. 370.

[3] Sir Roger Manley, *History of the Rebellion in England, Scotland and Ireland (1691)*, p. 63.

[4] Walter Money, *The First and Second Battles of Newbury* (2nd edn., 1884), pp. 56 and 83.

[5] Thomas Fuller, *The Worthies of England*, Vol. I (1840), p. 216.

[6] Lloyd, p. 369.

KING CHARLES THE FIRST
(1600-1649)

'SAD STORIES of the death of kings' recur in English history. Charles I's story is unique for he is our only sovereign to have perished on a public scaffold at his subjects' hands.

The second son of James VI of Scotland and I of England and his Danish queen, Anne, Charles became heir to the throne on his brother's death in 1612. Deeply religious, chaste and temperate, carefully trained in book learning and athletic accomplishments, with a love of pictures which developed into rare connoisseurship and discerning patronage of the arts, assiduous in attending the House of Lords, at his accession in 1625 Charles might have seemed to possess qualities conducive to a peaceful reign. Unfortunately these were offset by the antagonism of an aggressive, turbulent, and largely Puritan House of Commons, which found a legitimate target in the King's undue reliance upon the extravagant Duke of Buckingham, assassinated in 1628. By 1629 the dead-lock was complete: Charles dissolved Parliament and entered upon eleven years' personal rule.

Despite the benevolence of his aims, Charles's government, as conducted through Strafford and Laud, aroused widespread opposition to its 'tyranny'. The resulting revolution was sparked off by the King's ill-considered religious measures in Scotland, which led to two brief wars, both fiascos for lack of funds. In 1640 an empty exchequer forced him to summon a Parliament which, after redressing grievances, proceeded to undermine the power of the monarchy. Charles's consent, extorted against his will, to Strafford's execution in 1641, brought his darkest hour, and was to cloud his conscience for the rest of his days.

The violence of the Commons created a Royalist party and fortified the King in his refusal to abandon control of the militia. England drifted into war. In August 1642, Charles, who had left London in January after his failure to arrest the Five Members and had since been recruiting in Yorkshire and the Midlands, set up his standard at Nottingham.

Thus at the age of forty-one Charles was compelled to assume the unenviable rôle of Commander-in-Chief of an army raised to suppress 'this damnable rebellion'. Naturally, the King relied upon professional advice. But he shirked neither responsibility for policy, being the most diligent member of his Council of War, nor exposure in the field. If his courage usually displayed itself in fortitude rather than in *élan*, his presence nonetheless was enheartening. Notable engagements in which he participated were Edgehill, First and Second Newbury, Cropredy Bridge, Lostwithiel, and Naseby. The brilliant Lostwithiel campaign of 1644 was a personal triumph for him.

The shattering defeat of Naseby (14 June 1645) could not shake Charles's conviction that, although he might perish, God would ultimately give victory to his cause. His last years were a mounting nightmare. In April 1646 he left Oxford, the Royalist capital, and surrendered to Parliament's military allies, the Scots, at Southwell. Borne thence a prisoner to Newcastle, for nine months Charles was 'strangely and barbarously threatened', but he resolutely refused to take the Covenant and abolish episcopacy. Handed over by the Scots to commissioners of the English Parliament, the King was carried south, only to be seized by the rebel Army, now at loggerheads with its paymaster. He strove to play them off. Flight to the Isle of Wight (November 1647) led to a year's imprisonment at Carisbrooke, whence, after the abortive Treaty of Newport with Parliament, the King was removed by the Army in stages to stand his 'trial' at Westminster before an illegal tribunal. Charles displayed splendid courage in refusing to plead. On 30 January 1649 he was beheaded at Whitehall. He had told his young daughter Elizabeth 'that it would be a glorious death that he should die'. And so indeed it proved. By his queen, Henrietta Maria of France, Charles had nine children, six of whom survived him.

KING CHARLES II
(1630-1685)

PRINCE CHARLES was born in St James's Palace on 29 May 1630. As Prince of Wales he was fortunate in having for his tutor a nobleman of the calibre of the Earl of Newcastle. At Edgehill, though only twelve, he wanted to charge the enemy. He was in nominal command of the army of the West from 1645 till 1646 when he retired to Jersey and eventually to France. Proclaimed King in Edinburgh on his father's death, he sailed in 1650 for Scotland where he unashamedly took the Covenant and was crowned at Scone. In 1651 he invaded England with an army which was defeated on 3 September at Worcester. For the next 44 adventurous days he was a hunted man, saved only by the loyalty of poor Catholic woodcutters, and others like Father Huddleston, Jane Lane, and several old Cavalier colonels, till he and Wilmot found a ship to carry them to France. The next nine years he spent in exile, keeping in touch, through Hyde and the Sealed Knot, with Royalist conspirators in England. In 1656 he concluded the Treaty of Brussels with Spain by which 6000 Spanish troops would be landed in England if a port could be secured. But in 1660 Monck's free Parliament invited him to return. He entered London in triumph on 29 May, his 30th birthday, having previously signed the Declaration of Breda which promised that the Army should be paid and disbanded, that all but the regicides should be pardoned, that those who had acquired land during the Commonwealth should keep it, and that there should be 'liberty of conscience' for everyone. Although the first three promises were kept, the strongly Anglican Cavalier Parliament refused to consider the King's Declaration of Indulgence, passing instead those acts against dissenters known as the Clarendon Code.

Parliament never granted the King enough money to fight the Dutch, our trade rivals. He gained some pecuniary relief by marrying Catherine of Braganza, who brought for her dowry more than half a million in cash, Bombay, and Tangier ; and by the profitable sale of the almost indefensible Dunkirk. But the Great Fire added to the nation's bankruptcy, the fleet was laid up because there was no money to pay the men, and the Dutch fleet sailed up the Medway and burnt Chatham. The Triple Alliance with Holland

and Sweden was popular but Charles, still desperate for money, negotiated, through his beloved sister Minette, the Treaty of Dover, promising to be Louis XIV's ally against Holland in return for an annual war subsidy and £1 50,000 when he should declare himself a Roman Catholic. Louis invaded Holland in 1672 and Charles issued a Declaration of Indulgence. The Protestant opposition, led by the Earl of Shaftesbury, forced him to withdraw it and next year pass the Test Act against Catholics. Charles handled with prudence the 'Popish Plot' invented by Titus Oates, the Exclusion Bill, and the Protestant efforts to proclaim his bastard, the Duke of Monmouth, as the legitimate heir to the throne. In 1681 he dissolved the Parliament which he had summoned to Oxford and committed Shaftesbury to the Tower. The discovery in 1683 of the Rye House Plot to murder him and the Duke of York gave him a further opportunity to crush his enemies, and the last years of his reign passed in peace, without his summoning another Parliament.

To him on his deathbed Father Huddleston, the man who, in the Duke of York's words, had once saved his life and now came to save his soul, administered the last sacraments of the Roman Church. He died 6 February 1685. He had learned to live and let live in exile, but came home to find a Parliament deaf to his appeal 'to look forward and not backwards'[1]. Yet the poor hand dealt him he played dexterously and with considerable ability. Though notorious for indulging his many mistresses (from whom are descended the Dukes of Grafton, St. Albans, and Richmond), he was never happier than when walking or sailing, at Newmarket, or in the tennis court, in his laboratory, or listening to music. Three memorials to his reign are the Royal Society, Chelsea Hospital, and St. James's Park.

NOTES

[1] Arthur Bryant, *King Charles II* (1931), p. 138.

SIR HUGH CHOLMLEY or CHOLMONDELEY, BART
(1600-1657)

HUGH CHOLMLEY was one of those 'northern men' who quarrelled with Strafford, and therefore with the King, over Ship Money and the billeting of soldiers in Yorkshire. Indeed the King threatened to hang him and his cousin Sir John Hotham if they ever meddled again. Even so Cholmley called the 19 Propositions which he, with the Parliamentary committee, presented to the King at York 'the most unjust and unreasonable ones as ever I think were made to a King.'[1] He himself believed that the King should enjoy 'his just rights as well as the subjects theirs.' This explains his later conduct.

He was the son of Sir Richard Cholmley of Roxby, Yorkshire, and was educated at Beverley Free School and Jesus College, Cambridge. In 1622 he married Elizabeth, daughter of Sir William Twysden of East Peckham, Kent, and frequently extols her courage and domestic virtues in the *Memoirs* which he wrote after her death, recalling, as he wrote, her black eyes, chestnut hair, and pretty little mouth which she would purse up 'especially when in a muse or study.'[2] In 1626 he was knighted, and in 1641 created a baronet. He sat for Scarborough in James I's last Parliament and the first two of Charles I, as well as in the Short and Long Parliaments.

When the War broke out Essex urged Cholmley to raise a regiment and secure Scarborough Castle. Although still hoping for a peaceful solution, he desided that he could better 'advance a treaty with my sword in my hand ... than by sitting in the House of Commons where I had but a bare vote.[3]' By November 1642 he had 400 foot and some horse at Stamford Bridge where they were destroying the water-mills between there and York. He disobeyed Fairfax's order to oppose Newcastle's entry into Yorkshire, but did win a minor victory in January 1643 at Guisborough over Colonel Guilford Slingsby (once Strafford's secretary) who was mortally wounded – a personal loss for Cholmley and he were cousins. The Queen's arrival at Bridlington in February finally decided him to change sides since Parliament had failed 'in performing those particulars they made the grounds of war, viz., the preservation of religion, the protection of the King's person, and the liberties of the subject'.[4] Newcastle gave him command of all

PLATE 9   Maj. Gen. Sir Richard Browne, Bart.   *attributed to Edward Bower*

PLATE 10   John, 1st Lord Byron   *William Dobson*

PLATE II   Arthur, Lord Capel   *Henry Paert after an unknown artist*

PLATE 12   Robert Dormer, Earl of Carnarvon (with his wife Anne Sophia)
From a portrait of the Herbert family, c. 1635-6
Sir Anthony van Dyck

PLATE 13   King Charles the First   *Sir Anthony van Dyck*
"The King's Matie in Armoure upon a White Horse" with his riding
master, Monsieur de St. Antoine, 1633. This painting was especially
designed to hang at the end of the long gallery in St. James' Palace.

PLATE 15   Prince Charles (later Charles II)   *William Dobson*
The armour he wears was made at Greenwich and is now in the
Armouries at H.M. Tower of London. The trophies at the Prince's
feet include some of the Earl of Essex's orange-tawny colours captured
at the Battle of Edgehill (1642), which is depicted in the background.

PLATE 14   King Charles the First with Sir Edward Walker

Sir Hugh Cholm
of Whitby

PLATE 16   Sir Hugh Cholmley, Bart.

maritime affairs between Tees and Bridlington Bay and he became a formidable foe of Parliamentarian trade. His wife and their two younger daughters now came up from London to Scarborough by sea.

In July 1643 Cholmley joined Newcastle at the second Siege of Hull with 700 horse and foot. The next time these two met was a year later when Newcastle came to Scarborough Castle as a fugitive from Marston Moor before taking ship for Holland. In February 1645 the castle was besieged by Meldrum. Cholmley sent his daughters to Holland but his wife stayed with him, sharing all the hardships of a twelve-months' siege and making him promise never to surrender on her behalf. In a heated correspondence between the two commanders the last word came with Meldrum's threat to bring 'great ordnance to make your strong walls spue you out at the broad side, and the issue will bear witness which of us has been most out of square.'[5] Three months later Meldrum was mortally wounded (or, as some said, he fell from a rock when the wind got under his cloak) and died a lingering death shortly before Cholmley surrendered, in July 1645, to Sir Matthew Boynton. He was ill and went overseas, to settle in Rouen. Returning in 1649 to Whitby, he was arrested but escaped from his escort on the way to York by jumping a hedge and galloping off on his 'little Galloway.' Thereafter he lived at his wife's old home in Kent. After eight weeks' imprisonment in Leeds Castle during Charles II's incursion into England in 1651, he and his family returned to their Whitby home, the first time that they had all been together for seven years. But his wife died in 1655 on a visit to London, and two years later he died at Peckham, 30 January 1657. Instead of being buried 'in his own country among his ancestors he chose to be laid by her by whom he had six children.'[6]

NOTES
[1] *Memoirs of Sir Hugh Cholmonley* (1787), pp. 66-7.
[2] *Ibid.*, p. 83.
[3] *Ibid.*, p. 67.
[4] *Ibid.*, p. 69.
[5] H.M.C. Xth Report, Appendix vi, p. 157.
[6] *Memoirs*, p. 82.

EDWARD HYDE, 1st EARL OF CLARENDON
(1609-1674)

HISTORIANS ARE FOREVER indebted to Edward Hyde for his monumental *History of the Rebellion* and the Clarendon State Papers. The son of Henry Hyde of Dinton, Wiltshire, he entered Magdalen Hall, Oxford, in 1622 and the Middle Temple in 1626. In the Short Parliament he represented Wootton Bassett and in the Long Parliament Saltash, and took a prominent part in attacking the Ship Money judgment and the prerogative courts. But his opposition to the Root and Branch Bill and the Grand Remonstrance brought him into close touch with the King. From the autumn of 1641 he was his confidential adviser and, with Falkland and Culpeper, managed his affairs in Parliament. In 1642 he joined the King at York and for the next three years worked in All Souls, Oxford, drawing up all Charles's declarations and constantly urging him to act constitutionally and stand on his legal rights. In 1643 he was knighted and became a Privy Councillor. In the same year his closest friend, Falkland, was killed at First Newbury which called forth this passionate cry : 'if there were no other brand upon this odious and accursed civil war than that single loss, it must be the most infamous and execrable to all posterity.'[1] During the peace negotiations at Uxbridge in January 1645 Hyde resisted all proposals from the Scots Commissioners that the King should embrace Presbyterianism, and stressed his master's determination to preserve episcopacy, for which he was violently attacked by Loudoun, the leading Scots Commissioner. In March, with others who opposed the bringing in of an Irish army to help Montrose, he was sent with the Prince of Wales to the West. In April 1646 he accompanied him to Scilly where he began his *History*, and thence on to Jersey. Here he continued to oppose the Queen's plans of conceding to the Scots, and also her demand that the Prince should join her in Paris. When the Prince himself decided to go, Hyde declined to go with him. He worked away on the *History*, only interrupting it to remonstrate against Jermyn's miserable proposal to cede the Channel Isles to France in return for help. In 1648 he rejoined the Prince in Holland and once more advised him to reject the Scottish alliance for which Lauderdale was pressing.

In the spring of 1649 Hyde went as ambassador to Spain,

returning in 1651 to become Charles II's chief adviser and Secretary of State. From then on he kept in close touch with Royalist conspiracy in England by regular letters, in code, and through the Sealed Knot which embraced his policy of reliance on the Old Royalists, without foreign aid or religious compromise. There was too much wait and see about his attitude for the more ardent conspirators. But by 1660 politics had replaced conspiracy and the Declaration of Breda which he, as Lord Chancellor, drafted, was accepted by the Convention Parliament. With the Restoration he became Baron Hyde and his daughter, Anne, married the Duke of York. In 1661 he was created Earl of Clarendon and elected Chancellor of Oxford University. His aim, as the King's chief minister, was to maintain the balance between the Crown and Parliament. The promise of liberty of conscience in the Declaration of Breda was rejected by the Cavalier Parliament, and the Clarendon Code re-established the Church of England. Abroad Clarendon favoured the French alliance and in 1662 negotiated the profitable sale of Dunkirk. Three years later he opposed the war with Holland, but was held responsible for its mismanagement and in 1667 was impeached. He fled to France and on 9 December 1674 died in Rouen, having completed his *History*. His tomb is in Westminster Abbey, but he is universally commemorated by the Clarendon Building in Oxford and, as Lord Chancellor, in the pages of English history for his loyalty to Crown and Church and his reverence for the Constitution, as well as for being grandfather of two Queens of England, Mary II and Anne. He married first Anne Ayscliffe, who died six months later ; and secondly Frances, daughter of Sir Thomas Aylesbury, who bore him three sons and one daughter, Anne.

NOTES
[1] Clarendon, Bk. VII, § 217.

35

SIR WILLIAM COMPTON
(1625-1663)

THE THIRD SON of the 2nd Earl of Northampton, at the age of eighteen he joined his father and brothers in the field. He distinguished himself at the taking of Banbury in 1642, leading three attacks and having two horses shot under him, and became Governor of the town and its castle, under his father. He was knighted in 1643 and next year was besieged in Banbury. He refused two summonses, counter-mined eleven times, and never took off his clothes for thirteen weeks. His religious devotions and unremitting vigilance prevented any mutiny in town or garrison. The siege was raised in October 1644 by his brother James, 3rd Earl of Northampton since their father's death at Hopton Heath. Banbury was once more besieged in 1646 and Compton only surrendered after an investment of ten weeks. He took part in the Kentish rising of 1648 and was Major-General of the Royalist forces during the Siege of Colchester where, by his example, he kept up the spirit of the troops. On its surrender he was imprisoned in Windsor Castle but escaped, on the night before the King's execution, to Rotterdam.

In 1651 Compton married Elizabeth, the widow of William, Lord Alington of Horseheath near Cambridge, and sister of Sir Lionel Tollemache. Two years later he became one of the six members of the Sealed Knot, three of whom lived in Cambridgeshire – himself at Linton, John Russell at Shingay, and Sir Richard Willys at Fen Ditton, within easy riding distance of each other. Although neither they nor East Anglia took any evident part in the regional risings of 1655, Compton was sent to the Tower for a spell. In August 1656 he and Willys were instructed to meet John Wildman, the leading Leveller in England, to discuss a Royalist-Leveller rising. Compton met Wildman twice in 1657 and, in a letter to Hyde, expressed himself 'abundantly satysfied', and expecting 'something to be done speedily'.[1] He would have been less confident had he known that the wretched Wildman, ex-major of Parliamentarian horse, 'agitator', and speculator in forfeited Royalist estates (who survived to 'see two generations of his accomplices die on the gallows')[2], was even then in the pay of Cromwell's secretary, Thurloe. After this discovery further

36

negotiations were abandoned. The abortive risings of 1658, in which Compton was responsible for the area south of Trent, but did nothing, brought him again to the Tower for three months, together with Russell and Willys. He was released in August and warned that no mercy would be shown him if he plotted again. The formation of the Great Trust in March of this year, to replace or revitalize the Sealed Knot, had been coldly received by Compton, Willys, and Russell who did not come forward to lead the East Anglian rising planned for July 1659, although Lady Compton's sister-in-law (the Countess of Dysart, Tollemache's wife, and once 'the supposed mistris of Oliver Crumwell')[3] dispensed lavish hospitality that month to local Royalists in her home at Helmingham, near Ipswich. However, the potential leaders were ordered to surrender and the Cambridge authorities sent Compton up to London to appear before the Council. It was now that Willys was publicly accused by Morland, Thurloe's assistant secretary, of having supplied Thurloe with information ; and Morland sent as evidence to Charles II letters Willys was said to have written to Thurloe under a pseudonym. Compton, and others, refused to believe in Willys's guilt and ignored the King's order to break with him, demanding to see the incriminating letters, which Hyde refused. Willys's guilt is still unproven.

At the Restoration Compton became M.P. for Cambridge and Master of the Ordnance. He died suddenly in Drury Lane 18 October 1663 and was buried in Compton Wynyates church. 'One of the worthyest men and best officers of state now in England', wrote Pepys, 'of the best temper, valour, abilities of mind, integrity, birth, fine person and diligence of any man he hath left behind him in the three nations.'[4] Even Cromwell had called him, after Colchester, 'the sober young man and the godly cavalier.'

NOTES
[1] *Calendar of Clarendon State Papers* Vol. III, p. 335.
[2] Macaulay, *History of England* (The New Universal Library), Vol. I (1908), p. 456.
[3] Sir John Reresby, *Memoirs*, ed. Andrew Browning (1936), p. 126.
[4] Pepys, *Diary*, 19 October 1663.

OLIVER CROMWELL
(1599-1658)

Cromwell, our chief of men.

JOHN MILTON

None climbs so high as he who knows not whither he is going.

OLIVER CROMWELL

OLIVER CROMWELL, the second son of Robert Cromwell and Elizabeth Steward, was born at Huntingdon 25 April 1599. He was descended from one Richard Williams who, having been advanced by Thomas Cromwell, Henry VIII's minister, had adopted his patron's name. Oliver was educated at the Free School, Huntingdon, and at Sidney Sussex College, Cambridge, where we are told, he was 'well read in Greek and Roman story,'[1] but 'took more delight in horse and field exercise.' In 1620 he married Elizabeth, daughter of Sir James Bourchier, a wealthy City merchant. He first sat in Parliament in 1628, as member for Huntingdon. Legends surround the early years of his private life. In 1631 he sold most of his Huntingdon property, and rented grazing land at St. Ives. In 1636 he succeeded his uncle, Sir Thomas Steward, as farmer of the Cathedral tithes and lived at Ely.

About this time he saw the light and became the spokesman of the sectaries. 'My soul is with the congregation of the first-born, my body rests in hope, and if here I may honour my God either by doing or suffering, I shall be most glad', he wrote to Mrs St. John in 1638. 'You know what my manner of life hath been. Oh, I lived in and loved darkness, and hated the light. I was a chief, the chief of sinners.' He represented Cambridge in the Short and Long Parliaments and spoke out, among other things, for annual Parliaments and against episcopacy. At this period Sir Philip Warwick, a Cavalier, says of him : 'His stature was of a good size . . . his countenance swolen and reddish, his voice sharp and untuneable, and his eloquence full of fervour.'[2] When the Civil War began he was forty-three with a family of seven children. But he became a captain of horse and threw himself into the task of training and disciplining his men. He had a low opinion of the majority of the Parliamentarian cavalry and said 'You must get men . . . of a spirit that is likely to go on as far as gentlemen will go, or else I am sure you will be beaten still'.[3] Cromwell's solution was to get religious

38

men into his troop, who were of greater understanding than common soldiers and therefore more apprehensive of the importance and consequences of war. In the selection of his officers he describes the type he sought, 'a plain russet-coated captain that knows what he fights for, and loves what he knows.'[4]

Cromwell had successes in 1643 at Grantham (13 May), Gainsborough, (29 July), and Winceby (11 October) where one gallant, Sir Ingram Hopton, made a dead set at him, but was killed in the attempt to terminate his career. Not long afterwards he was made Lieutenant-General of the Horse in the army of the Eastern Association, and led the left wing of horse at Marston Moor (2 July 1644). Although slightly wounded, he contributed very greatly to that victory, and Prince Rupert regarded him as the best cavalry officer in the Parliamentarian Army. In the New Model Army, in which he served as second-in-command to Sir Thomas Fairfax, he greatly distinguished himself at Naseby and elsewhere.

In the Second Civil War Cromwell took Pembroke Castle and won the Battle of Preston (17 August 1648) against long odds. From this time forwards to relate his career is to retell the History of England : his part in bringing the King to the scaffold, his conduct of the war in Ireland, his victories at Dunbar and Worcester, and the rule of the Major-Generals. But the Cromwellian government was too narrow-based to survive, depending as it did upon the Army – 'You can do anything with bayonets except sit on them' – and his sweet-natured son Richard was not the man to succeed when Oliver died 3 September 1658. 'I have no mind to give an ill character of Cromwell', wrote Sir Philip Warwick. As a soldier he must stand high in the esteem of his countrymen. Of his foreign policy Pepys wrote : 'What brave things he did and made all the neighbour princes fear him.' Clarendon thought him 'a brave bad man' ; John Lilburne and his friends thought him a hypocrite. But his steward, Maidstone, said, 'A larger soul, I think, hath seldom dwelt in a house of clay.'

NOTES
[1] The authority is Edmund Waller.
[2] *Memoirs of the Reign of King Charles the First* (1813), p. 273.
[3] These words, spoken to Hampden, were recalled by Cromwell in a speech of 1657.
[4] Letter of 29 August 1643.

JOHN, 1st BARON CULPEPER or COLEPEPER
(d. 1660)

AFTER MILITARY SERVICE abroad John Culpeper, only son of Sir John Culpeper of Wigsell [sic], Sussex, and Elizabeth Sedley, married Philippa, daughter of Sir John Snelling, and settled down to country life. 'A man of an universal understanding, a quick comprehension, a wonderful memory',[1] he was often chosen to sit at the Council board when country matters were discussed. He was M.P. for Rye in the Short Parliament and for Kent in the Long Parliament, spoke against monopolies, and was on the committee of defence appointed by the Commons. He also spoke against Strafford, the Root and Branch Bill, the Grand Remonstrance, and the Militia Bill, but defended the Prayer Book. Although 'his person and manner of speaking were ungracious', writes Clarendon, 'he prevailed only by the strength of his reason, which was enforced with confidence enough.'[2] In 1642 he became Chancellor of the Exchequer and a Privy Councillor, and advised the King to move north and secure Hull. At the end of May he joined him in York. In August he and Southampton went with the King's final offer to negotiate with Parliament, and had to deliver it from the bar and not from his seat, 'looking more like a culprit than a Privy Councillor'.[3] He charged gallantly at Edgehill with Rupert, and after the battle vigorously opposed the decision to withdraw under cover of darkness instead of holding the field. The King made him Master of the Rolls in January 1643, intending him to hand over the Chancellorship to Hyde. His delay in doing so caused a coolness between the two men. As one of the two Privy Councillors in the Oxford Parliament his influence with the King in military matters was resented by the generals, especially his good advice to besiege Gloucester. After reading the King's letter to Rupert of 14 June 1644 commanding him to relieve York and 'beat the rebels' army of both kingdoms which are before it,' he asked the King if it had already been sent and, when told that it had, remarked 'Before God you are undone, for upon this peremptory order he will fight, whatever comes on't.'[4] Which Rupert did, on Marston Moor, and there lost the North for the Royal cause.

In October 1644 Culpeper was created Baron Culpeper of Thoresway and in March next year his appointment to the Prince of Wales's Council effected a reconciliation with Hyde, and both men went with Prince Charles to the West. At Brecon in August the King commissioned him to take the Prince to France in case of danger. They first went to Jersey whence, in May 1646, the Prince's Council sent Culpeper and Capel to persuade the Queen to stop asking her son to join her. But she won Culpeper over and, when the Prince himself decided to go, he accompanied him to Paris and, two years later, to Holland. Here his approval of religious concessions to the Scots was opposed by Hyde, as it had been by the King in an earlier letter. When, in July 1648, Prince Charles put to sea with that part of the Fleet which had revolted, and showed himself off the south-east coast of England, Culpeper sailed with him as chief adviser and was blamed for the expedition's failure. In 1650 he was sent to Russia to borrow money from the Tsar and had several audiences in Moscow with him, refusing to kiss his hand, but kissing the hem of his garment instead. He returned with a loan of 20,000 roubles in corn and furs, repayable at 100% after three years. In 1652 he was sent to Holland, then at war with England, to seek armed aid, but two years later in consequence of a treaty between Cromwell and Mazarin, was expelled from France. On Cromwell's death in 1658 he wrote to Hyde suggesting that Monck should be approached as the man most likely to restore the King.

Culpeper died 11 July 1660. His first wife, who died in 1630 bore one son and one daughter; his second wife, Judith, daughter of Sir Thomas Culpeper of Hollingbourne, bore seven children, her eldest son, Thomas, succeeding to the title. Ability in debate, fertility in counsel, but changeability and uncertainty of temper are characteristics of Culpeper on which Sir Philip Warwick and Clarendon both agree, the latter drily adding that 'his person and manner of speaking were ungracious enough'.

NOTES
1 Clarendon, Bk. IV, § 122.
2 Ibid.
3 J. L. Sanford, Studies and Illustrations of the Great Rebellion (1858) p. 529.
4 Marston Moor, p. 87.
5 Clarendon, Bk. II. § 122.

MAJOR-GENERAL and ADMIRAL RICHARD DEANE
(1610-1653)

AS A YOUNG man Richard Deane probably made mercantile voyages under the patronage of his great-uncle Sir Richard Deane (Lord Mayor 1628-9). He was the son of Richard Deane of Temple Guiting, Gloucestershire, and on his mother's side was related to Cromwell. In 1642 he joined one of the Parliamentarian artillery trains, and commanded the artillery under Essex in Cornwall until the Earl abandoned his army in August 1644, surrendering the 49 brass cannon and 'the great basilisco of Dover.'[1] In the New Model Army Deane was commissioned Comptroller of Ordnance, fought at Naseby, and commanded the artillery at Langport. He was highly commended for his services at the capture of Sherborne Castle and afterwards took part under Fairfax in a series of sieges where artillery was needed, culminating in the second Siege of Oxford. After the Army had abducted the King from Holdenby, Deane was one of the senior officers who kissed his hand at Newmarket, and had hopes of winning him over, in opposition to Parliament. But the Second Civil War, in which he commanded the right wing at Preston, made him change his mind, and he is presumed to have drafted the Remonstrance of the Army which urged Parliament to proceed against the King as 'a man of blood', and to search out all those responsible for bringing the Scots into England. When, on 2 December, the unpaid Army entered London, Deane was ordered by Fairfax to seize the treasuries of the Goldsmiths' Hall and Weavers' Hall, and removed £20,000. As one of the Commissioners nominated to try the King he both examined witnesses and, with four others, chose the time and place for the execution. His firm signature is 21st on the death warrant.

When Warwick was removed from the office of Lord High Admiral in February 1649 the command at sea was divided between Popham, Blake, and Deane. Deane convoyed Cromwell's army to Dublin, and then patrolled the North Sea to cut off Charles II from Holland. He joined Cromwell, after Dunbar, in Edinburgh, and in May 1651 took a command ashore. As a Major-General he pursued Charles II and his army down to Worcester where, with Lambert, he secured Upton Bridge, thus cutting off the Royalists' retreat to the south. Returning to Scotland as Commander-in-

Chief to settle the country, he captured the Bass Rock, which commanded the navigation of the Forth, and made an agreement with Argyll for the pacification of the Highlands, patrolling Loch Ness with an armed pinnace and establishing garrisons in other parts of the Highlands. When Dunottar Castle fell and the regalia could not be found, Deane imprisoned Ogilvie, the Governor, and the minister, Mr Granger, as well as both their wives. For it was whispered that Mrs Granger, entrusted with the jewels by Mrs Ogilvie, had smuggled them out of the castle and given them to her husband who buried them in his church.[2] Deane was accused of torturing the Grangers and causing the death of Mrs Granger. But there is no evidence to support this. Recalled to the Fleet in December 1652, Deane, with Blake, fought the Dutch off Portland where Blake was wounded. Deane and Monck now commanded the Fleet and correspondence reveals Deane's meticulous care over its refitting, and the welfare and training of the officers and men.

When Cromwell dissolved Parliament in 1653 Deane was largely responsible for drawing up the *Declaration of the Generals at Sea and the Captains under them* which pledged the Fleet to take no part in political activities on shore. The Fleet finally located the

Dutch Fleet off Solebay and defeated it on 3 June off the Gabbard. But a shot cut Deane nearly in two at the beginning of the battle, and Monck threw a cloak over his mangled remains lest the sailors might be discouraged. After lying in state in Greenwich, he was buried with pomp in Henry VII's Chapel, Westminster Abbey, on 24 June, but exhumed at the Restoration. He had married Mary Grymesditch of Nottingley, Yorkshire, and had one daughter. Essex called this amphibious warrior 'an honest, judicious and stout man.'

NOTES
1 Rushworth, Vol. V, p. 108.
2 Related by Sir Walter Scott in *Antiquities of Scotland* (1826), p. xxvii.

JAMES STANLEY, 7th EARL OF DERBY
(1607-1651)

KNOWN AS 'THE MARTYR EARL' this eldest son of William, 6th Earl of Derby and Lady Elizabeth, daughter of Edward de Vere, 17th Earl of Oxford, was privately educated in France and Italy, and became M.P. for Liverpool in 1625, and a K.B. on Charles I's coronation in 1626. In the same year he married Charlotte de la Trémoille (q.v.). Called to the Lords in 1628, he became Lord Lieutenant of North Wales. But he preferred his farm and his library to court and parliamentary life. In 1639 he joined the King at York and by 1642 had mustered more than 6000 men in Lancashire,

44

sensibly, but in vain, urging the King to raise his standard there rather than at Nottingham. His first orders were to recover Manchester, which was strongly fortified. He made two attempts, first through his friendly relations with leading citizens, then by assault in September, both of which failed. Next year he took Preston, and Lancaster which he burnt. Defeated by Brereton at Whalley, he retired to York and thence to the Isle of Man to quell disturbances there. By 1644 he was back in Cheshire with Rupert, whose approach caused Rigby to raise the Siege of Lathom House, valiantly held by Derby's wife. He went on with Rupert to capture Bolton where he led the assault, giving little quarter. After the taking of Liverpool Rupert inspected the defences of Lathom, and pressed Derby to return to the Isle of Man. In September he was still at Lathom, then undergoing its second siege, but later joined his family in Man, staying there for the next six years.

In July 1649 he rejected Ireton's summons, declaring his intention to hold the island 'where we will unanimously employ our forces to the ruin of the Regicides and their final destruction by land and sea.'[1] In 1650, though disliking Charles II's concessions to the Scots, he prepared to join him in Lancashire and landed at Wyre Water on 15 August with 250 foot and 60 horse. Presbyterian support, hoped for in Warrington, was not forthcoming because Derby had refused to take the Covenant, and he was heavily defeated at Wigan by Robert Lilburne. Though severely wounded, he made his way south and stayed two days at Boscobel before joining Charles on the eve of the Battle of Worcester. After that disastrous battle he guided Charles to Boscobel, and then rode north with other fugitives. They surrendered, on quarter, to a Captain Edge near Nantwich, but Derby wrote to his wife that he wished he had been killed and 'put out of reach of envy and malice.'[2] He was court-martialled, and sentenced to death, at Chester where his two younger daughters, Catherine and Amelia, were imprisoned. After attempting to escape by rope from the leads of the castle, he was retaken on the banks of the Dee. A final petition to the Speaker, praying that he might not be beheaded in Bolton, as if he were a sacrifice for all the blood he had spilt there, was carried by his son, Lord Strange, riding post, but not read in Parliament till he had already been taken to Bolton. Here Strange

45

rejoined him, and helped to attire him for his death, promising to return his 'George' to the King. The scaffold, built partly of timber from Lathom, had been erected at Bolton Cross but the block was not ready, so Derby had to sit in a chair and wait till it was. He was no orator and this, together with the tumult, prevented him from saying what he had intended. He first tried his neck on the block and asked for it to be moved so that he could face the church, which was done. He then knelt down and gave the executioner the sign, but a servant interrupted and he had to repeat it. Strange carried his father's body away that night (15 October) in a wagon to Ormskirk church where it was later buried.

Clarendon calls him a 'man of great honour and clear courage' whose defects and misfortunes 'proceeded from his having lived so little amongst his equals, that he knew not how to treat his inferiors.'[3] Nor indeed his foes, for his brutal method of warfare had offended many of the Lancastrian Royalists.

NOTES
[1] *Tracts Relating to Military Proceedings in Lancashire during the Civil War*, ed. George Ormerod: Chetham Society, Vol. II (1844), p. 284.
[2] *Ibid.*, p. 311.
[3] Clarendon, Bk. XIII, § 68.

CHARLOTTE, COUNTESS OF DERBY
(1599-1664)

THIS REMARKABLE WOMAN was the eldest daughter of Claude de la Trémoille and Charlotte, third daughter of William the Silent. It was while she was staying with her cousin Frederick of Bohemia and his Queen, Elizabeth, that her marriage with James, Lord Strange, was arranged by her mother who had come to England in the train of Henrietta Maria. She was eight years older than James whom in 1626 she married at The Hague and 'brought him down upon the nail a portion of £24,000, he making her but £12,000 a year jointure',[1] as one gossip wrote. For the next sixteen years they lived quietly in Lancashire, at Knowsley or Lathom House, and she bore him five sons and four daughters. When her husband joined the King in 1642 she was at Lathom and stayed there even when next year he had to go and quell disturbances in the Isle of Man. The *Scottish Dove* (which had the lowest common multiple of London readers) reported her as having 'stolen the Earl's breeches when he had fled . . . into the Isle of Man, and hath in his absence play'd the man at Lathom.'[2] She was still doing so in February 1644 when a factious preacher in Wigan, on a text from *Jeremiah*, XIV, verse 15, denounced her as 'the scarlett Whore and the Whore of Babylon whose walls and seven towers (like the seven hills of Rome) would fall down flatt'[3] before the guns of Fairfax, who invested it two days later. Special prayers for the success of the siege were offered up in all the Puritan churches of Lancashire, which the garrison answered with resolute sallies. When Rigby, who had succeeded Fairfax, summoned the Countess to surrender in May she told 'that insolent rebel' that she would fire the house first. But a 13in. mortar, which threw stones and grenadoes, so 'frighted 'em from their meate and sleepe'[4] that they determined to capture it. In a dawn sally, with the loss of only two men, the Cavaliers seized and dragged it with ropes back to the House where it lay 'like a dead lyon' among them. Such was her Ladyship's 'very skurvy answer' to Rigby on the very day that he had invited all his friends to come and see him destroy the House. But reports of Rupert's approach caused him to raise the siege and withdraw to Bolton. Here Derby (as he now was), who had joined Rupert, wreaked his revenge on the besiegers, and the Countess was presented with twenty-two of their colours which three days before were 'proudly flourish't before her house.'[5] Throughout the siege she had attended public prayers every day with her two young daughters, and issued orders through the Major of the House, drawing by lot the captains for each sally, who then chose their own lieutenants.

P.S.W.B

By the time that the second Siege of Lathom began, in July 1644, Charlotte and her family had, on Rupert's advice, moved to the Isle of Man. But Lathom held out for the next seventeen months. By the terms of surrender (December 1645) the Countess was allowed a third of the Earl's estate and conveyance of his goods to Knowsley. She remained in Man, but in 1647 her eldest son, Charles, two of his brothers, and three of his sisters, visited England to petition for a fifth of the estate. This was granted and they were put in possession of Knowsley, but next year they were removed to Liverpool, imprisoned there, and threatened with worse if their father continued to hold Man and treat his prisoners harshly. By 1651, when Derby had landed in Lancashire to join Charles II's march south, Henrietta, Edward, and William were with their

PLATE 17 Edward Hyde, 1st Earl of Clarendon *after Adriaen Hanneman*

PLATE 18   Sir William Compton   *Henry Paert after Sir Peter Lely*

PLATE 19   Oliver Cromwell   *Sir Peter Lely*
"Mr Lilly *(sic)*, I desire you would use all your skill to paint my picture
truly like me and not flatter me but remark all these ruffness, pimples,
warts and everything as you see me; otherwise I never will pay a farthing
for it."

PLATE 21   James Stanley 7th Earl of Derby c. 1636-7 *after Sir Anthony van Dyck*

LATE 20   Maj. Gen. and Admiral Richard Deane   *Robert Walker*

Charlotte, d. of C
de la Tremouill
de Thouars: m 16
James Stanley (
Strange of Knoc
7ᵗʰ Earl of Derby
ted for her defe
Lathom House;
to surrender Isle
B. 1599 D. 1661

PLATE 22   Charlotte, Countess of Derby c. 1657

PLATE 23   Maj. Gen. John Desborough

ROBERT DEVEREVX EARLE OF ESSEX HIS EXCEL
lency &c Generall of ẙ Army

PLATE 24   Robert Devereux, 3rd Earl of Essex   *Wenceslaus Hollar*

mother in Man, Charles was married and living elsewhere in England, and Caroline and Amelia were removed to Chester for greater security. Here they, alone of the family, were able to see their father before he was taken to Bolton for execution. The Countess held Man until November 1651 when she surrendered to superior forces. She moved to Knowsley and lived there till she died, 21 March 1664, still lamenting the ingratitude of the King who had refused a bill passed by Parliament to restore the family estates to her. She was buried with her husband in Ormskirk church.

NOTES

[1] *Complete Peerage*, quoting John Pory to Joseph Mead, 1 July 1626.
[2] *Tracts relating to Military Proceedings in Lancashire during the Civil War*, ed. George Ormerod: Chetham Society, Vol. II (1844), pp. 163, 167.
[3] *Ibid.*, p. 176.
[4] *Ibid.*, p. 179.
[5] *Ibid.*, p. 183.

MAJOR-GENERAL JOHN DESBOROUGH, DESBROW, or DISBROWE
(1608-1680)

JOHN DESBOROUGH, married Cromwell's sister Jane in 1636 and although bred an attorney, was more interested in his farm. Wood calls him 'a great lubberly clown who by Oliver's interest became a Colonel.'[1] In *Hudibras* he is Colon, a farmer, rougher even than his horse. His father was James Desborough whose timbered house still overlooks the village green of Eltisley, near Cambridge, and his mother was Elizabeth Hatley of Over, Cambridgeshire. As a captain in Cromwell's horse he did distinguished service during 1642-3, fought as a major at Langport and Hambledon Hill (1645), and at the Siege of Bristol where he commanded the horse. He took part in the Siege of Colchester (1648) but kept clear of the King's 'trial' and execution. As a major-general he fought against Charles II at Worcester. Subsequently the fugitive King in disguise passed right through a regiment of his horse near Salisbury, with a kinswoman of Colonel Wyndham riding pillion behind him, and further on met the major-general himself without being recognized.

49

In 1653 Desborough was a member of Cromwell's Council of State and one of the four generals of the Fleet with Blake, Monck, and Penn. Next year he was Constable of St. Briavell's Castle in the Forest of Dean, and M.P. for Cambridgeshire. Sent to suppress Penruddock's rising in 1655, he found nearly all the conspirators already in Exeter gaol. He subsequently became Major-General for the South-West, M.P. for Somerset, a Privy Councillor, and a commissioner for managing affairs at home, with Blake and Montagu. Although strongly opposed to the offer of the crown to Cromwell, he became one of the new Lords. On the Protector's death he, with others, forced Richard Cromwell to dissolve Parliament in April 1659. But Parliament, restored next month, appointed him one of seven commissioners to revise the list of officers and nominate them to each regiment. In August he was sent to the West to suppress any risings in sympathy with Booth's in Cheshire. Because Parliament rejected the soldiers' petitions Lambert, Fleetwood, and Desborough expelled it and were appointed by the Army Major-General, General, and Commissary-General of Horse respectively, forming a Committee of Public Safety to govern the country for the time being. Monck's declaration for a free Parliament however upset their calculations, and Desborough marched north to join Lambert in opposing his entry into England. But Monck outmanoeuvred them and by the time Desborough reached London again petitions for a free Parliament were being circulated. Defections increased daily and on 29 December Desborough wrote a letter of submission and apology to the Speaker. The restored Rump of January 1660 cashiered and relegated him to his country home.

At the Restoration Desborough tried to leave the country but was arrested on the Essex coast. Although exempted from the Act of Indemnity, he was freed, but rearrested on suspicion of plotting to kill the King. Released for lack of evidence, he fled to Holland and tried to unite the remnants of the republican party. For this the government ordered him to return before July 1666 or be declared a traitor. He did return, was liberated after examination, and lived quietly till he died in 1680 in Hackney. His first wife, Jane, who bore him one daughter and seven sons, had been buried in Westminster Abbey, but was exhumed at the Restoration. His second wife was probably Anne, daughter of Sir Richard Everard of Much Waltham, Essex. It is said that his ambition had been to found a military despotism, with himself in high command, which is borne out by a contemporary cartoon depicting him as 'the grim Gyant', club in hand, helping Lambert to remove by force 'the meek knight',[2] Richard Cromwell.

NOTES

[1] Anthony Wood, *Fasti*, ed. Bliss (1820), Pt. II, p. 155.
[2] Frontispiece to *Don Juan Lamberto, A Comical History of our late Times*, by Montelion, Knight of the Oracle etc. (1661).

ROBERT DEVEREUX, 3rd EARL OF ESSEX
(1591-1648)
Old Robin.

ROUNDHEAD SOLDIERS' NICKNAME FOR ESSEX

ESSEX WAS CAPTAIN-GENERAL of the Parliamentarian Armies from 1642 until the formation of the New Model Army in 1645. Lethargic by nature, he was no great strategist and an indifferent administrator. Nevertheless, he has one important success to his credit, the relief of Gloucester in 1643. He was the eldest son of Robert, 2nd Earl of Essex (1566-1601) and Frances, daughter of Sir Francis Walsingham and widow of Sir Philip Sidney. Although his father had died attainted, he was restored to the earldom by Act of Parliament only three years later (1604). In 1606, when he was only 15, King James arranged his marriage to Frances Howard, a younger daughter of the Earl of Suffolk. From 1607 to 1609, while he was travelling abroad, the King's favourite, Sir Robert Carr, took a liking to Essex's young wife – which she returned. In 1613 she procured a sentence of nullity of the marriage on the grounds that Essex was incapable of consummating it. Carr, who was created Earl of Somerset, wedded her soon after. Essex went to serve under Sir Horace Vere in the Palatinate; and was vice-admiral of the Cadiz expedition of 1625. Six years later he married Elizabeth, daughter of Sir William Paulet. A child was born but died in infancy. Then the Earl's attendants, jealous perhaps of Elizabeth's influence over him, accused her of adultery and a separation followed.

In the First Scots War Essex was second-in-command, but thereafter he threw in his lot with Parliament and the King attempted in vain to win him over. On 12 July 1642 he was given command of the Parliamentarian Army. The King now declared him a traitor. On 9 September Essex joined his army, taking with him his coffin, winding-sheet, and scutcheon to prove his fidelity to the cause. In the 1642 campaign he dispersed a number of his regiments and allowed the King to get between him and the capital. He fought bravely, pike in hand, in the indecisive Battle of Edgehill, and managed to get his army back to London in time to face the King at Turnham Green and foil the most dangerous Royalist threat to the capital. On 13 April he laid siege to Reading, which he captured after a short siege. He then sat down in Buckinghamshire, observing Oxford, the Royalist capital, and excusing his inactivity on the grounds that his men were sickly and ill-paid. Rebuked by Pym, he tendered his resignation (28 July) which was refused. The threat to Gloucester stirred him into life. Reinforced by regiments of the London Trained Bands, he succeeded in relieving the city (8 September) only to be cut off on his way home at Newbury, and having to fight with the enemy between him and his base. Here, however, he fought his best battle (20 September), and when the next day dawned he found the Royalists gone, and with them the King's greatest chance of destroying the main Parliamentarian Army. Despite his victory Parliament entrusted independent armies to Manchester and Waller, but, though mortified, Essex remained faithful to his trust. In May 1644 he advanced on Oxford from the east, while Waller assailed the city from the south and west. King Charles eluded them by his famous night march, and thereafter the two Parliamentarian commanders parted company. They permitted their personal jealousies to overrule strategic sense. Essex, after relieving Lyme, invaded Cornwall, where his army was hemmed in and compelled to surrender. He ingloriously escaped by sea leaving Skippon to arrange the capitulation. Thereafter he played no part in the War and on 2 April 1645 he formally laid down his command. He died at Essex House, Strand, 14 September 1646.

He was a good-hearted, muddleheaded sort of man, not lacking in dignity or a sense of duty, but devoid of any real grasp of strategy. What other modern general has fought all his major battles with the enemy between him and his base?

53

LIEUTENANT-GENERAL JAMES KING, LORD EYTHIN

(1598?-1652)

He had throughout the whole course of his life been generally reputed a man of honour, and had exercised the highest commands under the King of Sweden with extraordinary ability and success, so he had been prosecuted by some of his countrymen with the highest malice from his very coming into the King's service; and the same malice pursued him after he had left the kingdom, even to his death. CLARENDON.

THE PORTRAITS which Clarendon paints of the soldiers of his day are seldom flattering. Yet there are those who will think his character of Lord Eythin unduly charitable. The son of David King of Warbester Hay in Orkney,[1] the future general joined the Swedish service. In 1638 he lent the Swedish contingent to the Elector Palatine for the ill-fated invasion of Westphalia, which ended in disaster at Vlotho or Lemgo. On that occasion Prince Rupert, at the age of 18, was colonel of a regiment of cuirassiers. He led an impetuous charge and was taken prisoner. King did not hesitate to lay the whole blame for the defeat upon the Prince's shoulders.

Whilst Rupert was still languishing in prison, King left the Swedish service and went to England, where he was well received by King Charles and given a pension of £1000 per annum. When, in about March 1643, Newcastle dismissed the Earl of Newport, who was no soldier, he made King Lieutenant-General of his army in his place. It was a sound choice for Newcastle was wholly lacking in military experience. As a wealthy 'grandee' he had the power to raise an army, but he needed a real soldier to train and administer it. King was made a Scots peer with the title of Lord Eythin on 28 March 1643.

The tide turned against the Northern Royalists in October when they lost Winceby Fight and were compelled to raise the Siege of Hull. It has often been said that had Newcastle, instead of besieging Hull, invaded the Eastern Association after the victory at Adwalton Moor (30 June 1643) the whole course of the War might have changed to King Charles's advantage. But we do not know to what extent we must blame Lord Eythin, as Newcastle's chief professional adviser, for the latter's failure to adopt it. No doubt Eythin was consulted on all important questions of strategy, but one cannot imagine a grandee of Newcastle's calibre accepting military advice that conflicted with his personal inclinations.

The advent of Prince Rupert and the relief of York (1 July 1644) momentarily transformed the affairs of the Northern army. Rupert was convinced that King Charles's vague instructions gave him no alternative but to offer battle. Hence the unpleasant scene between the Prince and Eythin at Marston Moor on the afternoon of 2 July which is related by Sir Hugh Cholmley.[2] Clarendon's version is that Rupert asked his colleagues their opinion of the battle as he meant to fight it. Eythin's comment is said to have been 'By God, Sir, it is very fine on paper, but there is no such thing in the field,' with the added taunt 'Sir, your forwardness lost us the day in Germany when you yourself were taken prisoner.' We have no direct evidence as to the part Eythin played in the battle. It is probable that he commanded the foot in the centre. He was among the officers who accompanied Newcastle to Hamburg after the disaster, and he played no further part in the First Civil War. Indeed it is evident that there were those who did not venture to criticize the Marquess, but were very willing to make a scapegoat of Eythin.

In a little-known letter written in Hamburg in January 1646 to the Prince, Eythin pleads ignorance of an order he was said to have received recalling him from Scarborough (whither he had first fled) and asks Rupert's pardon : 'If yor Hgs at my teaking my leave from you had leavyd Yor least commands or desyrs upon me, they should heave been obeyed.'[3] Although this letter has the ring of truth about it, there is no evidence that it brought any reconciliation between the two men. It seems that in March 1650 Eythin still had some reputation left, for on the 19th Montrose made him his Lieutenant-General. However his soldiering days were done. He died in Stockholm on 9 June 1652.

NOTES
1 *D.N.B.* gives his date of birth as 1589? but I venture to suggest that 1598 is more probable. (P.Y.).
2 *Marston Moor*, pp. 116-17. He was Governor of Scarborough Castle and his account was based on those of the fugitives, including Newcastle and Eythin, who reached his garrison soon after the battle.
3 *The Pythouse Papers*, ed. W. A. Day (1897), No. 22.

FERDINANDO FAIRFAX,
2nd LORD FAIRFAX OF CAMERON
(1584-1648)

FERDINANDO FAIRFAX was the son of Thomas, first Baron Fairfax[1], of Denton, Yorkshire, and Ellen Aske. His father wanted him to be a soldier and sent him to the Netherlands, only to be told that 'he makes a tolerable country justice, but is a mere coward at fighting.'[2] He married in 1607 Mary, daughter of Lord Sheffield. In the last two Parliaments of James I and the first three of Charles I he represented Boroughbridge, and in 1640 succeeded to his

56

father's title. Like most other Yorkshire gentlemen he desired the downfall of Wentworth – 'that great engine . . . who hath . . . battered down the laws and liberties'[3] of the kingdom – and was one of those who had, as he put it, 'framed a short Bill to convict him of treason, which was the speedier way', as indeed it proved to be. In the First Scots War he commanded a regiment of the Yorkshire Trained Bands, but he does not seem to have played any part in the Second. Then, representing Yorkshire in the Long Parliament, he threw in his lot with the popular party. He was one of the committee charged to present the Grand Remonstrance, and favoured some limitation of episcopal power. When King Charles established himself at York in 1642, Fairfax was one of the committee sent by Parliament to observe his movements.

In September Fairfax's selection to command the Parliamentarian forces in Yorkshire was confirmed, and he was commissioned by Essex (December). He began his operations with a treaty of neutrality, which was annulled by Parliament. For this Clarendon, unjustly, accused him of perfidy. He attempted to blockade York, but with the arrival of Newcastle's army was compelled to act on the defensive and from his headquarters at Selby accused Newcastle of invading the county with an army of papists, while Newcastle retaliated by publishing a list of Yorkshire traitors which included Fairfax and his son Sir Thomas. His strength lay in the West Riding, and he was forced to withdraw to Leeds. Newcastle greatly outnumbered him, but he held out for some time, thanks to the courage and enterprise of Sir Thomas. But at Adwalton Moor (30 June 1643) his army was utterly defeated, partly because he failed to launch his reserve. Without telling his son that he was withdrawing, he made his way to Hull for, 'like an old Gamester, he knew the hazard of venturing still upon hard luck'.[4] He was made Governor of Hull (22 July) which Newcastle began to besiege on 2 September. At first it was a matter of work and counterwork, the defence advancing their artillery emplacements to silence the longer-range Royalist guns. But on 14 September Fairfax opened the sluices to let in the water from the Hull and the Humber, flooding the countryside, and the Royalists out of their trenches. On 11 October he ordered a sally in force which overran the Royalist works and captured one of the two great 'Brasse demy Cannon', Gog and Magog. Next morning Newcastle raised the siege, which had immobilized for six weeks his army so much needed by the King, and allowed the Parliamentarians to get better organized. Next spring Fairfax and his son joined forces and inflicted a heavy defeat on the Royalists at Selby, thereafter going on to besiege York. In the ensuing Battle of Marston Moor Fairfax, in command of the Allied armies, was carried away by the flight of his troops and was said to have fled as far as Cawood, but there is evidence that in fact he returned and was in the field at the end of the day. When York surrendered (16 July) he was made Governor, but the Self-Denying Ordinance of December 1644 compelled him to relinquish his command and he resumed his seat in Parliament. In 1647 he remarried, but next year on 14 March he died of blood poisoning from a corn on his toe.

Fairfax was no great soldier, but without him the Roundheads of the West Riding would scarcely have made progress against the Earl of Newcastle and his great host.

NOTES
1 In the peerage of Scotland.
2 Sir C. R. Markham, *The Life of the Great Lord Fairfax* (1870), p. 12.
3 *Fairfax Correspondence*, ed. G. W. Johnson, Vol. II (1848), p. 104.
4 Slingsby, p. 97.

THOMAS FAIRFAX, 3rd LORD FAIRFAX
OF CAMERON
(1612-1671)

The man most beloved and relied upon by the rebels in the north.

SIR EDWARD NICHOLAS

SON OF FERDINANDO, second Lord Fairfax (q.v.), he was born at Denton, Yorkshire, 17 January 1612. He matriculated from St. John's College, Cambridge, in 1626 and in 1629 went to serve under Sir Horace Vere in the Low Countries, where he took part in the Siege of Bois-le-Duc. He then travelled in France, and in 1637 married Anne Vere (his commander's daughter) after being at first coldly received in London by her mother and having to write to his father and ask how he should now proceed.[1]

In the First Scots War Fairfax served the King, commanding a company of 160 Yorkshire dragoons and being knighted in 1640. As one of the leading Yorkshire magnates he attempted to present a petition of the Yorkshire gentry and freeholders at Heyworth Moor, near York, in June 1642 but the King refused to accept it. When the fighting began he served as his father's second-in-command, and greatly distinguished himself. His exploits at Leeds (23 January) and Wakefield (21 May) were offset by his defeat at Seacroft Moor (30 March). But, when he stormed Wakefield with only 1500 men, he took Goring, who had three times his numbers, by surprise, capturing 28 colours and 1400 prisoners. His resolution after the disaster at Adwalton Moor (30 June) enabled the Roundheads to hang on to their important base at Hull. At Winceby (11 October 1643) Fairfax began the charge with 'Come let us fall on, I never prospered better than when I fought against the enemy three or four to one.' At Naseby, in command of the New Model Army, after leading several charges, he actually took a colour with his own hands ! But though severely wounded at the Siege of Helmsley Castle (August 1644) when a musket-ball broke his shoulder, he was on the whole fortunate. The wound he received at Marston Moor was a sword slash in the face which soon mended. At Torrington he had a narrow escape 'where great webs of lead fell thickest' when the Royalist magazine blew up.

In the period after Naseby Fairfax successfully conducted a

number of sieges and other operations, of which the most important were the Battle of Langport (10 July 1645), the storming of Bristol (10 September) and of Torrington (16 February 1646), the surrender of Hopton's army at Truro (14 March), and of Oxford (24 June). In the Second Civil War he added to his laurels by crushing the Kentish Royalists in Maidstone (6 June 1648) and his 76-day Siege of Colchester. Unfortunately for his reputation, he permitted the Cavalier leaders, Sir Charles Lucas and Sir George Lisle, to be shot after the surrender.

There were those, including the poet Milton, who hoped that Fairfax would settle the kingdom and clear it of avarice and rapine. Unhappily Fairfax's talent was for battle; as a statesman he was completely out of his depth. He did not approve of the King's 'trial' and beheading, and was instrumental in bringing about the Restoration, when he neither desired, nor received, any reward. Indeed he courageously declared 'that if any man deserved to be excepted [from pardon] he knew no man that deserved it more than himself who, being general of the army,' had 'power sufficient to prevent the proceedings against the King'. In his last years he was a sick man. During that time his cousin, Brian Fairfax, tells us that 'he sat like an old Roman, his manly countenance striking awe and reverence into all that beheld it.' He wrote two autobiographical works: *A Short Memorial of the Northern Actions in which I was engaged*, and *Short Memoirs of some things to be cleared during my Command*.

Fairfax was silent in council, but in battle 'so highly transported that scarce any man durst speak a word to him, and he would seem more like a man distracted and furious . . . than of his ordinary mildness.' He loved learning, and the Bodleian Library profited from his generosity and his protection. Although towards the end of the Protectorate his relations with Cromwell were extremely strained, the continual reports that he was involved in plots are apparently unfounded. Lady Fairfax died in 1665 and her husband who had succeeded his father in 1648, followed her six years later to their grave in Bilbrough church, on the hill which was his favourite viewpoint. He died 12 November 1671.

NOTES
1 Bodleian, Western MS. 31065, f. 84.

LUCIUS CARY, 2nd VISCOUNT FALKLAND
(c. 1610-1643)

'TO LIVE LIKE Clodius and like Falkland fall.' Byron, contrasting vice and virtue in this line, echoed the verdict of history. Lucius, born at Burford, probably in 1610, was the son of Sir Henry Cary, 1st Viscount Falkland, and Elizabeth, daughter of Sir Lawrence Tanfield. In 1621 he was entered at St. John's College, Cambridge, but he accompanied his parents to Ireland when in 1622 his father became Lord Deputy and later went to Trinity College. Dublin Between 1629 and 1631 he married Letice, daughter of Sir Richard Morison of Tooley Park, Leicestershire. He married for love, not money, which so angered his father that Lucius offered to surrender his claim to the family estate when he succeeded his father in 1633. That winter his mother tried hard to convert him, and his sisters, to Catholicism and blamed his refusal on the Socinian heresy which he had adopted, denying the Divinity of Christ.

Falkland continued to live at Great Tew, about seventeen miles north-west of Oxford, rejoicing in the country life, in his books, in writing, and in the company and conversation of his many friends from Oxford and elsewhere who gathered round him, attracted by his wit. But he was no idle dreamer and as member for Newport, Isle of Wight, in the Short and Long Parliaments, he opposed arbitrary power in any form, particularly Strafford's policy, and the subservient judiciary which had, by upholding the King's right to collect Ship Money, allowed him to be 'the sole power in necessity, the sole judge of necessity, but had enabled him to take from us what he would, when he would, and how he would.'[1] He also opposed Laud's ecclesiastical policy, but not to the extent of advocating the abolition of episcopacy and substituting Presbyterianism. Although he was the only member of the Commons to plead for more time to be allowed Strafford to prepare his defence, he finally voted for his attainder. In the First Scots War he had applied for a commission to command a troop of horse, and when this was refused, joined the Earl of Essex as a volunteer. In January 1642 he was offered a vacant Secretaryship of State which his great friend Hyde persuaded him to accept. After the Royal Standard was raised at Nottingham he carried a conciliatory message from the King to Parliament, to which Charles privately added that he was prepared to consent to a thorough reformation of religion and to any other reasonable demand. It was Parliament's rejection of this overture that finally threw Falkland into the Royalist camp.

He was present at Edgehill where he so far forgot his Secretaryship as to take part in Wilmot's charge. In August 1643 he was at the Siege of Gloucester where the agony of this fratricidal war so obsessed him that he could not sleep, and longed only for death. His chance came at First Newbury, 20 September. Early that morning he dressed in clean linen, received the Sacrament from the rector of Newbury, and, as a volunteer, joined Sir John Byron's troop of horse. When it was held up by enemy fire from a hedge with a gap in it, only wide enough for one horse to pass at a time, he spurred straight through and was instantly killed.[2] His body was found next morning, stripped and identifiable only by a mole on his neck. Laid over a horse, the corpse was escorted by a detachment of the King's own troop to Newbury Town Hall, and thereafter taken for burial in the church at Great Tew, where his widow was buried beside him three years later.

The day after Falkland was killed Hyde received the reply to a letter he had sent to him at Gloucester, imploring him as a Privy Councillor and a Secretary of State not to endanger himself in the trenches. In it Falkland said that 'so much notice had been taken of him for an impatient desire of peace that it was necessary he should make it appear that it was not out of fear of the utmost hazard of war' and that he hoped that the battle soon to be fought 'would put an end to the misery of the kingdom.'[3] It put an end only to his own misery, and a friendship which Hyde called 'the joy and comfort of his life.' They had in the past sat side by side in the Commons, and so regularly that if one were absent a place was always left vacant for the other to fill when he came.

NOTES
[1] C. V. Wedgwood, *The King's Peace* (1955), p. 379.
[2] Walter Money, *The First and Second Battles of Newbury*, 2nd edn. (1884), p. 52.
[3] *Life of Edward, Earl of Clarendon*, Vol. I (1857), pp. 164-5.

NATHANIEL FIENNES
(1607-1669)

NATHANIEL FIENNES had an enviable start in life. The second son of William, 1st Viscount Saye and Sele of Broughton, Oxfordshire, he was educated at Winchester and New College, Oxford, where, as founder's kin, he was admitted a perpetual Fellow and stayed up five years without taking a degree. Thereafter he visited Switzerland which, according to Clarendon, increased 'his disinclination to the Church with which milk he had been nursed.'[1] He sat for Banbury in both the Short and Long Parliaments, and in December 1640 spoke against the Canons issued by Convocation and in February 1641 against episcopacy. In June he reported to Parliament some hearsay evidence of Wilmot's implication in the Army Plot to seize the Tower, and of Strafford's offer of £20,000 to the Lieutenant of the Tower to connive at his escape, which produced such an uproar that Speaker Lenthall had to adjourn the House. On the outbreak of war, commanding a troop of horse under Essex, Fiennes failed to prevent Lord Northampton from removing the guns sent by Lord Brooke to Banbury. He fought bravely at Powick Bridge, and showed more military skill than Brown, his professional officer. At Edgehill his troop was under Balfour on the right, and he wrote *A True and Exact Relation* of both this battle and of Powick Bridge. In February next year he was sent to Bristol to investigate the misconduct of the Governor, Colonel Essex, whom he at once arrested. Discovering that a rising was imminent, he also arrested the conspirators only two or three hours before the gates were to be opened to Rupert, and executed the leaders. In May he was appointed Governor by the Earl of Essex and found himself with insufficient money or men since Waller had taken much of his garrison and lost it at Roundway Down. When Rupert summoned the city on 24 July Fiennes had only 300 horse, 1500 foot, and nearly 100 guns to hold the five forts and a line some four miles long. But he rejected the summons. The assault began at 3 a.m. on 26 July and by the evening, after bitter fighting, Fiennes, short of ammunition, sent to ask for a parley. By the terms of surrender he abandoned the remainder of his ammunition, arms, and 60 guns, and was allowed to march out. On 5 August he delivered his report to Parliament which charged

63

him with treachery and cowardice. Like Rupert, after he surrendered Bristol two years later, Fiennes angrily demanded a court-martial. This, held at St Albans, sentenced him to death, but he owed his life to the good sense of Essex.

Fiennes's military career, however, was ended and he seems to have gone abroad. Rupert's surrender of Bristol in September 1645 brought a change of opinion which induced Fairfax and Cromwell to sign a certificate exonerating him. He reappeared in September 1647 on the Committee of the Army. Because he said that the King's concessions over the Treaty of Newport constituted grounds for a peace, he was excluded from Parliament by Pride's Purge (6 December 1648) and he took no more part in political life until the Protectorate when he became a member of Cromwell's Council of State. He sat for Oxfordshire in 1654, for the University in 1656, was one of the Keepers of the Great Seal, and on the committee which urged Cromwell to accept the crown, becoming a new Lord in 1658. In two important speeches, one in Oliver's last Parliament, the other in Richard's, he emphasized the religious features of Cromwell's domestic and foreign policy. At the Restoration his public career ended, and he died 16 December 1669 at Newton Tony, Wiltshire, where he was buried. His first wife, Elizabeth, daughter of Sir John Eliot, bore him one son, William, 3rd Viscount Saye and Sele. By his second wife, Frances, daughter of Richard Whitehead of Tudeley, Kent, he had three daughters. According to Wood, he was the author of *Monarchy Asserted*, published in 1660.

NOTES
1 Clarendon, Bk. III, § 33.

PLATE 25   Lt. Gen. James King, Lord Eythin c. 1623

PLATE 26   Ferdinando Fairfax, 2nd Lord Fairfax of Cameron   *Edward Bower*

PLATE 27   Thomas Fairfax, 3rd Lord Fairfax of Cameron
Engleheart after Edward Bower
The medal about his neck was awarded after Naseby.

PLATE 28   Lucius Cary, 2nd Viscount Falkland   *John Hoskins*

PLATE 29   Nathaniel Fiennes c. 1642-3
The colours he wears are those of the Earl of Essex. The armour is
painted black to prevent rust, and the arm guard is to protect the bridle
arm. Michiel Jansz van Miereveldt died 1641.

PLATE 30   Maj. Gen. Charles Fleetwood

PLATE 31   Patrick Ruthven, Earl of Forth and Brentford

PLATE 32   Colonel Sir Henry Gage   *perhaps after William Dobson*

MAJOR-GENERAL CHARLES FLEETWOOD
(d. 1692)

CHARLES FLEETWOOD became one of the military triumvirate which ruled England for the second half of 1659, but lost the last throw of the game. The son of Sir Miles Fleetwood of Aldwinkle, Northamptonshire, and Anne Luke of Woodend, Bedfordshire, he was a member of Gray's Inn in 1638, and Essex's Lifeguard in 1642. Wounded as a captain at First Newbury, next year he was rewarded with the receivership of Court wards forfeited by his Royalist brother, Sir William. He was a notorious favourer of the sectaries, and the regiment which he commanded in Manchesters' army was described as 'a cluster of preaching officers and troopers.[1] When they murmured he invited them to pray, falling on his knees before them. He commanded a regiment of horse at Naseby, and in August helped to reduce the Dorset Clubmen who were threatening Fairfax's supplies. Next year, by preventing the Oxford cavalry from joining Astley, he contributed to his surrender at Stow-on-the-Wold. He was recruiter M.P. for Marlborough in 1646, and in the wrangling of 1647 between Parliament and the Army acted both as parliamentary commissioner and army representative. He contributed to the surrender of Colchester by capturing Mersea Island and cutting off supplies. As Cromwell's Lt-General of Horse he fought at Dunbar in 1650 and next year became a member of the Council of State. When Charles II marched into England, Fleetwood gathered the militia of twenty counties at Banbury and, after securing the bridges over Severn and Teme at Upton and Powick south of Worcester, drove the Royalists into a trap. Two deaths this year touched him closely, that of his wife, Frances Smith of Winston, Norfolk; and that of Ireton, for next year (October) he succeeded him as Commander-in-Chief in Ireland, and married his widow, Bridget, Cromwell's eldest daughter.

In 1654 Fleetwood became Lord Deputy and was mainly concerned with the transportation of condemned Irish landowners to Connaught, and the settling of disbanded soldiers on their estates, a task for which his hatred of Roman Catholic priests well fitted him. Recalled to England in 1655 he took a leading place in his father-in-law's Court, and became Major-General for the

Eastern counties. He approved of the Cromwell's limitation of parliamentary powers, and of his foreign policy as being divinely inspired to protect persecuted Protestants against the common enemy, but opposed the offer of kingship to him though becoming one of the new Lords. On Oliver's death he supported Richard, but when the latter refused the Army's demands, he assembled his forces at St. James's and compelled him to dissolve Parliament, in return for which the Army made him Commander-in-Chief. Parliament was again forcibly dissolved in October by Lambert who, with Desborough, went north to oppose Monck's entry into England, leaving Fleetwood in London to maintain order. He made repeated efforts to treat with Monck, who would not reply; but, when advised by his brother and Bulstrode White-locke to come to terms with Charles II before Monck did, said he must first consult Lambert. By then it was too late. The Rump was restored and Fleetwood, after appearing before it to answer for his conduct, was deprived of his command. At the Restoration he was merely incapacitated from holding any office of trust. Two years later his wife, Bridget, died and he married his third wife, Dame Mary Hartopp, widow of Sir Edward Hartopp and daughter of Sir John Coke of Melbourne, Derbyshire. They lived in Stoke Newington, where he died 4 October 1692 and was buried in Bunhill Fields cemetery. When this cemetery was turned into gardens in 1869 his altar-tomb was discovered, 7 feet below ground, and restored. By his first wife he had one son and one daughter, and by his second one son and two daughters.

NOTES
1 *The Quarrel between the Earl of Manchester and Oliver Cromwell*, Camden Society, Vol. CXVII (1875), p. 72.

PATRICK RUTHVEN, EARL OF FORTH
and BRENTFORD
(c. 1573-1651)

IT IS UNCERTAIN when this 'hail man, made for the hardship of Souldiers'[1] was born. He was the son of William Ruthven of Ballindean and Katherine, daughter of John, Lord Stewart. He left Scotland in 1606 for the Swedish service, possibly because he wished, as a younger son, to follow the career of arms. By 1618 he was colonel of a regiment of Scottish horse. After the Battle of Dirschau in 1627 he was knighted before the whole army by Gustavus Adolphus, who appreciated him not only as a soldier but also as a man who could 'drink immeasurably and preserve his understanding to the last', and so could extract secrets from his military and political opponents 'in their more cheerful hours.'[2] He was also of an ingenious turn of mind and could communicate with beleagured cities 'by significant Fireworks formed in the air in legible characters.'[3] After being garrison commander of Ulm, he finally left the Swedish service in 1638, returning to England where Charles I made him his Muster-Master in Scotland. Next year he was created Baron Ruthven of Ettrick. He became Governor of Edinburgh Castle which he held against the Covenanters for nine weeks till 15 September 1640 when, with his water supply destroyed, more than two hundred casualties, and himself stricken with scurvy and having lost most of his teeth, he had to surrender.

Early in 1642 Ruthven went to Germany on private business and returned with twenty-two officers, joining the King at Shrewsbury. He was created Earl of Forth and, at Edgehill, was ordered by the King to draw up the army in battle, which so greatly incensed Lindsey, the Commander-in-Chief, that he swore he would fight as a colonel at the head of his regiment, where he was killed. After the battle Forth urged the King to march on London, and took a leading part in the capture of Brentford. In April 1643 he made a vain effort to relieve Reading, and in August was wounded at the Siege of Gloucester. Next year, in March, although suffering from gout, he was in command at the Battle of Cheriton, against Waller, where his caution restrained Hopton from delivering an outflanking attack which might have given the Royalists the victory. Forth retired to Oxford and it was probably on his advice that the King withdrew the garrison from Reading, thus strengthening his own army, and did not give battle to the combined armies of Essex and Waller which had occupied Reading. He was now created Earl of Brentford and went with the Royal army when it marched out of Oxford on 3 June to beat Waller at Cropredy Bridge on the 29th. He was also at Lostwithiel when Essex surrendered in September, and at Second Newbury, where he was wounded in the head. After the battle his third wife, a German Baroness, was captured in her coach.

P.J.W.B.

Because of his increasing deafness, wounds, old age, and perhaps his drinking (he was nicknamed 'Pater Rotwein'), the King decided in November to replace Brentford by Rupert. He was made Chamberlain to the Prince of Wales and in 1646 accompanied him to Jersey and then to France. In February 1649 he went from St. Germain to Sweden to ask Queen Christina for aid, and returned with arms and ammunition which he paid for out of his Swedish estates. He sailed with Charles II to Scotland in 1650, despite the objections of the Scottish Commissioners. But the Scottish Parliament excluded him from his estates so he retired to Perthshire. He died in Dundee 2 February 1651 and was buried in Grange Durham's aisle in the parish church of Monifieth. By his first wife (name unknown) he probably had two daughters; by his second, Joanna, sister of Colonel John Henderson, he had a son and daughter both of whom died in infancy. His third wife was Clara Berner of Mecklenberg.

Although this 'Scotch man and therefore an excellent souldier'[4] was seventy when the War began, he acted as Charles I's Chief of Staff for the next three years by which time the King, under his guidance, had become a competent commander in the field. He was a man of honour, a brave and skilful officer, and one whose faults have been exaggerated by writers who neither like nor understand professional soldiers.

NOTES
[1] Lloyd, p. 674.
[2] Walter Harte, *The History of Gustavus Adolphus*, Vol. I (1807), p. 177.
[3] Lloyd, *loc. cit.*
[4] *Ibid.*

COLONEL SIR HENRY GAGE
(1597-1645)

THIS *Alter Britanniae Heros*, as Edward Walsingham[1] calls him, was the son of John Gage of Haling, Surrey, and a strong Roman Catholic. At the age of 20 he was sent to be educated in Flanders and later went on to Italy to hear the philosophical discussions of the famous scholar Piccolomini. In 1619 he entered the Spanish service and trailed a pike for a year in Antwerp. He was then given a company by the 7th Earl of Argyll and spent the next 12 years soldiering in the Netherlands, distinguishing himself at the Sieges of Bergen-op-Zoom in 1622 and Breda in 1624. When hostilities broke out between England and Spain he returned to

England and resumed his favourite pursuit, the study of war, translating Hugo's Latin account of the Siege of Breda into English, and Vincent's *Heraldry* from English into French. In 1630 he returned to Spanish service in the Netherlands as Captain-Commandant of an English regiment, and was commissioned to raise a regiment of his own for the defence of St. Omer in 1638.

When the English Civil War broke out, Gage used his influence to intercept supplies to Parliament from Flanders. In the spring of 1644 he came over to England and was made a member of the military council formed to advise the Governor of Oxford. As Deputy-Governor he infused a new spirit of determination into the garrison. On 12 June he captured Boarstall House, having first made certain that Lady Denham, who owned it, had made her escape 'in private Habit'. And in September, with 800 horse and foot, he relieved Basing House in one of the most remarkable exploits of the whole War. His plan was to march through Parliamentarian country with his men wearing 'Orange Tawny scarfs'. But the advanced guard forgot to wear their Roundhead colours and came in conflict with the enemy at Aldermarston. The main body had therefore to make a forced march by night, the foot riding pillion or taking a turn in the saddle. Reaching Basing 'extreamly surbated and weary'[2] in the early hours of 11 September the Royalist horse drove off the enemy while the foot, advancing from hedge to hedge, at last gained an entry into the House. They captured a colour inscribed with the motto *Non ab Equo sed in Aequo Victoria* which Gage considered more appropriate to his own cause whose justice had given them the victory. Leaving 100 Whitecoats behind, he marched on to Basingstoke whence he sent back to the House quantities of food, arms and ammunition, horses and carts. By the success of this operation he cut the link between London and the wool of the Wiltshire Downs. As the enemy began to rally he decided to withdraw by night, fording the Kennet, since the bridge had been broken, with his musketeers riding en croup. He had lost only 11 men and taken 100 prisoners. In October he commanded a contingent of foot from the garrison of Oxford in the relief of Banbury Castle. Next month Basing was again besieged, but the news that the King from Marlborough and Gage (who had been knighted for his services) were on their way to relieve it, broke up the siege. On Aston's removal from the Governorship of Oxford after his accident, he told the King that Gage, who succeeded him on Christmas Day, was 'the most Jesuited Papist alive'.[3] But Gage, when asked by the King not to display his religion too zealously, replied, with impish satisfaction, that although he did hear Mass every day, he had heard only one sermon and that, when pressed to do so, at the house of Aston's daughter. That might well have been his last, for in an attempt in January to capture Abingdon from the south side over Culham Bridge he was mortally wounded on the 11th. He was buried on the 13th in Christ Church Cathedral where, on a small stone under his monument, are the words *AETERNA PRAEPONE CADUCIS* (prefer things Eternal to things Temporal). His wife, Mary Daniel, two sons and four daughters, survived him. Clarendon, writing of the King's 'wonderful loss' by his death, calls him 'a man of great wisdom and temper, amongst the very few soldiers who made himself universally loved and esteemed'.[4]

NOTES
[1] Edward Walsingham, *Alter Britanniae Heros, or the Life and Death of Sir Henry Gage*, Oxford (1645).
[2] Sir Edward Walker, *Historical Discourses* (1705), pp. 90-5. For full account: Dugdale, *Diary*, ed. W. Hamper (1827), pp. 72-3; *Mercurius Aulicus*, p. 1222.
[3] Clarendon, Bk. VIII, §§ 1665.
[4] *Ibid.*, Bk. VIII, § 166.

SIR THOMAS GLEMHAM
(c. 1595-1649)

Of courage and integrity unquestionable; but he was not of so stirring and active a nature as to be able to infuse fire enough into the phlegmatic constitutions of that people' (of Yorkshire) 'who did rather wish to be spectators of the war than parties in it, and believed if they did not provoke the other party they might all live quietly together.

CLARENDON

HE WAS BORN about 1595, the son of Sir Henry Glemham of Little Glemham, Suffolk, and Anne, daughter of Thomas Sackville, 1st Earl of Dorset. In 1610 he was entered as a commoner at Trinity College, Oxford. James I knighted him on 10 September 1617. In the first two Parliaments of Charles I Sir Thomas was M.P. for Aldburgh. He then took to soldiering and was in the ill-starred Rhé and Rochelle expedition (1627), being taken prisoner in the retreat. He served as a volunteer at the Siege of Bois-le-Duc (1629) and in both Scots Wars, commanding his own regiment in the Second.

When, in August 1642, King Charles moved south from York, he left the Lord Lieutenant, Henry Clifford, 5th Earl of Cumberland, in command, with Glemham as his military adviser, and as Governor of York. But though Glemham showed himself more active than Clarendon would have us believe, he was not remarkably successful in his first operations against the Yorkshire Parliamentarians. When, on 13 October 1642, he led a force to garrison Pontefract Castle, Captain John Hotham obliged him to retreat. Not long after this Cumberland sent Glemham with a party of horse and dragoons to beat up Sir Thomas Fairfax's quarters at Wetherby, which he did with some success. But when, in December, Newcastle came to their relief, the Yorkshire Royalists were practically beleagured in York. It was now that Newcastle appointed Glemham to be Colonel-General of his army. His activities during most of 1643 are obscure. Certain it is that in December he was Commander-in-Chief of the Royalist forces in Cumberland, Westmorland, Northumberland, and the Bishopric of Durham. His Headquarters were at Newcastle, and it fell to him to make the first resistance to the Scots invasion in January 1644.

After the defeat at Marston Moor (2 July) Newcastle departed for the Continent, leaving Glemham in command at York. He was compelled to surrender soon after (16 July), but, so far from abandoning the struggle, made his way to Carlisle. Here he put up a prolonged resistance to the Scots. 'He was', according to Lloyd, 'the first man that taught soldiers to eat cats and dogs',[1] but was eventually forced by starvation to capitulate (28 June 1645). With the remnants of his garrison he joined the King at Cardiff and his foot were given the privilege of marching as the King's Lifeguard.[2] A week later, in Brecknockshire, they were converted to dragoons, no doubt by commandeering the local Welsh cobs.[3] On 2 October he was sent to be Governor of Oxford in place of Colonel Will. Legge.

Glemham took over Oxford on 8 October, and immediately began to prepare for a vigorous defence. About the same time he succeeded Lord Astley as Sergeant-Major-General of the Foot. In the summer of 1646 Oxford was besieged by Sir Thomas Fairfax. By that time the King was in the hands of the Scots. Nevertheless, when the Privy Council ordered Glemham to surrender, he and 24 of his officers made a strong protest.[4] He ultimately surrendered on very good terms on 24 June 1646, it being agreed that he and his garrison should march out with the honours of war.[5] Despite the articles Glemham was imprisoned in the Fleet, but, upon application to Sir Thomas Fairfax, was released by the House of Commons on 21 August 1646. He and his son, Captain Sackville Glemham, compounded for their estates on the Oxford Articles, being fined £951 :15 :0 (25 March 1647). Even so Glemham took the field once more in 1648, assisting Sir Philip Musgrave to capture Carlisle.

It is not certain when he died, but his Will was proved on 13 March 1650. He was the best type of Cavalier officer, experienced and resolute.

NOTES

[1] Lloyd, p. 552, n.

[2] Richard Symonds, *Diary of the Marches of the Royal Army during the Great Civil War*, ed. C. E. Long, Camden Society, Vol. LXXXIV (1859), p. 219 (7 August 1645).

[3] *Ibid.*, p. 223.

[4] Dugdale, *Diary*, p. 88.

[5] Joshua Spriggs, *Anglia Rediviva* (1647), pp. 261-2.

GEORGE, LORD GORING
(1608-1657)

IT WAS HOPED that this wild young son of Lord Goring (later Earl of Norwich) would settle down in Ireland after his marriage in 1629 to Lady Lettice Boyle, daughter of Richard, Earl of Cork. But he soon left her and joined the Dutch service, where he was given a regiment of foot. In 1637 he was wounded in the ankle at the Siege of Breda, and lamed for life. In 1639 he became Governor of Portsmouth. In the two Scots Wars he commanded first a regiment, and then a brigade, under the Earl of Holland. The gross mismanagement of these campaigns led him to intrigue for the post of Lt-General of the North. Failing in this, he headed the Army Plot of 1641, inspired by the Queen during Strafford's trial, to occupy London and seize the Tower. But then, deciding it was too risky, he betrayed both plot and plotters.

At the outbreak of war Parliament thought that Goring was on its side, but he chose to follow the King. He could not, however, hold Portsmouth, blockaded by land and sea, and sailed to Holland. Returning to Yorkshire, he joined Newcastle, who made him General of Horse. In March 1643 he defeated Sir Thomas Fairfax at Seacroft Moor but was captured by him at Wakefield in May and imprisoned in the Tower for nine months. When released, he joined Rupert and in the ensuing Battle of Marston Moor commanded the left wing where the Northern Horse drove Sir Thomas Fairfax's cavalry off the field but, returning in disorder, were themselves scattered by Fairfax and Cromwell. After the battle Goring retreated with Rupert into Lancashire and in August rejoined the main army and succeeded Wilmot, who was dismissed, as General of Horse in the West where Essex's army was surrounded in Lostwithiel. He occupied St Blazey in order to cut Essex off from supplies by sea but was blamed, unfairly, for letting his cavalry escape. Advancing east with the army after Essex's surrender, he drove Waller out of Andover, and at Second Newbury led a gallant charge. In March 1645 Prince Charles came to take command in the West. But Goring became more interested in supplanting Hopton as Lt-General of the Western Army than in prosecuting the Siege of Taunton. From Bath, where he went to take the waters, perhaps because of ill-health, he was ordered to join the Royal

Army about to leave Oxford. At a Council of War at Stow-on-the-Wold, where Rupert's plan to march north and Goring's and Digby's to fight Fairfax on his way to relieve Taunton were bitterly argued, the King tried to please both by sending Goring back to the West and marching north himself. But Goring failed to intercept either Fairfax, or the forces which had in the meantime relieved Taunton. He resumed the siege and, when ordered by Rupert to rejoin him in Leicestershire, replied that he would when Taunton was reduced. Hearing, however, that Fairfax was again approaching, after Naseby, with an army twice the size of his own, he abandoned the siege. But, by a feint towards Taunton, he drew off 4000 of Fairfax's troops to follow him, and then took up a strong position at Langport. Here, on 10 July, he was heavily defeated and retired to Exeter. In November he applied for leave to go to France, and left before receiving an answer. Next year he was given command of the English regiments in the Spanish service and in 1650 went to Spain and was present at the Siege of Barcelona. In 1655 he wrote to Charles II apologizing for his four years' silence and offering his services, but died two years later in Madrid, 25 July 1657.

According to Clarendon he was a master of dissimulation, insatiably ambitious, and loved debauchery more than victory.[1] He may have drunk to drown the pain of his wounds, but his courage, bold leadership, and quickness of decision in the field, and the inspiration he gave to his men, were never in doubt.

NOTES
[1] Clarendon, Bk. VIII, § 169.

P.B.

COLONEL SIR BEVILL GRENVILE
(1596-1643)

'I CANNOT CONTAINE my selfe within my doores when the King of England's standard waves in the field upon so just an occasion, the cause being such as must make all those that dye in it little inferiour to Martyrs.'[1] So wrote Sir Bevill to his friend Sir John Trelawny on the outbreak of the War. He was the son of Sir Bernard Grenvile and Elizabeth Bevill of Kellygarth, Cornwall, and grandson of Sir Richard Grenvile of the *Revenge*. In 1611 he went up to Exeter College, Oxford, where, as he wrote thirty years later to his eldest son, Richard (then at Gloucester Hall, Oxford), 'I was left to my own little discretion and so fell upon the sweet delights of reading poetry and history . . . and troubled no other booke ; and doe finde my selfe so infinitly defective by it . . . as I would give a limbe it were otherwise.'[2] A progressive landowner and lover of learning, he was devoted to his wife, Grace, daughter of Sir George Smith of Maydford in Heavitree, Devonshire, and their family of seven sons and five daughters. He became a staunch friend of Sir John Eliot and, as M.P. for Cornwall and later Launceston, loyally supported him in Parliament and during his long imprisonment in the Tower until his death there in 1632. In 1639 he abandoned the opposition to the King, who knighted him in June, and enthusiastically supported him in the First Scots War.

When the Civil War broke out Grenvile published the King's commission of array in Cornwall, disregarded the Parliamentary order to arrest him, and drove the Roundhead forces out of Launceston. In January 1643, serving under Hopton, he faced Ruthin's army drawn up on Braddock Down. 'After sollemne prayers at the head of every division', he wrote to his wife, before putting off his armour, 'I ledd my part away who followed mee with so gratt courage both downe the one hill and up the other that it strooke a terror in them.'[3] This victory was followed in May, after the unsuccessful Siege of Plymouth which he had opposed, by another victory at Stratton over Stamford. In this Grenvile played a decisive part, throwing in his local reserves to check a counter-attack by General James Chudleigh whom he captured. Stamford fled, leaving 300 dead and 1700 prisoners. In June Grenvile joined Prince Maurice's army which marched into Somerset and in July attacked Waller on Lansdown Hill. Here, Grenvile 'lead up his pike in the midle and gain'd with much gallantry the brow of the hill, receiving all their small shott and cannon from their brest-worke, and three charges of horse, two of which he stood, but in the third fell with many of his men.'[4] He was struck to the ground by a blow from a pole-axe and died the next day, 6 July, at Cold Ashton parsonage, four miles off. In his pocket was found a treasured letter which the King had sent him the previous March. He was buried on 26 July at Kilkhampton. 'Maddam', wrote Trelawny to his widow, 'hee is gone his Journey but a little before us, wee must March after when it shall please God, for your Lady-ship knows that none fall without his Providence which is as great in the thickest showre of Bulletts, as in the Bedd.'[5]

A memorial to Sir Bevill on Lansdown Hill, marking the centre of the position which he so gallantly attacked, was erected by his grandson, Lord Lansdown, who also erected another at Stratton and a third at Kilkhampton. On the south tablet of the Lansdown Hill monument are inscribed Clarendon's words: 'A brighter courage and a gentler disposition were never married together to make the most cheerful and innocent conversation.'[6] In a collection of poems published at Oxford, entitled '*Verses on the death of the right valiant Sir Bevill Grenville Knight*', two lines are often quoted:

'Where shall the next Grenville's ashes stand?
Thy grandsire fills the seas, and thou the land !'

His death was a very great loss to the Royalist cause in the West for he had laid the foundation of all that was done in Cornwall and was himself the ideal leader of men. His two eldest sons had died before the War and his third son, John, was created 1st Earl of Bath.

NOTES
[1] Roger Granville, *History of the Granville Family*, p. 213.
[2] *Ibid.*, p. 224.
[3] *Ibid.*, p. 249.
[4] Sir R. Hopton, *Bellum Civile*, ed. C. E. H. Chadwyck-Healey: Somerset Record Society, Vol. XVIII (1902), p. 95.
[5] *History of the Granville Family*, p. 95.
[6] Clarendon, Bk., VII, § 108.

JAMES HAMILTON, 1st DUKE OF HAMILTON
and 2nd EARL OF CAMBRIDGE
(1606-1649)

JAMES HAMILTON, described as the most disastrous of all the King's friends whom 'opportunity made a fool and accident a villain',[1] was the son of James, 2nd Marquess of Hamilton and Anne Cunningham. One of Charles's pages, he was at the age of fourteen married to Mary Feilding, daughter of Lord Feilding and a Lady of the Bedchamber. He matriculated from Exeter College, Oxford, in 1621 and seven years later succeeded Buckingham as Master of the Horse and was appointed a Privy Councillor. Financed by the King, he led a force of 7000 in 1631 to help the Protestant cause in Germany, but plague and famine incapacitated his army and he returned in 1634. In 1638 he went to Scotland as the King's commissioner to pacify the Scots by promising a temporary suspension of the Prayer Book if they would repudiate the Covenant. Just before he left his wife died suddenly, leaving him with three small sons and two daughters. The Assembly, meeting in Glasgow Cathedral, was so hostile to episcopacy that he dissolved it and the King, on hearing his report in January 1639, resolved on war. In this Hamilton was to command the Fleet with orders to land, at Aberdeen, the 5000 men he embarked at Yarmouth. But this order was countermanded. His role in the Second Scots War was to land troops from Ireland on the west coast of Scotland, a dubious manoeuvre which never materialized and for which, understandably, he had no enthusiasm. With the King's consent he now began to correspond with the Covenanters, thereby arousing suspicion. He was in fact planning an agreement between the King and Argyll on the basis of the King's acceptance of Presbyterianism in return for Scottish help. When the King came to Edinburgh in August 1641 Montrose, whom Argyll had imprisoned for communicating with him, now wrote again offering to prove Hamilton a traitor. 'The Incident', an alleged Royalist plot to kidnap Hamilton and Argyll at Holyrood, cast even more suspicion over the doings of these two noblemen. The King, however, continued to trust Hamilton rather than Montrose who advised him to strike at Argyll while he was still vulnerable. By August 1642 it was too late, for Argyll was in effect the ruler of Scotland. Not until Montrose came to Oxford in 1643 did the King at last heed his words; and by the time Hamilton arrived in December the Scottish Alliance with Parliament had come into effect. He was arrested and sent to Pendennis Castle and later to St. Michael's Mount where he stayed till Fairfax released him in 1646.

He now waited on the King at Newcastle and urged him to accept Presbyterianism if the Scottish Army could secure better terms for him from Parliament. When, however, the Scots 'sold' the King a wave of revulsion swept over the Royalists in Scotland and in March 1648 Hamilton found himself with a majority over Argyll, in the Scottish Parliament, in favour of armed intervention in England. He was appointed commander of the 10,000 men, the 'Engagers', who assembled at Annan on 4 July. Hampered by the divided counsels of his generals, he moved slowly south, his army spread over fifty miles, while Langdale ahead of him had to face Cromwell alone at Preston, and was defeated (17 August 1648). Hamilton marched on south, pursued by Cromwell, but when his exhausted troops mutinied at Uttoxeter on 25 August he surrendered. He was confined in Windsor Castle where, on 23 December, he saw the King on his way to his 'trial'. Cromwell tried to extract, as the price of his life, the names of those Englishmen who had invited him to cross the Border. But he refused to talk. In March he was tried by Bradshaw and, with Capel and Holland, sentenced to death. On his way through Westminster Hall to his execution on 9 March he 'seemed yet to have some hope of a reprieve, and made some stay in the Hall, till the earl of Denbigh came to him; and after a short whisper, in which he found there was no hope, he ascended the scaffold.'[2]

The Parliamentarian editor, Marchamont Nedham, wrote of him

'. . . Rather than he his ends would miss
Betray'd his master with a kiss. . .'[3]

Clarendon wrote that 'his natural darkness and reservation in his discourse made him to be thought a wise man . . . and his continued discourses of battles and fortifications, made him be thought a soldier'[4]— mistakes for which he paid with his life.

NOTES
[1] C. V. Wedgwood, *The King's Peace* (1955) p. 213.
[2] Clarendon, Bk. XI, § 262.
[3] *Digitus Dei* (1649).
[4] Clarendon, *loc. cit.*

JOHN HAMPDEN
(1594-1643)

JOHN HAMPDEN, chosen by Gray in his *Elegy* and Edmund Burke in his *Speech on American Taxation* in 1774, as a champion of liberty, was the son of William Hampden of Great Hampden, Buckinghamshire, and Elizabeth, daughter of Sir Henry Cromwell of Hinchingbrooke and aunt of Oliver Cromwell. He was educated at Thame Grammar School and Magdalen College, Oxford, matriculating in 1610. In 1619 he married Elizabeth Symeon of Pyrton, Oxfordshire, and went to live at Great Hampden. He was M.P. for Wendover in 1625, 1626, and 1628. In 1636 he refused to pay Ship Money, for which he was assessed at 20/- for lands in Stoke Mandeville (though with his other properties this would have been nearer £20). When the case was tried in 1637, seven of the twelve judges decided in favour of the King which, as Clarendon

Ætat 39
1640.

Anglorum Magnanimus BEVILLIVS
GRANVIL Cornubiensis Eques Auratus.

PLATE 34   Colonel Sir Bevill Grenvile

PLATE 35   James Hamilton, 1st Duke of Hamilton and 2nd Earl of Cambridge
Daniel Mytens

PLATE 36   John Hampden   *style of William Dobson*

PLATE 37   Maj. Gen. Thomas Harrison

PLATE 38   Queen Henrietta Maria   *Sir Anthony van Dyck*

William Seymour, 1st Marquess, 2nd Earl of Hereford,
2nd Duke of Somerset   *Engleheart after Sir Anthony van Dyck*

PLATE 40   Henry Rich, Earl of Holland   *after Sir Anthony van Dyck*

says, 'left no man any thing which he might call his own.'[1] As M.P. for Buckinghamshire in the Short Parliament, Hampden was one of the committee to consider Ship Money and the King's alternative demand for twelve subsidies if he were to abandon it, but Vane, the Secretary of State, so bungled the matter that it came to nothing. In the Long Parliament, again sitting for Buckinghamshire, he played an important part as a moderator, unwilling to proceed against Strafford by Act of Attainder, and in favour of the monarchy if it were guided by Parliament. He 'showed a flowing courtesy' to all men and it was his calming words that averted a brawl during the discussion over the Grand Remonstrance. As one of the four commissioners attending the King on his visit to Scotland in 1641, he learned of his intrigues with the Scottish nobility. This, and the attempt to arrest the Five Members (of whom he was one) in January 1642, brought an end to his moderation.

Hampden was on the Committee of Safety formed in July, and promised to raise a regiment of foot for Parliament. Known as the Greencoats, this was to become one of the best of the Parliamentarian regiments, perhaps as a result of that recorded conversation between Hampden and Cromwell on the necessity to recruit 'such men as had the fear of God before them.'[2] He was escorting artillery from Worcester at the time of Edgehill, but fought at Brentford and pressed Essex, in vain, to follow up the Royalist retreat. During the winter of 1642-3 he was a 'hawk' among the 'doves' who were anxious for peace, even on unsatisfactory terms. As Clarendon says, 'when he first drew his sword he threw away the scabbard.'[3] He took part in the Siege of Reading and after its capture counselled a direct attack on the King's Headquarters at Oxford. Essex got as far as Thame where Rupert surprised him and scattered his forces. Reorganized by Sir Philip Stapylton, they tried to cut off Rupert's retreat, but he turned and routed them on Chalgrove Field (18 June). Here Hampden, not waiting for his own regiment to arrive, fought with the cavalry and was mortally wounded. He rode off the field, to die six days later in Thame. He was buried in Great Hampden church where, in 1714, a monument depicting the battle and a genealogical tree was erected. When Lord Nugent came to write his *Memorials* (published in 1832) he found himself confronted by a legend that Hampden had not been wounded by a bullet in the shoulder, but had had his hand shattered by an overloaded pistol. 'To remove all doubts' Hampden's body was exhumed and both arms amputated. Further examination favoured the pistol theory, but when it transpired that the body might not after all have been Hampden's, Nugent suppressed the story.

Hampden's first wife bore him nine children of whom John, the eldest, died during the War as a captain in his regiment. His second wife, Letitia, daughter of Sir Francis Knollys, survived him. He was 'possessed with . . . the most absolute facilities to govern the people of any man I ever knew',[4] wrote Clarendon, and all historians agree that his death was an irreparable loss not only to the Parliamentarian Army but also to the nation.

NOTES
1 Clarendon, Bk., I, § 150.
2 Thomas Carlyle, *Oliver Cromwell's Letters and Speeches*, ed. S. C. Lomas (1904), Speech XI, p. 114.
3 Clarendon, Bk. VII, § 84.
4 *Ibid.*, § 83.

MAJOR-GENERAL THOMAS HARRISON
(1606-1660)

THOMAS HARRISON, the son of a butcher or grazier of Newcastle-under-Lyme, was well educated and became clerk to an attorney in Lincoln's Inn. In 1642 he enlisted in Essex's Lifeguards and fought as a major at Marston Moor, being dispatched after the battle to report the glorious victory in London, a sure sign that he had distinguished himself. He fought at Naseby, and Langport after which battle he poured forth rapturous praises to God, and took part in the capture of Winchester and the Siege of Oxford. As a colonel at the storming of Basing House he is said to have slain in cold blood Major Robinson, an ex-Drury Lane comedian, crying 'Cursed be he that doeth the Lord's work negligently.'[1] He was M.P. for Wendover in 1646 and next year, on 11 November, his demand that the King, as 'a man of blood', should be prosecuted caused Cromwell to warn Whalley at Hampton Court of a rumoured Levellers' Plot to seize the King, who escaped, probably with Whalley's connivance, that night. Harrison, with his mutinous regiment which paraded three days later on Corkbush Field, Ware, with copies of *The Agreement of the People* stuck in their hats, now joined Lambert in the North. He was wounded in August 1648 at Appleby, capturing a colour single-handed from a cornet of Langdale's horse.

Still determined to secure the King, with three other colonels Harrison wrote to Hammond at Carisbrooke in November, adjuring him to prevent Charles's escape by all means in his power. *Mercurius Pragmaticus*[2] was already reporting libellous rumours of Hammond's instructions from the Army 'to make away with the King by poyson or otherwise' and Harrison's subsequent arrival at Hurst Castle to escort him to Windsor, confirmed Charles's worst fears. He was reassured only by Harrison's soldierly bearing and honest look. But he still entertained hopes of escape, for 'the fleetest horse in England'[3] stood in Lord Newburgh's stables at Bagshot where they were to dine. But the horse was lame and the King, noting the well-armed, well-mounted escort, which Harrison made a point of showing him, gave up the idea. Harrison was one of the committee of five to draw up the King's sentence, and the seventeenth to sign the death warrant. During Cromwell's absence in Scotland in 1650 he was Commander-in-Chief of forces in England, but failed next year at Knutsford to check Charles II's march south. He fought at Worcester and followed up the fugitives so vigorously that few escaped. At the conference to settle the kingdom, Cromwell complained that 'he will not wait for the Lord's leisure but hurries me on to that which he and all honest men will have cause to repent.'[4] He was co-opted a member of Barebones Parliament, but with its extinction his political career ended. Next year he was deprived of his commission and, for his relations with the Anabaptists, imprisoned in Carisbrooke for a year till 1656, when he was allowed to live with his family in Highgate. On suspicion of being implicated in a dangerous plot in 1658 he was sent to the Tower. At the Restoration Harrison refused to take refuge in flight. As a fanatical Fifth Monarchy man he had firmly believed in the millenial rule of the Saints on earth and abhorred Cromwell's government. At his trial on 11 October 1660 he defended the execution of the King as the shedder of his people's blood, and said of himself 'I followed not my own judgment; I did what I did, as out of conscience to the Lord . . . Maybe I might be a little mistaken, but I did it all according to the best of my understanding.' At his execution on 13 October at Charing Cross, 'looking as cheerful as any one could do in that condition',[5] he told the onlookers that the trembling of his hands and knees, which he had suffered from for 12 years, was 'by reason of much blood I have lost in the wars.' To a scoffer who shouted 'Where is your Good Old Cause now?', he replied, clapping his hands to his breast, 'Here in my bosom, and I shall seal it with my blood.'[6] Of such stuff were the true old Ironsides made.

NOTES
1 James Wright, *Historia Histrionica* (1699).
2 *Mercurius Pragmaticus*, 24 and 25 September 1648.
3 S. R. Gardiner, *History of the Great Civil War*, Vol. III (1893), p. 549.
4 Edmund Ludlow, *Memoirs*, ed. C. H. Firth, Vol. I (1894), p. 171.
5 Pepys, *Diary*, 13 October 1660.
6 *State Trials: Trial of Charles I and some of the Regicides*, pp. 291, 333, 331.

QUEEN HENRIETTA MARIA
(1609-1669)

FEW QUEENS HAVE experienced greater contrasts of fortune than Henrietta Maria, consort of Charles I. 'The happiest woman in the world' of her husband's period of personal rule, she sank to 'la reine malheureuse' of her tragic widowhood.

The youngest child of Henry IV of France and his second wife, Marie de Medicis, Henrietta was an infant when her father was assassinated, but she took pride in being his daughter and in emulating his courage. Brought up by her possessive and intriguing mother, she was indifferently educated. On her arrival here in 1625, the 15 years-old bride was singularly ill-equipped for her difficult position, not least by her ignorance of English, which she was slow to learn. As a 'Papist', an object of aversion to the Puritans, the young Queen was on the defensive for her persecuted religion, which she sought to propagate and which her French suite encouraged her to flaunt. Their mischievous influence and the King's infatuation for Buckingham together nearly wrecked the marriage. The dismissal of the bulk of her attendants and the murder of Buckingham saved it. Thenceforward the mutual devotion of this Royal couple was renowned.

Secure in the love of an indulgent husband and finding fulfilment in her growing family, Henrietta, naturally vivacious, blossomed into a charming if not strictly speaking beautiful mistress of the cultured Stuart Court. Her fondness for masques and plays increased her unpopularity with the Puritans. With the Scottish revolt the Queen began to concern herself with politics.

Henrietta's influence over Charles, although never allowed to shake his religious principles, was profound and it was constantly exercised, seldom wisely, in favour of bold and resolute courses. Nor did she confine herself to exhortations. In February 1642, when civil war loomed ahead, she crossed to Holland in order to sell jewels and buy arms and ammunition for the Royal cause. A year later she landed at Bridlington, where, undaunted after a hazardous voyage, she unflinchingly encountered inaccurate bombardment by the rebellious Fleet. After a long stay at York, Henrietta marched south to join the King, a gallant 'generalissima' commanding sizeable reinforcements. She entered Oxford in triumph.

What the elements and the enemy could not accomplish, sickness achieved. An inopportune ninth pregnancy, productive of intense suffering, broke Henrietta's spirit. In April 1644 the King and Queen parted, never to meet again : in June a daughter was born at Exeter. Under threat of enemy attack, Henrietta managed to reach Falmouth and sail for France in the teeth of a storm and cannonading by hostile craft : she always had bad luck at sea.

For sixteen years she was an exile in her native land, subsisting on charity as a poor relation at the French Court. During the Fronde she endured bitter privations which coincided with the arrival of the terrible news of Charles's decapitation, a crushing blow. His wife had corresponded with him as long as possible. Her letters, in the main a consolation, had at times aggravated the King's distresses, as when she repeatedly urged him to accept the abolition of episcopacy. Such small comfort as Henrietta knew after January 1649 was derived from two sources : the companionship of her youngest daughter, also named Henrietta, smuggled over to France in 1646, whom she reared in her own faith : and the foundation of a Visitation convent at Chaillot. With her sons, all three of whom found temporary asylum in France, she proved difficult. Towards the boy Duke of Gloucester, who withstood her efforts to convert him, she displayed positive cruelty, born of her increasing religious intolerance.

In 1660 Henrietta returned briefly to England, with its poignant associations. She paid her last visit here from 1662 to 1665; a back number at the Restoration Court and a victim of our climate. She died at Colombes 31 August 1669.

WILLIAM SEYMOUR, 1st MARQUESS, 2nd EARL OF HERTFORD, 2nd DUKE OF SOMERSET
(1587-1660)

WILLIAM'S CAREER BEGINS with a romantic yet tragic tale. As the son of Edward Seymour, Lord Beauchamp, and Honora, daughter of Sir Richard Rogers, he was in the Suffolk line of succession to the throne. It was his tragedy that another possible claimant to the throne, Arbella Stuart, although twelve years his senior, formed an attachment for him, probably before he went up to Magdalen College, Oxford, in 1605. They plighted their troth at Woodstock

87

in February 1610, and were secretly married at Greenwich in June, but without the King's consent. James I was so much alarmed by this union, for Arbella was his first cousin, a niece of Lord Darnley, and often considered by Elizabeth as her possible successor if she was not satisfied with James's conduct, that he ordered her to be confined in Lambeth and sent William to the Tower. Arbella escaped from Barnet, whither she had been moved, and rode in man's attire thirteen miles to the Thames where she took ship for Calais. William also escaped, disguised as his own barber, missed Arbella's ship, boarded a collier, and sailed after her. But contrary winds landed him at Ostend and he went on to Bruges to await tidings. In the meantime Arbella had been captured by an English frigate just off Calais, and was taken back and put in the Tower where, five years later, she died of grief. William remained abroad until 1616 when he made his peace with the King, and in 1617 he married Frances Devereux, daughter of the 2nd Earl of Essex.

In 1621 William succeeded his grandfather as Earl of Hertford. In 1640 he was made a Privy Councillor and next year was created Marquess of Hertford. In 1642 he joined King Charles at York with the Prince of Wales, whose governorship he took over from Newcastle, and was appointed commissioner of array and Lt-General of the Western counties. Raising 2000 men in Wales, he drove Stamford out of Hereford and joined Prince Maurice and Hopton at Chard. He was with Hopton when he beat Waller at Lansdown. After Rupert stormed Bristol three weeks later, he asserted his authority by appointing Hopton Governor of the city. But Rupert had already asked the King for this appointment. Hopton tactfully agreed to serve as Rupert's deputy and Hertford, who loved his ease, retired from command in the field to be one of the King's advisers in Oxford and a Gentleman of the Bedchamber. At Uxbridge, as one of the Royal Commissioners, he favoured the peace overtures made by the Scots and Essex, his brother-in-law, which were unacceptable to the King. On the surrender of Oxford in 1646 he compounded and went home, but attended a Council at Hampton Court when the King was a prisoner there. He was with him in the Isle of Wight and was one of his Commissioners at the Treaty of Newport. During the King's 'trial' he and three other peers – Richmond, Southampton, and Lindsey – offered themselves and their estates to Parliament if it would free the King and acknowledge his Royal title. All they were granted was permission to bury him in St. George's Chapel, Windsor, and each held one corner of the black velvet pall as they crossed in the snow from the Deanery to the chapel.

In 1660 Hertford welcomed Charles II at Dover and next day received from him the Garter at Canterbury. Charles also revived for him the Dukedom of Somerset and Barony of Seymour. But the new Duke did not live long to enjoy his new honours. He died 24 October and was buried at Bedwyn Magna, near Marlborough, leaving by his second wife two daughters and one son, John; the elder son, Henry, predeceased him. From the adventurous young lover caught up in the dynastic web he matured into the scholarly 'grandee', universally esteemed and living 'in great splendour'. Despite 'hard measures from the court' in both reigns and 'notwithstanding all his allies and those with whom he had the greatest familiarity and friendship were of the opposite party',[1] he was 'steady for the King' who trusted him as much as 'any man in the three kingdoms.'

NOTES
[1] Clarendon, Bk. IV, § 294.

HENRY RICH, EARL OF HOLLAND
(1590-1649)

HENRY RICH successively enjoyed the favour of James I, Charles I, and last, but by no means least, of Henrietta Maria. His father was Robert Rich, 1st Earl of Warwick, and his mother Penelope Devereux, immortalised as 'Stella' by Sir Philip Sidney. He matriculated from the puritanical Emmanuel College, Cambridge, in 1603 and later served as a volunteer at the Siege of Juliers. After his marriage to Isabel, daughter and heiress of Sir Walter Cope, they lived in the house which her father had built in Kensington. In 1623 Rich was created Baron Kensington and next year was sent to France to negotiate a marriage between Prince Charles and Henrietta Maria, whom he charmed, as he did all women, thereby gaining a somewhat unenviable reputation. He was now created Earl of Holland and a Knight of the Garter. In 1627 he took command of the fleet and army sent to reinforce Buckingham on the Isle of Rhé but sailed too late, for which delay he was, unjustifiably, blamed. After Buckingham's assassination in 1628 he succeeded him as Chancellor of Cambridge University. In 1630 he became the first Governor of the Providence Company, a puritanical venture designed to prey on Spanish ships in the Caribbean. Because of his intrigues at Court against the pro-Spanish Lord Portland he was temporarily arrested. In 1636, through the Queen's influence, Holland was appointed General of the Horse instead of the more capable Essex, and exhibited his incompetence at Kelso in the First Scots War. During these years he was adding sumptuously to his Kensington home with money borrowed from the wealthy Sir Arthur Ingram, whose daughter Elizabeth became his second wife in 1641.

Next year, although Groom of the Stole, Holland refused to accompany the King to York and thereby forfeited the Queen's patronage and was deprived of this office. In July he carried the declarations of Parliament to the King who, not unnaturally, received him coldly. After Edgehill he exhorted the citizens of London to defend it against a Royalist attack. He became one of the leaders of the peace party in the Lords but, discouraged by Essex in August 1643, joined the King at the Siege of Gloucester and fought bravely for him at First Newbury. But when Hertford was made a Gentleman of the Bedchamber instead of him he re-embraced the Parliamentary cause and had the effrontery to claim compensation for the pecuniary losses he had sustained by leaving the King's service. But he turned Royalist once again when a proposal to give him a pension of £1000 was rejected, and tried to mediate between the Scots Commissioners and the English Presbyterians, suggesting that the King should take refuge with the Scots Army. In the Second Civil War he rose in arms for the King and, as Commander-in-Chief, took the field at Kingston on 5 July 1648, intending to relieve Colchester. But, defeated at Reigate, he rode by hidden ways with 300 horse to St. Neots where he was cornered in the archway of an inn, cut off by the river from escape. He surrendered on condition that his life be spared, and was sent to Warwick Castle. Although Parliament agreed to banish him, the Army insisted on bringing him to trial in February 1649. Despite intercessions by Fairfax and Warwick, his elder brother, he was condemned to death by thirty-one to thirty votes. On 9 March he, Capel, and Hamilton were taken to a room off Westminster Hall where they had to wait for an hour till their execution in Old Palace Yard. Holland, who went second, drank a little wine, while Capel, the last to go, smoked his pipe. Holland left a son, Robert, who became the 5th Earl of Warwick (1673), and four daughters.

In Clarendon's view 'he took more care to be thought a good friend to parliament, than a good servant to his master' and 'too much desired to enjoy ease and plenty when the King could have neither, and did think poverty the most insupportable evil that could befall any man in this world.'[1] At least he did not lack courage. Unhappily the glories of Holland House, destroyed in the blitz of 1940, no longer survive to redeem his memory.

NOTES

[1] Clarendon, Bk. XI § 263.

DENZIL, 1st LORD HOLLES OF IFIELD
(1599-1680)

DENZIL HOLLES was one of the Five Members whose attempted arrest in January 1642 precipitated the Civil War. The second son of John, 1st Earl of Clare, after matriculating from Christ's College, Cambridge, in 1613 and going to Gray's Inn, he sat for St. Michael, Cornwall, in 1624, for Dorchester in 1628 and again in the Short and Long Parliaments. It was he who, when in 1628 the Speaker was about to adjourn the House on the King's command, held him down in his chair 'till we please to rise', for which he was fined 1000 marks and imprisoned. He escaped and lived in banishment for seven or eight years. When Strafford, his brother-in-law, was on trial, he sought in vain to save his life by trying to get the King to abolish episcopacy if Parliament dropped the attainder. In the House he opposed Buckingham's foreign policy, invoked aid for the Elector Palatine, supported the Root and Branch Bill, the Grand Remonstrance, and Parliamentary control of the militia. On the outbreak of war he raised a regiment of foot who wore red coats and fought well at Edgehill, where he held them together when the fleeing Parliamentarian horse rode over them. But the regiment was cut up at Brentford and never recovered.

Thereafter Holles led the peace party in the House and was one of the Parliamentarian Commissioners sent to Oxford in November 1644 to propose a treaty with the King, who privately consulted him and Whitelocke on the best means of ending the War. In December Holles, with Essex and other leaders of the peace party, discussed with the Scottish Commissioners the Scottish proposals to accuse Cromwell (whom he detested and whose conduct at Marston Moor he strongly criticized in his *Memoirs*)[1] of being an incendiary between the two nations. But there was insufficient evidence. Holles himself was now accused by Lord Savile for his part in this, and earlier, negotiations in which he had worked for an alliance between the King and the Scots against the Army, to further which he had proposed that six regiments should be diverted to Ireland to crush the rebellion. He was also held responsible for the declaration of 1647 which stigmatized as enemies of the State all Army petitioners. This drew some 'rude expressions'[2] from Ireton in the House which fired Holles to challenge him to a duel and, when he declined, to tweak his nose – the nose of 'the third person of the army, and a man of the most virulent . . . nature of all the pack.'[3] Not surprisingly Holles and ten other M.P.s were now impeached for corresponding with the Queen and inviting a Scottish invasion. But the *Full Vindication* which they published reprieved them, and Holles found himself on a new Committee of Safety. When, however, the Army marched into London in August he fled to Normandy and was disabled. Allowed to return next year (1648), he was one of the Commissioners sent to negotiate the Treaty of Newport, and pleaded with the King to accept Presbyterianism for a period. Threatened with arrest on his return, he once more escaped to France.

At the Restoration Holles was made a Privy Councillor and created Baron Holles of Ifield (1661). From 1663 to 1666 he was English ambassador in Paris and negotiated the Treaty of Breda with Holland (1667). Later, in Parliament, he opposed Clarendon's banishment, the Test Act, the Exclusion Bill, and the King's foreign policy. He died 17 February 1680 and was buried in St. Peter's church, Dorchester. He had three wives: Dorothy, daughter of Sir Francis Ashley, who bore him one son, Francis; Jane, daughter of Sir John Shirley; and Esther, daughter of Gideon le Lou. Bishop Burnet sums him up as 'a man of great courage and of as great pride. . . . He had the soul of a stubborn old Roman in him.'

NOTES
[1] *Memoirs of Denzil, Lord Holles* (1641-8) (1699).
[2] Clarendon, Bk. X, § 104.
[3] *Ibid.*

93

RALPH, LORD HOPTON
(1598 - 1652)

'I WILL STRIVE to Serve my Soveraigne King', the motto on Hopton's banner, characterized his devoted career. The son of Robert Hopton of Witham, Somerset, he went up to Lincoln College, Oxford, about 1616 and by 1620 he was fighting in Bohemia. After the Elector's defeat at The White Mountain in November he escorted the pregnant Queen-Electress on her perilous seven-days flight from Prague to Breslau and, when the roads became impassable, took her pillion behind him. In 1623 he married Elizabeth Lewyn, the widowed daughter of Sir Arthur Capel, and next year was ordered by the Privy Council to embark 250 foot at Dover, as Lt-Colonel of Sir Charles Rich's Regiment, for use in Mansfeld's service. But political pressure was brought on him to join the Fleet in another attack on Cadiz. In the end he did neither, and was created a K.B. on Charles I's coronation in 1626, having been M.P. for Bath in his first Parliament. He was M.P. for Wells in 1628-9, for Somerset in the Short Parliament, and for Wells again in the Long Parliament in which he voted for the attainder of Strafford. In 1642 he became Hertford's second-in-command in the West and raised an army in Cornwall. In December he crossed the Tamar and tried to blockade Plymouth, but with insufficient forces. General Ruthin, the Parliamentarian commander, followed him back into Cornwall but on 19 January 1643 Hopton routed him at Braddock Down, taking 1250 prisoners and all his guns, baggage and ammunition. In April 1643 Chudleigh drove him off Sourton Down and in May crossed the Tamar and advanced to Stratton. But here Hopton, though heavily outnumbered, defeated him and marched on to join Prince Maurice's army at Chard. The day after an indecisive battle at Lansdown (5 July) with Waller, his old comrade-in-arms in Bohemia, he was severely burnt when an ammunition wagon blew up beside him. He was carried into Devizes and from his bed directed the defence of the town till Wilmot and Maurice beat Waller at Roundway Down (13 July) and raised the siege. When Rupert captured Bristol three weeks later Hertford named Hopton its Governor, an appointment which Rupert challenged, desiring it for himself. Hopton

94

offered to be Deputy-Governor under Rupert, and was recompensed by being created Lord Hopton of Stratton.

In December 1643 he took Arundel Castle. The Earl of Forth now joined him and, as his senior officer, must take the responsibility for their defeat by Waller at Cheriton (29 March 1644). In August the King appointed Hopton General of the Ordnance, one of the Prince of Wales's councillors, and Lt-General of the Western Army. Goring intrigued to obtain this post for himself, and his refusal to obey the Council's orders made effective control of the army impossible. On Goring's departure for France in November Hopton was left with a dissolute army which was defeated by Fairfax at Torrington. His troops refused to stand again at Bodmin and in March 1646 he had to surrender at Truro. The final blow came with the death of his wife who had often accompanied him on his campaigns. He now went with the Prince to Scilly, then to Jersey, and on to France. In July 1648 he sailed with young Charles from Holland with part of the Royalist Fleet to attempt a landing in England. This proved impossible, but next year he cruised with twenty ships off the Cornish coast, summoning the gentlemen of Cornwall to acknowledge Charles II. During the negotiations over the Scottish Alliance at Breda in April 1650 he was excluded from the Council for opposing Charles's surrender to Presbyterian demands, and when Charles sailed for Scotland in June Hopton retired to Wesel, feeling that he could do no more. After Charles's defeat at Worcester he contemplated returning to England and compounding but, being one of those excepted from pardon, decided not to do so. War wounds and six years of lonely exile had weakened him and on 8 October 1652 he died in Bruges 'of an ague, in whom all honest and well affected men had a loss, but none so great as the King.'[1] His body was carried to Helvoetsluys and remained there till it was brought home and buried at Witham.

A firm disciplinarian, Hopton paid his troops as regularly as he could, shared their hardships, and won and held their confidence. To Prince Charles, as a loyal adviser, he spoke his mind freely, in conformity with his Anglican principles. He had the rare distinction of being respected alike by friend and foe.

NOTES

1 Nicholas to Hatton, from The Hague, 8/18 January 1652: *The Nicholas Papers*, ed. Sir G. F. Warner, Vol. I (1886), p. 284: Camden Society.

SIR JOHN HOTHAM, BART.

(c. 1585-1645)

SIR JOHN HAD the dubious distinction of being declared a traitor by both King and Parliament, which fits in with the comment that he made enemies as easily as he made friends. Knighted by James I at York in 1617, like many other adventurous young men he joined Mansfeld's expedition to rescue the Protestant King Frederick and Queen Elizabeth of Bohemia (the beautiful 'Queen of Hearts') from the invading forces of the Catholic Emperor, and fought at the Battle of The White Mountain in 1620. Created a baronet in 1622, he was M.P. for Beverley in all Charles I's Parliaments, became Governor of Hull in 1628 and High Sheriff for Yorkshire in 1635. In this office he was zealous in levying Ship Money until, taking offence at the King's appointment of Legge instead of himself as military commander in Hull in 1639, he desisted. For this Wentworth took him to task, as did the King for joining in the petition against billeting soldiers in Yorkshire, and he and Henry Belasyse were sent to the Fleet in 1640 for their 'undutiful speeches'. Hotham's animosity towards Strafford (as Wentworth had become) was such that he gave evidence against him at his trial.

Hull, as a port and magazine, was vital to both sides in 1642 and Parliament ordered Hotham to secure it. His son, Captain John Hotham (q.v.), was sent down to do so, and when the King came to Hull in April Sir John refused him entry. However Digby,

PLATE 41   Denzil, 1st Earl Holles of Ifield

PLATE 43   Sir John Hotham, Bart. 1638

ft PLATE 42   Ralph, Lord Hopton   *School of Daniel Mytens*

PLATE 44   Sir John Hotham, Bart. 1645   *probably Thomas Simon*
Silver medallion struck after his execution.

PLATE 45   Colonel John Hutchinson   *Robert Walker*

PLATE 46   Henry Ireton   *attributed to Robert Walker after*
                                             Samuel Cooper and Sir Anthony van Dyck

PLATE 47   William Juxon, Archbishop of Canterbury c. 1640

PLATE 48   Maj. Gen. John Lambert   *after Robert Walker*

returning from a secret visit to the King at York in June, was captured in the Humber and brought before Hotham whom he persuaded to surrender Hull to the King if only a shot were fired 'to cover the betrayal.' But by the time the Royal Army did come in July Hotham had changed his mind. When, however, Newcastle was at Bridlington with the Queen, who had landed there with arms and ammunition from the Continent, he intimated through his son, ostensibly discussing the exchange of prisoners, that he might still be persuaded to surrender Hull in return for certain honours, specified as a viscountcy for himself, a barony for his son, and £20,000; and admitted in one letter to Newcastle 'I . . . doe intend to serve His Majesty but I cannot doe it so unseasonably as to make my soe doing of noe advantage to him and a dishonour to myselfe.'[1]

Suspicion first fell on young Hotham who, on 12 June 1643, was arrested at Nottingham. He escaped to Lincoln, and thence to

97

Hull where he was re-arrested. His father, hearing of this, slipped out of the town and galloped towards Scorborough, his fortified home, but could not cross the River Hull as the boat was on the far side and the ferryman refused to bring it over at low tide. He rode on to Beverley, where he was caught. But, wrenching the reins from his captor, he spurred on till finally struck down with the butt of a musket. He was taken back to Hull and put aboard the *Hercules* with his son. They were transported to the Tower and imprisoned there without trial till November 1644 when their correspondence with Newcastle, captured after Marston Moor, provided more than enough evidence. The court-martial took place in the Guildhall, with Sir William Waller as President. Hotham's main defence was that his pretended offers to surrender Hull had been made in order to gain time to strengthen the defences, a stratagem which he had learned while serving under Mansfeld. More damning was his sudden flight from Hull, and a letter he wrote to his son at Lincoln, praising his escape from 'those villanes' and hinting at 'the greate game' they had now to play. But his chances of acquittal were slim, and he was sentenced to die on 7 December, a date altered three times until 2 January was fixed. A final attempt to get a reprieve from Parliament, for which he waited several hours on the scaffold, failed. He was buried, with his son, in All Hallows, Barking. He had five wives and three sons: Katherine Rodes, the mother of John; Anne Rokeby; Frances Legard; Catherine Hamborough; and Sarah Anlaby. 'He was but one half for Parliament, and manly for the defence of the liberty of the subject,' wrote Sir Henry Slingsby, 'but was not at all for their new opinions in church government.'[2] Although with tactful handling he would probably have conformed to the King's pleasure, he would, to say the least, have been a doubtful ally.

NOTES

[1] B. N. Reckitt, *Charles the First and Hull* (1952). p. 74: Hotham MSS. 22 March 1642/3.

[2] Slingsby, p. 92.

LIEUTENANT-GENERAL JOHN HOTHAM
(d. 1645)

FEW FATHERS AND sons have been executed on consecutive days, yet this was the tragic, if well-deserved, fate of the Hothams. John's mother, the first of Sir John's five wives, was Katherine, daughter of Sir John Rodes of Barlborough, Derbyshire. He himself had three wives: Frances, daughter of Sir John Wray of Glentworth; Margaret, daughter of Thomas, Viscount Fairfax of Emley; and Isabel, daughter of Sir Henry Anderson of Long Gowton, Yorkshire. After serving in the Netherlands he became M.P. for Scarborough in 1640. On his father's appointment to the Governorship of Hull in January 1642 Parliament sent him down with £2000 for the garrison and instructions that all overtures from the King should be rejected. On receiving these orders he sprang to his feet and cried 'Mr Speaker, fall back, fall edge, I will go down and perform your commands.'[1] But the Mayor of Hull at first would not open the gates, and when Hotham was finally admitted the citizens refused his men billets and they had to camp out in wintry weather in the streets. Not till he had made his peace with the Mayor were they allowed indoors. Hotham 'was a very vigilant soulgier', wrote Slingsby, 'and often in the night would march 16 miles to take a delinquent out of his bed.'[2] In December he occupied Doncaster, and seized Cawood Castle from which Archbishop Williams, whose head he had threatened to cut off, had escaped a few hours earlier. He next helped Lord Fairfax to occupy Leeds and blockaded York until sent north to check Newcastle's advance. But, heavily outnumbered at Pierce Bridge, he had to make a fighting retreat in order to rejoin Fairfax at Tadcaster. In January 1643 Lord Fairfax made him Lt-General of Horse under his son, Sir Thomas, which Hotham took as an insult and behaved so insubordinately that Sir Thomas complained to his father 'No order will be obeyed by him but what he pleases, unless some order be to restrain him.'[3] In February he went to Bridlington to discuss with Newcastle the exchange of prisoners, and was presented to the Queen. He, and his father, had been corresponding with Newcastle since December, protesting their loyalty and readiness to change sides at some favourable opportunity. The terms on which they were prepared to do this are said to have included a barony for himself, and £20,000.[4] Hotham, in one letter, perhaps to ingratiate himself with Newcastle, somewhat tactlessly warned him of current Court gossip that he was 'a sweet General, lay in bed until eleven a clock and could till 12, then came to see the Queene and so the worke was done.'[5]

In April 1643 Hotham was routed at Ancaster Heath by Charles Cavendish and moved on to Nottingham where the plundering of his troops and the secret correspondence which he was carrying on with the Queen's forces in Newark, roused Cromwell to report him to Parliament. He was promptly arrested and lodged in Nottingham Castle whence he smuggled out a verbal message to the Queen promising her Hull and Lincoln when he had escaped. This he did from the escort taking him up to London and, collecting fifty troopers, rode to Lincoln and then on to Hull. In the early hours of 29 June, however, the day after his arrival, his house was surrounded and he was re-arrested. There was found in his room a letter which he had just written to Newcastle announcing his freedom and willingness to serve him. He and his father were now taken by sea to the Tower where they remained till their trial in 1644. On 9 December, two days after his father had been sentenced to death, he was court-martialled and received a like sentence. He was executed on 1 January. His brother, Durand, who had conducted his defence, was with him on the scaffold, and laid his head in the coffin. Father and son were buried in All Hallows, Barking. The baronetcy passed to Hotham's eldest son, John, who in Parliament supported the Test Act and Exclusion Bill. For this he once apologized to the Duke of York who roundly rebuked him, reminding him of the fate of his father and grandfather. To which young Sir John replied that he never recalled it without remembering at the same time the fate of the Duke's father.

NOTES
1 Rushworth, Vol. IV, p. 486.
2 Slingsby, p. 79.
3 *Fairfax Correspondence*, ed. R. Bell, Vol. III (1849) p. 36.
4 *Calendar of Clarendon State Papers*, Vol. II, p. 183.
5 The Hull Calendar, p. 308. Contemporary copies of 17 of these letters (December 1642–April 1643) are preserved at Dalton Hall, Yorkshire.

COLONEL JOHN HUTCHINSON
(1615-1664)

JOHN HUTCHINSON is best known from the *Memoirs* written by his wife after his death, for their eight children, four sons and four daughters. 'He stands out from her canvas,' wrote J. R. Green, 'with the grace and tenderness of a portrait by Van Dyck.' He was the eldest son of Sir Thomas Hutchinson of Owthorpe, Nottinghamshire, and Margaret, daughter of Sir John Byron of Newstead, and was educated at Lincoln Free School and Peterhouse, Cambridge. He entered Lincoln's Inn in 1637 but preferred playing his viol to studying the law. In 1638, after a romantic courtship, he married Lucy, daughter of Sir Allen Apsley, Lieutenant of the Tower. Next year she bore him twin sons, but their domestic bliss was disrupted when, in 1642, Lord Newark, the Lord Lieutenant of Nottinghamshire, came to seize the powder-magazine of the county Trained Bands which Hutchinson refused to hand over. He was now commissioned Lt-Colonel of Colonel Francis Pierrepoint's Regiment of Foot. Among the forces concentrated around Nottingham in May 1643 to check Newcastle's advance south, was that of young Hotham, whose 'rude Yorkshiremen' so pillaged the countryside that Hutchinson and Cromwell complained to Parliament and Hotham was arrested. In June Hutchinson was appointed Governor of Nottingham Castle and next month was commissioned by Lord Fairfax to raise a regiment of foot. To an offer from his cousin Sir Richard Byron of £10,000 if he would surrender the castle he replied that it would have been more seemly if he had come with 10,000 armed men to assault it. In January 1644 Sir Charles Lucas with a force from Newark ploughed through waist-deep snow to enter Nottingham, and tried to fire the town but they were driven back, leaving a trail of blood in the snow. Meldrum, besieging Newark next month and, plagued with jealous commanders who 'knew not how to obey orders,'[1] welcomed Hutchinson's visits to his leaguer. But Hutchinson had his own troubles with the County Committee in Nottingham whose mutinous intrigues compelled him to appeal to the Committee of Both Kingdoms, and later relate to the House what was going on in Nottingham. His enemies were confounded, and he returned in time to retake the fort and bridges lost during his absence. Early in 1646 he led a successful assault on Shelford Manor, outside Newark, and remained in the leaguer for the rest of that bitter winter. During this time he was elected M.P. for Nottinghamshire. Soon after his return to Nottingham his wife bore another child whom, after consulting the Scriptures, Anabaptist treatises, and all the local ministers, they decided not to have baptized.

Nominated one of the Commissioners to 'try' the King, Hutchinson was the thirteenth to sign the death warrant. Later in 1649 Cromwell, mistrusting Overton as Governor of Hull, offered Hutchinson the post, but he refused it; and when Cromwell dissolved the Rump, he retired to Owthorpe. Back in London in 1658 he learned of a plot to throw Cromwell, while he was reading a petition, out of a window in Whitehall overlooking the river, and then, if he had not broken his neck, to carry him off in a boat and 'sett up Lambert.' Hutchinson warned Fleetwood but, when summoned by Cromwell, refused to name the conspirators, and told him that 'he liked not any of his wayes since he broke the Parliament.' Only the Protector's death soon afterwards saved him from arrest.

In 1660 Hutchinson was returned to the Convention Parliament, but was expelled as a regicide. On 11 October, however, he was arrested in his home, by order of Buckingham, for suspected implication in a 'northern plot'. He was taken to the Tower and in May next year transferred to Sandown Castle and lodged in a damp unfurnished room. His wife stayed in Deal and every day walked to visit him. But while she was away for a short time he died of a fever, 11 September 1664. There had never been any evidence against him, and at the inquest it was said that 'the place killed him.'[2]

NOTES
[1] Lucy Hutchinson, *Memoirs of the Life of Colonel Hutchinson* (1904 edn)., p. 215.
[2] *Ibid.*, p. 448.

HENRY IRETON
(1611-1651)

Ireton... was of a melancholic, reserved, dark nature, who communicated his thoughts to very few, so that for the most part he resolved alone, but was never diverted from any resolution he had taken.   CLARENDON

THE ELDEST SON of German Ireton of Attenborough, near Nottingham, he graduated from Trinity College, Oxford, in 1629 and entered the Middle Temple, but was never called to the bar.

In 1642, living on his estate in Nottinghamshire, he was given command of a troop of horse to be raised at Nottingham (30 June) and led it at Edgehill. He shared in Cromwell's victory at Gainsborough (28 July 1643) and thereafter Cromwell made him his Deputy-Governor in the Isle of Ely, which he fortified. He served in the 1644 campaign as Quarter-Master-General of Manchester's army, and after Second Newbury joined in Cromwells' criticisms of Manchester's half-heartedness.

Soon after the formation of the New Model Army, Ireton was given command of a regiment of horse. On the eve of the Battle of Naseby he raided Royalist quarters in 'Naseby Town' and took many prisoners. As a result he was given command of the left wing in the battle, but was quickly worsted by Rupert whom he outnumbered by three to two. Leading his division, he was wounded and temporarily captured. He made a swift recovery, for he was at the Siege of Bristol in September. He was one of those who negotiated the treaty of Truro (14 March 1646) which led to the disbanding of Hopton's army, and thereafter he took part in June in the Siege of Oxford. On the 15th of this month he married Cromwell's eldest daughter, Bridget, a union which did much to further his influence with Cromwell. Not long afterwards his political influence was increased when he became M.P. for Appleby (October). In 1647 he quarrelled with Denzil Holles over the petition of the Army, which the House had declared seditious, but declined to fight him and had his nose pulled![1]

In April he was sent with Cromwell, Skippon, Fleetwood, and some M.P.s to Saffron Walden 'to quiet all distempers in the army.' In the subsequent quarrel between Parliament and Army he favoured the Army and was one of the two authors of *The Heads of the [Army] Proposals*. He opposed the Levellers' *Agreement of the People*, and was an opponent of universal suffrage. Nor did he wish at this period to do away with the monarchy or the House of Lords.

Charles's flight to the Isle of Wight convinced him that it was not possible to come to terms with the King, though for a time he supported the idea of deposing him and setting the Prince of Wales or the Duke of York on the throne. During the Second Civil War Ireton served under Fairfax in Kent and Essex, and was at the Siege of Colchester. Clarendon attributes the execution of Sir Charles Lucas and Sir George Lisle after its surrender to his 'bloody and unmerciful nature', though Fairfax must bear the responsibility. Ireton's Regiment was one of the first to petition for the trial of the King. During the 'trial' Ireton sat regularly amongst his judges and was one of those who signed the death warrant.

He was anathema to the Levellers, whose leader, Lilburne, denounced him in the pamphlet *Impeachment of High Treason against Oliver Cromwell and his son-in-law Henry Ireton* (10 August 1649). On 15 June he was appointed second-in-command of Cromwell's expedition to Ireland where he landed about the end of August.

When Cromwell was recalled he made Ireton his deputy (29 May 1650) after which he carried on the work of subjugation, and continued Cromwell's policy of replanting Ireland with English colonists. He worked himself to death, seldom ate until 9 or 10 at night when the work of the day was done, and 'never regarded what clothes or food he used, or what hour he went to rest.' He caught a fever, died at Limerick 29 November 1651, and was buried in King Henry VII's Chapel, Westminster Abbey.

Although considered by some a rigid Republican it seems that he was not so much moved by 'malice against regal government' (Clarendon's expression)[2] as by mistrust of Charles I. At the Restoration the Royalists had the bad taste to dig up his corpse, along with those of Cromwell and Bradshaw, and hang them, with various other indignities, at Tyburn.

NOTES
[1] Clarendon, Bk. X, § 104.
[2] *Ibid.*, Bk. XIII, § 175.

WILLIAM JUXON, ARCHBISHOP OF CANTERBURY
(1582-1663)

WILLIAM JUXON, the son of Richard Juxon of Chichester (who was receiver-general of the estates of the see) spanned in his life a dramatic period of English history from Armada days to those of the Restoration. He was educated at Merchant Taylors, and in June 1598 became a scholar at St John's College, Oxford, where he studied law. He left the Law for the Church, being appointed in 1609 vicar of St. Giles, Oxford, and in 1615 rector of Somerton in North Oxfordshire, where he built a new rectory. In 1621, however, he was elected President of St. John's and lived at Somerton only during the vacations. Six years later (1627) he became Vice-Chancellor of the University, and bought the manor of Little Compton in Warwickshire. He was also made Dean of Worcester. When Laud became Archbishop of Canterbury in 1633 Juxon succeeded him as Bishop of London. In all disputes over Laud's disciplinary regulations Juxon enforced the law, where necessary, with tact and without making enemies.

His appointment as Dean of the Chapel Royal (1633) began a close association with the King which was to endure to the end. In 1636 he was appointed Lord High Treasurer and was for two years on the Board of Admiralty. Also in 1636 the new library of St. John's College, the building of which he had directed in its early stages, choosing the marble for the columns from a quarry at Bletchington which he had noticed while hunting, was opened by the King and Queen in his presence. He now became a member of the Council of War Committee, and was one of those who advised the King not to assent to Strafford's attainder. He had resigned the Treasurership by the time the War broke out, and retired to his house in Fulham where he remained except for accompanying and advising the King whenever he treated with the Parliamentary Commissioners. Towards the end he supported the King's offer of a three-years trial of Presbyterianism, and was with him throughout the Newport negotiations and during his 'trial'. Early on the morning of the King's execution he visited him, read the morning service, and gave him his last Communion. He alone of Charles's friends was on the scaffold where 'it was much to see the King dye with so undaunted a spirit: it was more to see the Bishop behold him with so unmoved a countenance: but so it became him whom His Majesty had chosen as his Second in that great Duel'. Amid the roll of the drums the King said 'I go from a corruptible to an uncorruptible crown'[1] and, taking off his neck the 'George', the last of his jewels, he handed it to Juxon with the one word 'Remember'.

Afterwards Juxon was asked what the King had meant by that word, and had to hand over the sheet of paper from which Charles had read his last address. He attended the funeral, which was held in silence in St. George's Chapel, Windsor, and thereafter retired to Little Compton where he began to hunt once more and kept his own pack of hounds. Episcopacy was abolished, and the living of Little Compton was held by a Puritan, so Juxon used to walk to the nearby parish of Chastleton every Sunday and take service in the house of a loyalist named Jones.[2] His love of the chase offended some of his Puritan neighbours who complained to Cromwell that the hounds had run through Chipping Norton churchyard during a service one day. But Cromwell asked them whether they really thought that the Bishop had prevailed on the hare to run that line at that time, and bade them begone and make no more such frivolous complaints. 'Let him enjoy his diversion of hunting unmolested', so long as he gives not 'my government any offence.'[3] 'His recreations', writes Lloyd, 'were innocent and many, traversing Hills and Dales for Health, and for Instruction studying God at Home and Nature abroad.'[4] On 3 September 1660 he was recalled to public life to become Archbishop of Canterbury, and next year crowned Charles II. On 4 June 1663 'he went to see King Charles I crowned in Heaven', and was buried beside his old friend Laud in St. John's College Chapel.

NOTES

[1] Lloyd, p. 597.
[2] John Hobson, in *Country Life*, 7 December 1967. The house is open to the public and is still furnished much as it was in Juxon's day.
[3] *Ibid.*
[4] Lloyd, *loc. cit.*

MAJOR-GENERAL JOHN LAMBERT
(1619-1683)

JOHN LAMBERT, scion of an old Yorkshire family from Calton near Malham Tarn, after training (according to Whitlocke) in one of the Inns of Court, married in 1639 Frances, daughter of Sir William Lister of Thornton in Craven. He first showed his mettle in a bold sally during the Siege of Hull in 1643. In January next year he fought under Fairfax at Nantwich, and again at Marston Moor, where he commanded his second line of horse on the right wing. He was wounded covering the Siege of Pontefract in March 1645. In the New Model Army he commanded the regiment of foot which had fought under Edward Montagu at Marston Moor. During the wrangle of 1647 between Parliament and Army he acted as spokesman for the disaffected officers ; and when Agitators seized Poyntz in York in July took over his command. Next year he fought under Cromwell at Preston and pursued Hamilton until he surrendered at Uttoxeter. Thereafter he besieged Pontefract which fell on 22 March 1649. In July 1650 as Cromwell's second-in-command he was wounded at Musselburgh, and led in person the attack at Dunbar. In December he defeated and captured Colonel Ker at Hamilton. When Charles II invaded England in August 1651 he harried him on his march south and, seizing Upton Bridge, cut off the Royalists' way to escape to the south and west.

On Ireton's death in November Lambert was appointed Deputy of Ireland, but before he went Parliament abolished the office. He refused the diminished appointment of commander of the forces in Ireland, which Fleetwood accepted. Though suspecting Cromwell's hand in all this he became a member of his first Council of State and a leading light in drawing up the Instrument of Government. As Major-General of the Northern counties his rule was severe ; but he was the only one to speak up for Naylor, his old quartermaster, when Parliament was debating this Quaker's blasphemies. By now he was 'the army's darling', its Major-General and colonel of two regiments, financially endowed, and seemingly powerful enough to set Cromwell up, or bring him down, which some observers thought he intended. They became estranged after Lambert opposed the offer of the crown. Cromwell sought a reconciliation in the spring of 1658 when they met, but the gap was too wide to close. Six months later Cromwell was dead. Lambert, as M.P. for Pontefract, supported Richard Cromwell, suppressed Booth's Rising in August 1659, and was rewarded, but not with the rank of Major-General. The importunity of army petitioners demanding this drove Parliament to cashier him. He at once replaced the Parliamentary guards with men of his own regiment and excluded the Speaker and members of the newly reinstated Purged Parliament. The Council of the Army now made him Major-General, and the Royalists expected him to declare himself Protector, and even considered a match between his very pretty daughter and one of the royal brothers. But, 'bewitched with an itch of having all,'[1] he secured himself with neither side. When sent to oppose Monck's entry into England, his troops retreated and then disintegrated. He was allowed to retire to Yorkshire but, being unable to afford £20,000 bail, was sent to the Tower whence, in April, he escaped, collected six troops of horse, and appointed a rendezvous at Edgehill. But his men would not fight and he was sent back to the Tower and thence to Guernsey. However, when his daughter married the Governor's son, Richard Hatton, he was moved to the Isle of St. Nicholas in Plymouth Sound, where he died in 1683.

'Honest John' was a generous opponent, a robust, courageous soldier, and a fluent speaker. But, influenced perhaps by his ambitious wife (who bore him ten children), his political activities towards the end brought him nothing but distrust. He was a keen gardener and his name has been associated with the Guernsey Lily – John Evelyn's 'Garnsy lilly' – one bloom of which he had sent from Wimbledon on 29 August 1659 to Alexander Marshall who made a water-colour of it which now hangs in the Royal Library in Windsor Castle. As a prisoner after the Restoration, Lambert was lampooned on the *Eight of Hearts* in a pack of cards as the Knight of the Golden Tulip.[2]

NOTES

[1] David Underdown, *Royalist Conspiracy in England* (1960), p. 310.
[2] *The Countryman*, Winter 1972-3, p. 158.

MARMADUKE, LORD LANGDALE
(1598-1661)

THIS DOUR YORKSHIREMAN was the son of Peter Langdale of Pig-hill, near Beverley, and married Lenox, daughter of John Rodes of Barlborough, Derbyshire. He was knighted by Charles I in 1628 but in 1639, as High Sheriff of Yorkshire, refused to levy Ship Money. At the outbreak of the Civil War he raised a regiment of foot in the East Riding, arming them from the ships which the Queen had brought to Bridlington from the Continent. Newcastle asked him to try to persuade his old friend Sir John Hotham, the Governor of Hull, to hand the port over to the King, but without success. In February 1644 Langdale, commanding the Northern Horse, defeated the Scottish cavalry at Corbridge; and at Marston Moor fought on the victorious right wing with Goring. After the battle he retired with Rupert to the North-West, rejoining the main army at Oxford in November. In 1645 he beat Colonel Rossiter at Melton Mowbray and, though outnumbered, raised the Siege of Pontefract. He seized a strategic hill overlooking Leicester which made its capture (31 May 1645) inevitable, and commanded the left wing at Naseby where, heavily outnumbered, the Northern Horse were driven from the field by Cromwell. In an attempt to relieve Chester in September the King ordered Langdale to drive off the besiegers, but reinforcements under Poyntz defeated him with heavy loss on Rowton Heath. At a Council of War at Welbeck in October it was decided to answer Montrose's appeal for more cavalry by sending the Northern Horse, commanded by Digby under whom Langdale had surprisingly agreed to serve. In a con-fused fight with Poyntz at Sherburn-in-Elmet they were defeated, but pressed on as far as Dumfries. Forced back, they were scattered at Carlisle, and Digby, Langdale, and others took ship for the Isle of Man.

Soon after this Langdale joined the refugees in France whence he is said to have visited the King, in disguise, at Hampton Court. In 1648, commissioned by the Prince of Wales, he sailed for Scotland where, in Edinburgh, his name attracted many recruits. He surprised Berwick and, with Hamilton and the Scots lagging behind, advanced into England. But in August, near Preston, and still unsupported, he was defeated by Cromwell in a desperate six-hours battle and eventually captured and imprisoned in Nottingham Castle. From here he wrote to his old comrade-in-arms, Sir Henry Slingsby, an account of the battle and his subsequent march south until, deserted by the Scots, he was left with 100 men.[1] An attempt by Pontefract Royalists to capture Rainsborough at Doncaster, and exchange him for Langdale, failed when Rainsborough was accidentally killed. This made it imperative for Langdale to escape. He succeeded, disguised first as a Parliamentarian soldier, then as a milkmaid, and lastly, after swimming the Humber, as a clergyman, and made his way to London and thence overseas. In 1652 he took part with the Venetians in the defence of Candia against the Turks. When the Northern Royalist rising was being planned for 1655 the Yorkshiremen asked for him to be their leader. But the Court refused, probably because, as a Roman Catholic, his participation might offend the Presbyterian element. His absence was one of the main causes of the failure of that rising, for men followed him where they would follow no one else. Slingsby, who had served under him, likened him to Julius Caesar who shared all his men's hardships and trained them to be ready for swift action at a moment's notice.[2] However, Charles II created him a baron in 1658. The Parliamentarian Press made him out a coward and mocked his leanness – 'if he be vulnerable, it is but stitching up the Parchment-Carkesse and then all's well again.'[3] But his enemies in the field 'called him Ghost, and deservedly for they were so haunted by him.'[4] At the time of the Restoration his losses amounted to £160,000 and he could not afford to attend the coronation. But in recompense he had 'the conscience of having suffered in a good cause, acquitted himself bravely, and played the man.'[5] He died 5 August 1661 and was buried in the family vault at Sancton. His son succeeded to the title.

NOTES

[1] Slingsby, pp. 334-8.

[2] Ibid., p. 145.

[3] Mercurius Britannicus, p. 82: 5 May 1645.

[5] Lloyd, p. 550.

[4] Ibid.

WILLIAM LAUD, ARCHBISHOP OF CANTERBURY
(1573-1645)

'A MAN OF BOUNDLESS PRIDE, of meanest Birth'[1] is how the writer of a scurrilous epitaph saw Laud, whose father was a Reading clothier. He was educated at Reading School and St. John's College, Oxford, where he was elected Fellow in 1593 and President in 1611. More promotion followed: the King's Chaplain, Dean of Gloucester, and, in 1621, Bishop of St David's. He became a friend of Buckingham, and so of Prince Charles who, as King, made him Bishop of London in 1628. Their ideas of a uniform, ritualistic, hierarchical Church tallied, but brought protests from the Puritan-dominated Parliament. Laud was elected Chancellor of Oxford University in 1629 and four years later became Archbishop of Canterbury.

He could now start in earnest to discipline the clergy, dignify the services, and restore the beauty of holiness to the churches. The Communion Table was to be fixed at the east end and railed, the clergy were to be surpliced and bow to the altar. More aggravating to the Puritans than this ceremonial was the prohibition of all sermons except for one on Sunday, on non-controversial matters, for the pulpit had become a political platform. Some bishops imposed the new regulations with discretion; others, like the diligent Wren of Norwich, aroused bitter hostility, and many clergy and their congregations emigrated to New England. Without the

PLATE 49   Marmaduke, Lord Langdale

PLATE 50   William Laird, Archbishop of Canterbury c. 1636
after Sir Anthony van Dyck

PLATE 51
John Maitland,
Duke of
Lauderdale
(and his wife
Elizabeth)

Sir Peter Lely

General Leslie.

PLATE 54   Gen. Alexander Leslie, 1st Earl of Leven

PLATE 55   Lt. Col. John Lilburne

PLATE 56   Robert Bertie, Lord Willoughby de Eresby, 1st Earl of Lindsey
Cornelius Johnson

support of the Crown Laud's policy, which offended Parliament, the lawyers, and puritanically inclined gentry, could never have been enforced, and in order to carry it out he used the Court of High Commission. In May 1640 Convocation issued the new Canons which, among other things, caused all members of learned professions to swear not to subvert the rule of the Church by 'Archbishop, Bishops, deans, and archdeacons, etc.' It was the 'Etcetera Oath' which provoked the loudest outcry for there were mischief-makers who professed not to know that it did not include even the Pope. The King's attempt to enforce the Canons and the Prayer Book on Scotland, instead of the liturgy prepared by the Scottish bishops but rejected by Laud, hastened Laud's fall.

In February 1641 he was impeached and taken to the Tower, his journey there by water watched by hundreds of his poor neighbours praying for his safe return. He was still in the Tower when the King consented to Strafford's attainder and, in his Diary, wrote of their royal master that 'he knew not how to be or be made great.' As Strafford passed below the barred window of his room in the Tower to be beheaded, Laud stretched out his hands to bless him. His own trial did not begin until November 1643, two and a half years after his imprisonment. The main charges against him, ruthlessly pressed by Prynne, were of trying to subvert the laws and overthrow the Protestant religion. When the judges declared that none of the charges were treasonable, the Commons attainted him, as they had Strafford. On 10 January 1645 he walked to the scaffold on Tower Hill with notes in his hand for his last sermon. In it he defended the King and himself from the aspersion of popery. 'I was born and baptized in the bosom of the Church of England. In that profession I have ever since lived and in that I am come to die.' The Yellow Press satirized him as 'The Little Fireworke of Canterbury (who) was extinguished upon Tower Hill, whither being come he did more than he had done many years before ; he preached to the people.'[2]

'His portrait shows his character more clearly than any number of biographies',[3] wrote a modern archbishop, who saw in it conviction and courage and little wisdom or tact. This 'little low, red-faced man' was irritable and discourteous in Council, and to the outside world no more than an intolerant disciplinarian. But he worked for what he believed to be right and not for what was expedient. Although his methods died with him on Tower Hill, his work lived on.

NOTES
1 *Mercurius Britannicus*, No. 68, 27 January, 1645.
2 *Ibid*. No. 65, 6 January, 1645.
3 Cyril Garbett, Archbishop of York, *Church and State in England*, (1950), p. 77.

P.S.V.B.

JOHN MAITLAND, DUKE OF LAUDERDALE
(1616-1682)

WITH CHARLES I it had been Hamilton, with Charles II Lauderdale, who pressed the Scottish Alliance, so fateful for the Royal cause. John Maitland was the eldest surviving son of John, 2nd Lord Maitland of Thirlestane, and Isabel, daughter of Alexander, Earl of Dunfermline. He became a Covenanter as being the only way he could participate in public life, and in 1643 carried the Solemn League and Covenant to the English Parliament and attended the Westminster Assembly in November. In 1644 he became a member of the Committee of Both Kingdoms, and at Marston Moor commanded one of the Scottish regiments. As a Scottish Commissioner at Uxbridge, he tried to persuade the King to accept Presbyterianism. In 1647 he had interviews with him at Newmarket and Latimer, discussing plans for a Scottish invasion, but was prevented by the Army from seeing him at Woburn to complete them. He saw Charles at Hampton Court in October, and again in December at Carisbrooke where he was one of those who signed the 'Engagement', leaving thereafter for Scotland to rouse his countrymen. When, in July 1648, Hamilton led his army into England, Maitland was on his way to the Prince of Wales in the Downs with an invitation from the Committee of Estates to come to Scotland. Two years later he accompanied Charles II there, fought at Worcester, and was captured and imprisoned until 1660.

At the Restoration Maitland was rewarded by being made Secretary of State for Scotland and, by his skilful intrigues, overthrew his rival, Middleton. His aim now was to make the Crown absolute in Scotland both in Church and State and, by preventing the episcopate from becoming too strong and acting vigorously against the Presbyterians of Fife and the South-West, he maintained for the King preponderance over both parties. By instigating the disbandment of the army and the formation of a militia of 22,000, he placed a more powerful weapon in the King's hands. In England he became a Privy Councillor and 'had very much the ear of the King'. With other members of the Cabal, he signed in December 1670 the secret Traité Simulé, which was in reality the Treaty of Dover all over again except that the £150,000 for Charles's conversion was now disguised as part of the subsidy for the war against Holland.

Next year Maitland's first wife, Anne, daughter of the 1st Earl of Home, who had borne him one daughter, died in Paris. In 1672 he married Elizabeth Murray, daughter of the Earl of Dysart, widow of Sir Lionel Tollemache, and an avid political intriguer. He was now created Duke of Lauderdale and Marquess of March. The Test Act of 1673 dispersed the Cabal in which he had been more interested in supporting the King than in English politics, but its dispersal made men think that his influence was waning. As a result a series of attacks on him by Parliament ensued, from each of which he was saved, either by a dissolution or the rigging of votes, and in 1674, perhaps to remove his vulnerability as an English commoner, he was elevated to the English peerage as Earl of Guildford and Baron Petersham. In order to check the increasing number of conventicles in Scotland, he loosed in 1677 800 Highlanders on the West country, till a deputation of Scottish noblemen persuaded the King to recall them. But Lauderdale continued to retain his power until the Covenanters' insurrection of 1679, when he resigned his Secretaryship. Next year, after a fit of apoplexy, he moved to Bath and later to Tunbridge Wells where he died 24 August 1682 and was buried at Haddington, leaving no heir. Pepys might call him 'a very cunning fellow' who 'would rather hear a cat mew than the best musique in the world',[1] but he gave Scotland internal peace and 'did more without the sword than Oliver Cromwell, the great Usurper, did with it.'[2]

NOTES
[1] Pepys, *Diary*, 2 March 1664, 28 July 1665.
[2] W. C. Mackenzie, *Life and Times of John Maitland, Duke of Lauderdale*, quoting Robert Law.

COLONEL WILLIAM LEGGE
(1609?-1670)

THE ELDEST SON of Edward Legge, Vice-President of Munster (who died in 1616), and Mary, daughter of Sir Percy Walsh of Moyvalley, Co. Kildare, he was brought up from the age of seven by his godfather, the Earl of Danby. As a young man he served in the Dutch and Swedish armies, and in 1639 Charles I sent him to inspect the fortifications of Hull, the largest magazine in the country, with arms and ammunition for 16,000 men. Later in the year the King, after visiting Hull himself, made Legge military commander over the head of Sir John Hotham, the existing Governor, a political blunder as it transpired. Two years later Legge, back in London, was involved in the two Army Plots to seize the Tower and support the King against the increasing Parliamentary pressure. When the Civil War seemed inevitable, the King sent Legge and Newcastle to secure Hull. They entered, incognito and with no forces, but were recognized and brought before the Mayor. Parliament summoned Newcastle back to take his seat in the Lords.

In April 1642 the King advanced with troops from York to demand an entry into Hull which Hotham refused after an angry parley outside the Beverley Gate to which Legge ironically enough, had during his earlier inspection ordered a drawbridge to be added. On 1 July Lord Lindsey laid siege to Hull. During the siege Legge and Wilmot, another captain, led a night attack in force and fired two vital corn-grinding windmills outside the walls before being driven off by gun-fire which so terrified some of their men that they 'resolved never to come neare the Waft of a Windmill (again)'.[1] In August Lindsey abandoned the siege, and soon after this Legge was captured in a skirmish at Southam, but escaped next month and joined the King at Oxford. Captured again in 1643 at the Siege of Lichfield, and at Chalgrove Field, where 'his courage engaged him too far', he so distinguished himself at First Newbury that the King presented him with an agate-handled hanger set in gold which he himself had worn that day. He would have knighted Legge with it had he not refused. In January 1645 he succeeded Sir Henry Gage as Governor of Oxford and was there when Rupert (whose great friend he was) arrived, after surrendering Bristol, and received the King's letter banishing him. The King, believing the jealous

Digby's tales that he and Rupert were plotting to surrender Oxford, also ordered Legge's arrest. He was released when the King came to Oxford, and wrote to Rupert, 'I have not lost a day without moving His Majesty to recall you.' When Oxford surrendered in 1646 he went abroad but returned to wait on the King, then a prisoner at Hampton Court, and with Berkeley and Ashburnham, aided his flight to Carisbrooke Castle where they stayed till the King's attempt to escape by boat, when they were ordered to leave the island. For the next few months Legge lingered in Hampshire plotting to rescue the King, but in May 1648 he was seized and sent to Arundel Castle. On promising not to bear arms again, he was allowed to compound and went overseas. In the summer of 1649 Charles II sent him to Ireland, but he was captured at sea and imprisoned in Exeter Castle until May 1651. Two years later he rejoined the Royalist exiles abroad. In 1659 Legge returned to England, empowered by Charles II to treat with all rebels except the regicides, promising pardons to those who would assist the Royalist rising being planned for that year. Once more he was arrested and committed to the Tower.

At the Restoration he was offered a peerage which, as the father of a large family, he could not afford. But he was restored to the posts of Groom of the Bedchamber and Master of the Armoury, to which was added that of Lieutenant-General of Ordnance. He died 3 October 1670 at his house in the Minories and was buried in Trinity Chapel, survived by his wife, Elizabeth, daughter of Sir William Washington of Packington, Leicestershire, who bore him three sons and four daughters. His eldest son, George, was created Baron Dartmouth in 1682.

Clarendon praises his 'integrity and fidelity to his master' and the commendable qualities of being 'a very punctual and steady observer of the orders he received, but no contriver of them.'[2] He was a man whose virtues were uncommon in the age in which he lived.

NOTES
[1] *Advertisements from York and Beverly*, quoted by B. N. Reckitt, *Charles the First and Hull* (1952), p. 55 n.
[2] Clarendon, Bk. X, § 130.

GENERAL DAVID LESLIE
(d. 1682)

THE FIFTH SON of Sir Patrick Leslie of Pitcairly, Fifeshire, and Lady Jean Stewart, second daughter of Robert, 1st Earl of Orkney, he served under Gustavus Adolphus and rose to the rank of colonel. He was severely wounded in 1640 but was sufficiently recovered to return to England later that year. In November 1643, as Major-General under Leven at Marston Moor, he commanded three regiments of horse, acting as a reserve on the Allied left. While Cromwell was out of action having his wound dressed, he broke Rupert's counter-attack and, with his 'little light Scotch nags', drove the Cavaliers off the field (for which he got little credit from Cromwell), and later took part in the final attack on Newcastle's Whitecoats. After serving at the Siege of Newark, he was sent to Westmorland where he defeated Musgrave and Fletcher and then laid siege to Carlisle. When Glemham surrendered, starved out, on 28 June 1645, Leslie left a Scottish garrison in charge, a move which was viewed with grave dissatisfaction at Westminster. He now advanced into Scotland and defeated Montrose in a surprise attack at Philiphaugh on 13 September, a victory sullied by the subsequent massacre of camp-followers, among whom were three hundred Irish women, many with children. Fifty Irish soldiers were taken prisoner but, after remonstrations from 'churchmen and noblemen of the Covenant' against such clemency, Leslie ordered his men to slaughter them as they passed through Linlithgow.[1] Tradition relates that eighty Irish women and children who had survived were thrown from a nearby bridge and drowned, as English Protestants had been drowned at Portadown. Such however was the awe in which the invincible Montrose was held that Leslie was rewarded in Glasgow with 50,000 marks and a chain of gold. He rejoined Leven before Newark and took command on Leven's departure.

In 1647 Leslie was sent to extinguish insurrections in Scotland, captured the Gordon and Huntly strongholds, and drove Macdonald and his Irish allies out of the country. He joined the 'Engagers' in 1648 and after their defeat at Preston (17 August 1648) supported their opponents, Argyll and the Whiggamores. When Montrose landed in Scotland in 1650 he marched north and beat him at Invercarron, treating him 'with great insolence'[2] when he was betrayed and refusing to allow him to change out of the old clothes in which he had escaped. But as soon as Charles II became a Covenanted King, Leslie raised an army to support his cause and faced Cromwell at Dunbar. He blamed his disastrous defeat there on 3 September, in which he lost three thousand slain, on the failure of the men after leaving the hills to stand to their arms, and of the officers to stay with their troops and regiments, and was exonerated 'of all imputation anent the miscarriage at Dunbar.' When Cromwell bypassed the strong position which he then took up between Stirling and Falkirk, he joined Charles's march into England as his Lt-General of Horse. In the Battle of Worcester, fought on 3 September 1651, he was 'dispirited and confounded, and gave and revoked his orders, and sometimes contradicted them,[3] and instead of launching the Scots reserve, which might have saved the day, he made his escape. One explanation of such conduct may lie in a remark which he made privately to Charles on the march at Warrington, that though the army might look well, it would not fight. Another view is that Dunbar had unnerved him. With other fugitives he reached Yorkshire where one of them, Sir William Armorer, who heard him say which way he would go, said he would go by another for Leslie had betrayed both his King and the army.[4] A fortnight later he was taken at Chester and in October sent to the Tower where he remained until 1660. In 1661 he was created Lord Newark with a pension of £500 per annum. He died of apoplexy in February 1682. His wife, Jane, daughter of Sir John Yorke, had borne him three sons (of whom David, the eldest, succeeded to the title) and five daughters.

Despite the massacres after Philiphaugh, the scurvy treatment which he accorded the captured Montrose after Invercarron, and his fatal vacillation at Dunbar and Worcester, his military reputation has survived.

NOTES
[1] S. R. Gardiner, Vol. II (1893), *op. cit.*, p. 356.
[2] Clarendon, Bk. XII, § 135.
[3] *Ibid.*, Bk. XIII, § 74.
[4] *Ibid.*, Bk. XIII, § 80.

GENERAL ALEXANDER LESLIE, 1st EARL OF LEVEN
(1580?-1661)

HE WAS BORN the illegitimate son of George Leslie of Balquhain, Captain of the Castle of Blair Athol, and Ann (or Margaret) Stewart whom his father later married. His education was slim although he once exclaimed 'I got the length of the letter "g".'[1] By the time of the Civil War he had served more than thirty years under Vere and Gustavus Adolphus, who knighted him in 1626. As a colonel he had distinguished himself by his defence of Stralsund in 1628 for which the King of Sweden gave him a medal of solid gold (still preserved in the family) and made him Governor of the cities of the Baltic coast. He fought at Lützen and had reached the rank of Field-Marshal by 1636, retiring from the Swedish service in 1638. Coming to England, he was presented to Charles I and offered to lead an expedition to restore the Elector Palatine. He had already taken the Covenant and when, in the following year (1639), the Covenanters raised their army his assistance in organizing, officering, and arming it was invaluable. It was thanks to a stratagem of his that Edinburgh Castle fell into the Covenanters' hands, and, as Lord-General of all Scottish forces, he crossed the Border in May 1640 with an army of 30,000 horse and foot to win the so-called Battle of Newburn. Next year he entertained Charles I when he visited Edinburgh, and was created Earl of Leven. The King had introduced his nephew the Elector Palatine to the Scottish Parliament, but the 10,000 Scottish foot, which Leven reported would be sent to help him, were diverted to quell the Irish rising and he went with them, taking, however, little active part.

Leven led the Scottish invasion of England through the snows of January 1644 and in April, with Lord Fairfax, laid siege to York. He commanded the Allied forces at the Battle of Marston Moor. But his right wing collapsed before Goring's onslaught, and much of the centre, too, from Blakiston's charge. Unable to rally the fugitives, he galloped off the field and 'never drew bridle till he came to Leeds, nearly 40 miles distant.' To which Sir James Turner added 'There was reason he should take the start . . . because he had furthest home !'[2] For the rest of the War his work was sieges – Newcastle, Hereford, and Newark. Early in December 1645 he left Newark for Newcastle and received the King when he came there as a prisoner next year. He tried to persuade Charles to take the Covenant, promising to serve him if he did. But because the King refused he disapproved of the 'Engagers' march into England in 1648. When they were beaten at Preston (17 August) he and David Leslie raised a new army in order to prevent Cromwell pursuing them across the Border, and secured Edinburgh Castle. When, however, Cromwell approached the city in peace, he entertained him sumptuously. In 1650 he raised another army for Charles II and, although very infirm, was in nominal command at Dunbar, a disaster from which he was exonerated. A more personal blow was the death next year of his wife, Agnes Renton, daughter of the Laird of Billy, who had borne him two sons (who predeceased him) and five daughters. In August he himself was captured by Monck's cavalry at Alyth, Forfarshire, and sent to the Tower. He was released, thanks to the intervention of Queen Christina of Sweden, in 1654, and died seven years later 4 April 1661, being buried at Markinch.

'Such was the wisdom and authoritie of that old little, crooked souldier,' wrote Baillie of him, 'that all, with ane incredible submission, from the beginning to the end, give themselves to be guided by him, as if he had been Great Solyman.'[3]

NOTES
1 David Masson, *Life of Milton*, Vol. III (1873), p. 55.
2 J. L. Sanford, *Studies and Illustrations of the Great Rebellion* (1858), p. 605.
3 Robert Baillie, *Letters and Journals*, ed. D. Laing. Vol. I (1844), p. 218.

LIEUTENANT-COLONEL JOHN LILBURNE
(1614?-1657)

FEW MEN HAVE STOOD for freedom against oppression with such courage and constancy as did John Lilburne. The son of Richard Lilburne of Thickley Punchard, Durham, and Margaret Hixon, he was educated at Newcastle and Auckland schools and then apprenticed to Thomas Hewson, a wholesale cloth merchant, who one day took him to see Bastwick in prison. It was for smuggling Bastwick's anti-prelatical *Letany* from Holland into England that in 1636 Lilburne was sentenced in the Star Chamber, although he was a gentleman, to be fined, whipped at the cart's tail, pilloried, and imprisoned. For having refused as a 'free-born Englishman' to take the Star Chamber oath he earned the name of 'Free-born John'. Shortly after he married Elizabeth Dewell, daughter of a London merchant, the War broke out, and he joined Lord Brooke's Regiment of Foot as a captain. He fought at Edgehill after which Warwick certified him as 'a man both faithfull, able and fit to be Captaine (of a Troop of Horse), having shewed his valour at the battell'.[1] He was soon afterwards captured at Brentford, tried in Oxford for high treason, and only saved from hanging when Parliament threatened reprisals. He took part in the storming of Lincoln (October 1643), and next year became a Lt-Colonel in Manchester's dragoons. Subsequently, encouraged by Cromwell, he bore witness against Manchester for his half-hearted conduct of the War. When the Self-Denying Ordinance came in 1645 he left the Army because he would not take the Covenant.

Lilburne now began his attacks on Prynne (whose clerk he had once been c.1632) for supporting Presbyterian intolerance and the supreme authority of Parliament; and then turned on Speaker Lenthall for his treasonable activities, a libel which landed him in Newgate. Here he wrote *England's Birthright Justified* (1645) exposing both the corrupt monopoly of the Merchant Adventurers who controlled the clothing trade, and the undemocratic government of the City. Next year in *The Just Man's Justification* he attacked Manchester again, for which he was sent to the Tower. There, also a prisoner, was the Royalist Sir Lewis Dyve with whom he discussed the possibility of a settlement with Charles I whose 'seventeen years misgovernment . . . was but a fleabite'[2] compared with that of a Parliament which seemed bent on disbanding the Army. But when the Army did enter London no release came for Lilburne, not even after Cromwell's visit to the Tower, until August 1648.

Lilburne disapproved of the King's 'trial' and execution, and also of those of Capel, Holland, and Hamilton to whom he offered legal advice. Infringement of the liberty of the subject was the theme of his next three pamphlets: *England's New Chains Discovered*, *The Hunting of the Foxes from Newmarket and Triplow Heaths to Whitehall by Five Small Beagles*, and *An Impeachment of High Treason against Oliver Cromwell and . . . Ireton* (all published in 1649). For these he was again committed to the Tower, where he prepared a final version of the *Agreement of the People* (1649). Levellers' activities finally determined Cromwell to bring Lilburne to trial for high treason. His acquittal in October 1649 was tumultuously cheered and a commemorative medal struck.

Two years later he supported his uncle George Lilburne against Sir Arthur Heselrige over family estates in Durham, and was fined £7000 for libel, and banished. News of the impending dissolution of the Rump reached him in Holland and inspired him to appeal (in *L.Colonel John Lilburne Revived*, 1653) to the people of England to elect defenders of their liberties against 'their present Tyrannical Riders' ; and in June he boldly returned without a pass. As a banished man, he was tried for his life but, although acquitted, was not freed, and in March 1654 was sent to Jersey and thence to Guernsey. Next year he was moved to Dover Castle where, among Quakers, he found a spiritual peace manifested in *The Resurrection of John Lilburne, now a Prisoner in Dover Castle* (1656).[3] His wife and children lived for a while in Dover. When they moved to Eltham he joined them on parole. Here, on 29 September 1657, the very day on which he was due back at Dover, he died. The Quakers buried him, simply, in Moorfields.

NOTES

[1] *Edgehill*, p. 251.

[2] Pauline Gregg, *Freeborn John* (1961), p. 169.

[3] A list of Lilburne's pamphlets (12 pages of them) appears in D. M. Wolfe, *Milton in the Puritan Revolution* (New York, 1941).

P.J.W.B.

ROBERT BERTIE, LORD WILLOUGHBY DE ERESBY, 1st EARL OF LINDSEY

(1572-1642)

ROBERT BERTIE, whose godmother was Queen Elizabeth, was the eldest son of Peregrine Bertie, 12th Lord Willoughby de Eresby, and Lady Mary Vere, daughter of the 16th Earl of Oxford. He went to Oxford where, in that happier age of non-specialization, he chose to study, with commendable reasons for his choice, history, mathematics, heraldry, geography, medicine, law, and divinity, and is said to have acquired a high proficiency in each. Fired with adventure and travel, he went with Essex on the expedition to Spain in 1597 and was knighted for bravery in the market place of Cadiz. In one sea-faring expedition he captured a carrick worth 1,000,000 crowns in sight of the Spanish Fleet. He took part in the Siege of Amiens in 1598 and thereafter, finding himself in straitened circumstances, asked leave to continue his travels until he had paid off his fathers's debts. After an advantageous marriage with Elizabeth, the only daughter of Edward, Lord Montagu of Boughton, Northamptonshire, he settled at Grimsthorpe Castle, near Stamford, and embarked on improving his fortunes by thrifty management, having learnt 'at Venice and Florence that merchandise was consistent with nobility'.[1] In 1605 he made a contract with other Lincolnshire landowners to drain the fens and received two-thirds of the 36,000 acres, on which he built farmhouses.

In 1621 Bertie inherited, through his mother's family, the office of Lord High Chamberlain. On the declaration of war against Spain in 1624 he left his rural pursuits to serve in the Low Countries where, as colonel of a regiment of 1600, he lived rough and 'seldom slept in a Bed ... hardening his body and knitting his soul'.[2] Being at war with Spain, it is not surprising that he declined to hand over 'a choice Gennet, managed for war and intended a Present to the King of Spain', even refusing the offer of £1000 down or a £100 pension for life. He was recalled to take part in Buckingham's naval expedition to relieve La Rochelle, and for his services was created Earl of Lindsey in 1626. After Buckingham's assassination in 1628 he succeeded him as Admiral of the Fleet dispatched in yet another unsuccessful attempt to relieve La Rochelle. The rottenness of the ships and low morale of the officers were mainly responsible for its failure. In 1638 he became Lord High Admiral of England, commanding the Fleet equipped by Ship Money to guard the Narrow Seas, and a year later Governor of Berwick. As Speaker in the House of Lords he acted as Lord High Constable at Strafford's trial.

When the Civil War broke out Lindsey was Commander-in-Chief of the Royal forces. But Rupert alone was exempt from all orders except those from the King, with tragic results. For at Edgehill (23 October 1642), enraged by the Prince's insistence on ordering the battle according to the Swedish rather than the simpler Dutch method, Lindsey threw his baton to the ground and said that if he was not fit to be a general he would at least die as a colonel at the head of his regiment – a prophetic utterance, for it was here that his son, Lord Willoughby de Eresby, found him with his leg broken by a musket shot. Bestriding him, pike in hand, Willoughby warded off all attacks until surrounded when, in order to look after his father, he surrendered. As Lindsey lay in a cottage on a heap of straw he was visited by Essex and other Parliamentarian officers whom he exhorted to return to their allegiance. But three days later, with eighteen wounds in his body, he died from loss of blood. He was buried in Edenham church, near Grimsthorpe Castle, where a black marble monument, consisting of a large double inscription plate surrounded by trophies of arms and other military symbols on white marble, was erected – a fitting memorial for a man whose hatred of Court life, which 'became a souldier . . . as a Bed of doun would one of the Tower lyons', and where 'the reptilia creep on the ground',[3] was well known.

NOTES
[1] Lloyd, p. 310.
[2] *Ibid.*, p. 106.
[3] *Ibid.*, p. 309.

MONTAGU BERTIE, LORD WILLOUGHBY DE ERESBY, 2nd EARL OF LINDSEY
(1608-1666)

MONTAGUE BERTIE, one of the four peers allowed to attend King Charles I in the Isle of Wight in 1648, was the son of Robert Bertie, 1st Earl of Lindsey(q.v.), and served as a captain of horse in the Low Countries. He married Martha, daughter of Sir William Cockayne. When the Civil War broke out he raised a regiment of horse for the King, and at Edgehill commanded the Lifeguard of Foot, in the second line. As soon as he heard that his father had fallen he went to his aid and found him lying ,badly wounded, in front of his regiment. He stood over him, warding off all attacks,

PLATE 57   Montague Bertie, Lord Willoughby de Eresby, 2nd Earl of Lindsey

PLATE 58   Sir George Lisle   *unfinished portrait after Sir Anthony van Dyck*

PLATE 59   Sir Charles Lucas   *William Dobson*
In his left hand he holds a wheel lock pistol, in his right a spanner for
winding it up. He wears a handkerchief about his neck in a fashion set
by Prince Rupert

PLATE 60   Edmund Ludlow

PLATE 61   Lt. Gen. Sir James Lumsden

PLATE 62   Charles Gerard, 1st Earl of Macclesfield   *William Dobson*

PLATE 63   Edward Montague, 2nd Earl of Manchester   *Sir Peter Lely*

PLATE 64   Maj. Gen. Sir Edward Massey   *Sir Peter Lely*

until choosing to surrender and stay with him till he died three days later. During his imprisonment in Warwick Castle he composed *A Declaration and Justification of the Earl of Lindsey, now a prisoner, wherein he makes apparent the Justice of His Majesty's cause in taking armes for the preservation of his Royal Person and Prerogative . . . etc.* Exchanged in 1643, he joined the King at Oxford where he became one of the Gentlemen of the Bedchamber, and was also one of the fifty peers who signed a letter to the Council in Scotland asking them to prevent the Scottish Army from invading England. He fought at First Newbury and Lostwithiel and commanded the King's Lifeguard at Naseby where he was wounded. Thereafter he accompanied the King into Wales ; thence, from the tranquillity of Raglan Castle, up through the mountains to Chester, pursued by Poyntz's army, and finally to Newark. During the negotiations in 1648 over the Treaty of Newport, when the King was a prisoner in Carisbrooke Castle, he was one of his advisers and, with the Duke of Richmond, strongly urged him to escape while he still could. But Charles, having given his parole to Parliament, refused. When the King was moved to Hurst Castle, Lindsey, Richmond, Hertford, and Southampton were no longer allowed to be with him. But towards the end of the King's 'trial' these four offered themselves and their estates to guarantee any terms on which the Army might be willing to free him and recognize his Royal title, which offer was rejected.

On the morning of the execution, 30 January 1649, the King entrusted to his attendant, (Sir) Thomas Herbert, his remaining books, including a copy to Lindsey, who was a French scholar, of the romance *Cassandra.* The four friends were to be permitted to attend the funeral provided they did not escort the body out of London. They had previously located the vault of Henry VIII in St. George's Chapel, Windsor, but only by stamping on the floor till they heard a hollow echo, for many of the tombs and inscriptions had been pulled down. When the vault was opened they saw a large leaden coffin of the King with a smaller one beside it, Jane Seymour's, and room for a third alongside. The funeral took place on 9 February, Lindsey, Hertford, Richmond, and Southampton each holding one corner of the black velvet pall. No word was spoken for the Prayer Book service was forbidden.

When in 1660 Lindsey and Southampton went back to find the grave, as Charles II wished to move his father's body to Westminster Abbey, they were unable to do so. There had been no inscription, and the interior of the Chapel was much altered.

Lindsey had compounded after the King's death and retired to Grimsthorpe Castle where he repaired the ravages wrought by Parliamentarian troops, improved his estates, doubling their value, and was universally popular with his tenants. In 1661 he was made a Knight of the Garter and restored to the office of Lord High Chamberlain. He died, twice widowed, 25 July 1666 at Campden House, Kensington, and was buried with his father in Edenham Church. 'His converse', wrote David Lloyd, 'gave the world a singular pattern of harmlesse and inoffensive mirth, of a nobleness not made up in fine cloaths and courtship.'[1] It was these qualities, and his unswerving loyalty, that endeared him to Charles also.

NOTES
[1] Lloyd, p. 316.

SIR GEORGE LISLE
(d. 1648)

GEORGE LISLE, the son of a bookseller, received his military training in the Netherlands and joined the Royalist cause early in the War. At First Newbury he led the forlorn hope and was wounded. At Cheriton, with an outpost of foot, he held the southern ridge of the horseshoe while the main body took up position on the northern ridge, and remained there till early next morning when the enemy's seizure of Cheriton Wood forced him to retire. At Second Newbury, holding the Royalist centre at Shaw House, he led three gallant charges, throwing off his buff coat so that his men could see his white shirt in the gathering darkness and stick close to him, 'the King being engaged in the next field in his royal person'. The Roundheads pretended to think that he was a witch! Words to describe his valour in this engagement failed even *Mercurius Aulicus*, the Royalist newspaper. In the winter of 1644-5 he was Governor of Faringdon and reported to Rupert that it was only one-third fortified and entirely unprovisioned. In April he was given an honorary D.C.L. by Oxford University, and next month took part in the storming of Leicester and was made Lt-General of the town under Loughborough. At Naseby, the tertia of foot which he commanded in the left centre bore the brunt of Cromwell's charge. In December he was knighted by the King at Oxford and became Master of his Household.

After the surrender of Faringdon in June 1646, Lisle compounded, and was allowed to go to London. It was not long, however, before he was raising men for a renewal of the War. He was one of the leaders of the Kentish Rising (May 1648) which Fairfax suppressed after bitter street fighting in Maidstone. With other survivors, he then joined Norwich's forces and crossed the Thames into Essex where they redezvoused with Lucas at Chelmsford. Thence, by a circuitous march, they moved towards Colchester which they occupied. During the siege that followed Lucas commanded the horse and Lisle the foot. In July the two made a dramatic sally with horse and foot (some of the foot crossing the river on planks) and seized the East mill and two guns before retiring in good order. Lisle was captured on this raid, but rescued almost at once. Although soldiers and citizens were reduced to a diet of horse, dog, and cat (sweetened, if one were lucky, with prunes), Norwich rejected all summonses. But when even this supply of food ran out he accepted, on 27 August, Fairfax's terms by which junior officers were to surrender at quarter (which meant their lives would be spared), but Lords, other officers, and gentlemen of quality were to surrender to the mercy of the Lord General, and some of them, especially the professional soldiers, would be 'set apart for the military execution'. Of these the Council summoned three : Lisle, Lucas, and Gascoigne, to appear before them, and ordered them 'to be immediately shot to death.'[1] Lisle's appeal for time to write to his father and mother, and more time for repentance, was refused. At 7 p.m. on 28 August the three men were brought out to the Castle Yard where three files of musketeers stood ready. As Lucas and Gascoigne embraced, protesting their innocence, Lisle added that it was God's will and that he only wished he could have seen the King, his master, on the throne again. Lucas was shot first, and as he fell, Lisle sprang forward, caught him in his arms, and kissed him. Then he took up his own stand and after drawing five gold pieces from his pocket – one for the executioners and the other four to be given to friends in London – he told the firing squad to come nearer. 'I'll warrant you, sir, we'll hit you', said one, to which he replied, with a smile, 'Friends, I have been nearer you when you have missed me.'[2] Gascoigne, who had watched the double execution and had taken off his doublet, ready to die, was told that he was reprieved. It was thought that the death of this Florentine, distinguished as he was, might be avenged on English visitors to Italy.

Lucas and Lisle were obscurely buried, but in 1661 were reinterred with great solemnity in the Lucas family vault in St. Giles's church, Colchester. Clarendon remarks that Lisle had all Lucas's courage and no man was ever better followed. But 'to this fierceness of courage, he had the softest and most gentle nature imaginable ... and without a capacity to have an enemy.'[3]

NOTES
1 Clarke Trials, f.33b.
2 Clarendon, Bk. XI, § 107.
3 *Ibid.*, § 108.

SIR CHARLES LUCAS
(d. 1648)

CHARLES WAS THE youngest of three brothers, sons of Sir Thomas Lucas of St. John's, Colchester, and Elizabeth Leighton. His youngest sister, Margaret, who became the Duchess of Newcastle in 1645, tells how her brothers used to fence, wrestle, and shoot together as young men, disdaining all music and dancing. So soldiering came naturally to Charles who, in Clarendon's disparaging words, was 'bred in the Low Countries, and always amongst the horse, so that he had little conversation in that Court, where great civility was practised and learned.'[1] In 1639 he was knighted, and commanded a troop of horse in the Second Scots War. He was wounded, though not seriously, in the skirmish at Powick Bridge, where his charge sent the enemy fleeing for seven miles to the Severn, which they swam. At Edgehill, with some 200 horse from at least three regiments, he charged Essex's rear and, as Lord Bernard Stuart reported, 'hath cut off four of their foot regiments and taken a whole bag full of their foot colours.'[2] He took part in the capture of Cirencester on 2 February 1643, and defeated Middleton at Padbury on 1 July, killing or capturing nearly half his force. In March 1644 he threw back some 3,000 Scottish horse at Hilton, near Sunderland, and when Newcastle was shut up in York in April he joined Rupert. As Goring's second-in-command on the left wing at Marston Moor, he swung the support line against the Allied foot, but was captured when, after several charges against the Scots squares, his horse was shot under him. After the battle his captors led him about the field to select any of the slain for private burial and, stern soldier though he was, he wept at the sight that met his eyes. Being exchanged in the winter, he was made Governor of Berkeley Castle where, in August next year, he was besieged by Rainsborough and swore that before he yielded he would 'eat Horse flesh first, and then Man's flesh when that was done'.[3] But after nine days he was forced to surrender. In November the King appointed him Lt-General of all his cavalry, but in March 1645 he was taken prisoner with Astley at Stow-on-the-Wold. Fairfax released him on parole, and he went to London and compounded.

In June 1648, commissioned by the Prince of Wales, Lucas

played a leading part in the Siege of Colchester where, according to Clarendon, who disliked him, his 'rough and proud nature . . . made him . . more intolerable than the siege.'[4] The garrison hoped for relief from Langdale who, from near Lancaster, wrote an encouraging letter to Lucas. But his defeat by Cromwell at Preston on 17 August forced it to surrender eleven days later, on terms by which the professional soldiers would be 'set apart for the military execution.'[5] Of these Lucas, Lisle, and Gascoigne were summoned before the Council of War, dominated by Ireton who 'was upon all occasions of an unmerciful and bloody nature.'[6] They were sentenced, by the Ordinance of Parliament which decreed that all found in arms were rebels, to be shot immediately. Five hours later, at 7 p.m. on 28 August, Ireton led the three to the place of execution. Lucas went first and, pulling his hat over his eyes and baring his breast, cried 'Rebels, do your worst !'[7] As he fell, Lisle sprang forward and embraced him. The two friends were buried in an obscure grave, but in 1661 were reinterred in the Lucas family vault in St. Giles's church, Colchester, under a marble slab which records that they had been 'in cold blood barbarously murdered' by Fairfax. Although Fairfax during the siege accused Lucas of breaking his parole, which Lucas denied, Gardiner says of the sentence that 'it was for a civil tribunal rather than a military tribunal to unravel the question of the guilt of the prisoners.'[8] Gascoigne was spared because he was a Florentine.

Lucas was a born soldier and, as a Royalist cavalry commander, second only to Rupert. He had, as his sister said, 'a practical genius to the warlike arts',[9] and wrote *A Treatise of the Arts in War*. But being in cipher, it was never decoded, and has since disappeared.

NOTES

[1] Clarendon, Bk. XI, § 108.
[2] *Edgehill*, p. 281 (Lord Bernard Stuart's letter, dated 28 October 1642, British Museum, Harl. MS. 3783, f.60).
[3] Lloyd, p. 476.
[4] Clarendon, *loc. cit.*
[5] S. R. Gardiner, *op. cit.* Vol. IV, p. 202.
[6] Clarendon, Bk. XI, § 109.
[7] James Heath, *A New Book of English Martyrs and Confessors* (1665?), p. 136.
[8] S. R. Gardiner, *op cit.*, Vol. III, p. 463.
[9] *Life of Margaret ,Duchess of Newcastle*, by herself, appended to her *Life of the Duke of Newcastle*, ed. C. H. Firth (1886), p. 158.

EDMUND LUDLOW
(1617?-1692)

'. . . A GRUFF, POSITIVE humour, resolutely bent upon whatever his own will suggested,' wrote Cromwell of the republican Ludlow who later became one of his bitterest opponents. Born in about 1617 at Maiden Bradley, Wiltshire, he was the son of Sir Henry Ludlow and Elizabeth Phelips. Educated possibly at Blandford, he matriculated from Trinity College, Oxford, in 1634, and in 1638 was admitted to the Inner Temple. Sharing the radical views of his father, M.P. for Wiltshire, he wrote that 'the question in dispute between the King's party and us is whether the King should govern us as a God by his own will . . or whether the people should be governed by laws made by themselves.'[1] He began his military career in Essex's Lifeguard and fought with them at Powick Bridge and Edgehill.[2] In May 1643 he was made Governor of Wardour Castle where he was besieged that winter, but after a spirited defence, had to surrender in May 1644. He was imprisoned in Oxford but quickly exchanged. Parliament made him Sheriff of Wiltshire, and Waller commissioned him to raise a regiment of horse. It was not a lucky regiment. Beaten at Warminster Heath, it

135

fought at Second Newbury, but in December was surprised at Salisbury and suffered 80% casualties.

In April 1645 Ludlow resigned his command, and in May next year became M.P. for Wiltshire, associating himself with the small 'Commonwealth' party described by Cromwell as 'a proud sort of people, and only considerable in their own conceits.'[3] Ludlow was a poor speaker but we know that he considered 'an accommodation with the King as unsafe to the people of England' and that only the blood of him that shed it 'could cleanse the land of the blood shed therein'. He played a leading part in Pride's Purge (6 December 1646), attended eleven meetings of the court which tried the King, and signed the death warrant. He was one of the five selectors of the new Council of State, and was himself added to that body. Although not a Leveller, he befriended Lilburne and was lampooned as 'Levelling Ludlow'. As second-in-command in 1650 in Ireland he approved of Cromwell's severity at Drogheda, 'to discourage others from making opposition'; and from Ireton's death in November 1651 until Fleetwood's arrival there in October 1652, he acted as Commander-in-Chief. He disapproved of Cromwell's expulsion of the Long Parliament, and in January 1656 Fleetwood discovered that he was circulating pamphlets against the government. Returning to England, Ludlow had two angry interviews with Cromwell and told him just what he thought of his government. Thereafter, for as long as Cromwell lived, he was closely watched. He represented Hindon, Wiltshire, in Richard Cromwell's Parliament, and on Richard's fall was given the command in Ireland and busied himself with replacing Cromwellian officers with staunch republicans. But events were moving too fast for him. The Convention Parliament, in which he sat for Hindon, was filling up with members expelled by Pride's Purge, and he was preparing to join Lambert in arms when that worthy was captured. He went into hiding and in August, with a price of £300 on his head, escaped to France. By 1662 he was settled, with other republicans and regicides, at Vevey where he completed his *Memoirs*.[4] But on 6 July 1689 he left them saying he had "received a call from the Lord to return to his native land . . . to deliver the nation from the house of bondage.'[5] On his arrival an address was delivered to William III demanding his arrest.

But he escaped and ended his days in Vevey, where he had a latin motto carved above his door : *Omne solvm forti partris quia patris.* Through thick and thin Ludlow had remained constant to his republican principles. He was no great genius in camp, or council. But for sheer obstinacy and 'unconquerable will' he had no equal in his own day, and few in any other.

NOTES

[1] *Memoirs,* ed. C. H. Firth, Vol. I (1894), p. xviii.

[2] After the battle he could not find his servant with his cloak and had to walk about all that frosty night 'with nothing to keep me warm but a suite of iron' (Peter Young, *The English Civil War Armies)* (1973), p. 37.

[3] *Memoirs,* Vol. I, p. 186.

[4] 'Those many reams of paper he had, whilst grumbling in Switzerland, emptied his galls into' (Geoffrey Ridsdill Smith, *Without Touch of Dishonour*) (1968), p. 168.

[5] *Memoirs,* Vol. I, p. vi.

LIEUTENANT-GENERAL SIR JAMES LUMSDEN (1598?-1660)

They that faucht stood extraordinarie weill to it . . .. These that ran away shew themselffs most baselie. I commanding the battel was on the heid of your Lordship's regiment and Buccleuches but they carryed not themselffs as I would have wissed, nather could I prevaill with them.

SIR JAMES LUMSDEN, writing of Marston Moor[1]

SIR JAMES, one of the three sons of Robert Lumsden, was Sergeant-Major-General of the Foot in the Scots Army which played such a vital part in the Parliamentarian victory at Marston Moor. He was an officer of good experience for he had commanded a Scots regiment under King Gustavus Adolphus of Sweden, and distinguished himself at the Siege of Frankfurt-on-Oder and at the Battle of Lützen in 1631. He had been Governor of Osnaburg [*sic*] in 1635. Returning to Scotland in 1639, he bought the estate of Innergellie in Fifeshire, and married a lady named Christianne Rutherford. His two brothers had also been in the Swedish service.

Robert seems to have been Major-General to Lord Callender in 1644 and was killed at the storming of Dundee in 1651. William, who is said to have fought at Marston Moor, was lieutenant-colonel of Lord Coupar's Regiment of Foot in 1645 and 1646.

Sir James's conduct at Marston Moor evidently contributed greatly to the Allied success. It was his duty to form up the foot in order of battle and, although compelled to do so in a hurry, he managed to arrange that, with them arrayed in three lines, he was able to plug the gaps when Sir William Blakiston's Royalist cavalry brigade counterattacked and caused panic in the front lines – 'so possessed with ane pannik fear that they ran for example to others and no enemie following', as Lumsden wrote in his dispatch. Not the least of his services, at any rate to historians, was to leave us a plan of the Allied dispositions appended to this dispatch to Lord Loudon which began 'These are to give your Lordship accompt of the victorie it hath pleased God to bestow on us far above our deserts, and the way was thus. Prince Rupert advancing for York we brak up our beleaguring to meet him, he haiffing ane order, which was intercepted, from the King that nothing but Impossibilities should stay him from beating the Scots,' an order which Culpeper had told the King would undo him, for Rupert would fight 'whatever comes on't'.

Early in 1644 Lumsden had been given command of a regiment of foot which had formerly belonged to Lord Gordon. By December, five months after Marston Moor, he was Governor of Newcastle. During the 1650 campaign in Scotland, in which Montrose was captured and hanged, he served as Lieutenant-General of Horse under David Leslie and, being taken prisoner by his former comrades-in-arms at Dunbar, was not released till 1652.

He could not have foreseen, as he wrote his dispatch three days after Marston Moor, with its detailed accounts of how each regiment fought, or ran, and how each commander carried himself, what interest it would arouse 300 years later. For, though the letter was printed as a broadside in Edinburgh under the title of *The Glorious and Miraculous Battel at York*, the appended plan was not. The accidental discovery of the very tattered original eight years ago gave us the first contemporary plan of the Parliamentarian battle order.

NOTES

1 Lumsden's account and the important plan which he drew are reproduced in *Marston Moor* and in Geoffrey Ridsdill Smith, *op. cit.*

CHARLES GERARD, 1st EARL OF MACCLESFIELD
(d. 1694)

IT IS NOT SURPRISING that this bold cavalry commander and friend of Rupert hated, 'without knowing why',[1] the scheming Digby. He was soon to learn. The eldest son of Sir Charles Gerard of Halsall, Lancashire, and Penelope, sister and heiress of Sir Edward Fitton, Bart., of Gawsworth, Cheshire, he entered Leyden University in 1633 and continued his education in France under John Goffe of Magdalen College, Oxford. He served in the Dutch army and in both Scots Wars, and joined the King at Shrewsbury in 1642. At Edgehill he commanded a brigade of foot, who fought courageously, and was himself wounded. He was wounded again at Lichfield in March 1643, and in July commanded a wing of cavalry at the Siege of Bristol. When Rupert sent him in to arrange terms with the Governor, he threatened to fire the town if shooting from the windows continued. He greatly distinguished himself at First Newbury, and in the relief of Newark, where he was wounded again and captured. As commander of the Royalist forces in South Wales his victory over Laugharne at Newcastle Emlyn in May 1645 gained him control of all the area except Pembroke and Tenby. But the violence of his ill-disciplined levies, and his own plain dealing, both with gentry and common people, had so offended the Welsh that they were unwilling to serve the King when he came among them after Naseby. In order to appease them Charles replaced Gerard by Lord Astley, compensating him with a barony, and the command of his Lifeguard when he left Wales in 1645. It was Gerard and Lichfield who led the cavalry sortie from Chester to rescue Langdale on Rowton Heath, but they were overwhelmed by Langdale's fleeing horse, Lichfield was killed, and Gerard wounded. When the army reached Newark, with Rupert and Willys, Gerard interrupted the King at dinner and remonstrated forcibly with him over his dismissal of Willys from the Governorship of Newark, and his own removal from his Welsh command for which he blamed Digby, calling him a traitor. Angrily dismissed, they submitted a petition demanding justice for Willys and for others like Rupert who had not been allowed to defend themselves. Next morning, the King being still adamant, they and most of the cavalry rode out of Newark, and out of the King's service. But next year Gerard rejoined the King at Oxford, raised a troop of horse, and scoured the countryside until Oxford surrendered. He then left England, probably with Rupert.

In 1649 Gerard was with the Prince of Wales in Jersey and next year, at Breda, advised him to come to terms with the Scottish Commissioners. By 1654 he was serving as a volunteer under Turenne at the Siege of Arras. Back in Paris, he quarrelled with Hyde for not urging Charles II to put work before pleasure; and encouraged his young cousin, John Gerard, in the plot to assassinate Cromwell. In 1660 he sailed with Charles to Dover, and rode at the head of the Lifeguard on his progress to Whitehall. In 1679 he was created Earl of Macclesfield but two years later was dismissed from the Bedchamber as an adherent of Monmouth whom he entertained at his Cheshire seat. Outlawed in 1684, he fled to the Continent. In 1688 he returned with William of Orange as commander of his bodyguard on the march to London, and the next year became a Privy Councillor, Lord President of the Welsh Marches, Gloucestershire, Herefordshire, Monmouth, and North and South Wales. His eventful, stormy career ended on 7 January 1694 and he was buried in the Exeter vault in Westminster Abbey. He was survived by his wife, Jane, daughter of Pierre de Civelle, a Frenchman living in England, who bore him two sons (the eldest of whom, Charles, succeeded to the title) and three daughters.

NOTES
[1] Clarendon, Bk. IX, § 121.

EDWARD MONTAGU, 2nd EARL OF MANCHESTER
(1602-1671)

A sweet, meek man.

ROBERT BAILLIE

Of a soft and obliging temper, of no great depth, but universally beloved, being both a virtuous and a generous man.

BISHOP GILBERT BURNET

CONTEMPORARY VIEWS of Manchester's character leave no doubt that he was a pleasant person, but by no means fit for great place. As an army commander it was his misfortune that his second-in-command, Cromwell, was in every way a better soldier.

Manchester was the eldest son of Sir Henry Montagu, 1st Earl of Manchester, by his wife, Catherine Spencer. He entered Sidney Sussex College, Cambridge, that hotbed of Puritanism, in 1618, and represented the county of Huntingdon in the Parliaments of 1624, 1625, and 1626. He was one of Prince Charles's entourage when, in 1623, he went to Spain in search of a bride, and was created a K.B. at the coronation (1626). That same year, after his father was created Earl of Manchester, he was known by the courtesy title of Viscount Mandeville. His second wife, Lady Anne Rich, being the daughter of the Puritan Earl of Warwick, he came to identify himself with the Puritans and became estranged from the Court. He was in constant touch with Pym, Hampden, Fiennes, and St. John. When the Five Members were impeached by Charles I for high treason (3 January 1642) his name was added to theirs.

In September 1642 Mandeville took command of a regiment of foot in Essex's army, a unit which fled with the first at Edgehill and was disbanded in November. In the same month he succeeded to his father's title. During the winter he was active, not only in raising money for the army but in endeavouring to bring about a truce. Parliament made him Lord Lieutenant of Huntingdonshire and Northamptonshire. On 9 August 1643 he replaced Lord Grey of Wark as Major-General of the Eastern Association, with Oliver Cromwell as his second-in-command and General of Horse. They were old acquaintances, both belonging to Huntingdonshire families and both educated at Sidney Sussex. The victory at Winceby (11 October) was a good beginning, and the storming of Lincoln (6 May 1644) secured possession of the county for

Parliament. Manchester took part in the Siege of York and the Battle of Marston Moor, where he took good care of his men, thanking them for their service and endeavouring to supply them with provisions. During the rest of the summer his operations were lethargic in the extreme, owing no doubt to the growing hostility between the Independents and the Presbyterians in his own command. At the Second Battle of Newbury he unsuccessfully attacked Shaw House too late in the day, and that night allowed the Royalists, who were within little more than musket shot, to slip away. In the quarrels that followed he declared 'If we beat the King ninety-nine times, he is king still, and so will his posterity be after him ; but if the King beat us once, we shall be all hanged, and our posterity be made slaves.'

This was too much for Cromwell who now denounced 'his Lordship's continued backwardness to all actions . . . . his neglecting of opportunityes and declineing to take or pursue advantages upon the enemy. . . .' With the formation of the New Model Army Manchester was relieved of his military command (4 April 1645). He was utterly opposed to the 'trial' of the King, retiring from public life except for being made Chancellor of Cambridge University in March 1649. In December 1657 he refused to take his seat in the Upper House, and worked hard for the Restoration of King Charles II, for which he was richly rewarded, being made Lord Chamberlain and a Privy Councillor, amongst other honours (1660), and created a K.G. (1661). At the coronation he carried the sword of state.

In the Dutch War Manchester was made a general (1667) but saw no action. In the same year he became a member of the Royal Society. He was married five times, and sired a numerous progeny. Dying on 7 May 1671, he was buried in Kimbolton church, Huntingdonshire.

MAJOR-GENERAL SIR EDWARD MASSEY
(1617/19?-1674/5?)

EDWARD MASSEY the fifth son of John Massey of Coddington, Cheshire, and Anne, daughter of Richard Grosvenor of Eaton in the same county, probably soldiered in the Low Countries before 1639 when he became a captain of pioneers in Legge's Regiment, and joined the King at York in 1642. But seeing little chance of promotion, he became Lt-Colonel of the Parliamentarian Earl of Stamford's Regiment of Foot in the West. Stamford was Governor of Gloucester, but when he marched out against Hopton in December 1642, he left Massey behind as Deputy-Governor. In March 1643 Waller retired there after beating Lord Herbert at Highnam, and held it while Massey led his force out to capture Tewkesbury by surprise, and break down Prince Maurice's bridge of boats. Waller, his men rested, now joined Massey in an effort to cut Maurice off from Oxford by seizing Upton Bridge over the Severn but they were defeated at Ripple Field in April. Massey withdrew to Gloucester where, with only one regular regiment and discontent rife among the citizens, he is said to have negotiated for surrender with Will. Legge, his old commanding officer. But he was probably only playing for time and rejected the King's summons on 10 August, from which date he held out stoutly until Essex relieved him four weeks later, when he had only three barrels of powder left. Throughout the winter of 1643-4 Gloucester was hard pressed by the surrounding Royalist garrisons, but in April 1644 Massey was able to break out and capture some of them, even as far afield as Monmouth. In April 1645, after being beaten by Rupert at Ledbury, he stormed Evesham, astride the Royalist lines of communication between Oxford and Worcester. As Major-General of the Western Association he now joined Fairfax, who was marching to relieve Taunton, besieged by Goring. But Goring abandoned the siege and Massey was detailed to follow him, with 4000 horse. He surprised some of the Royalist troops bathing at Ilminster, but Goring escaped to Langport. In the ensuing battle, Massey could take no part but joined Fairfax for the storming of Bridgwater in July 1645.

Next year Massey sat as M.P. for Gloucester but, as a Presbyterian, was obnoxious to the Independents who seized the opportunity of disbanding his two regiments which had refused to serve in Ireland. In April 1647 Parliament appointed him Lt-General of forces in Ireland, but his known opposition to the Army made many of the officers refuse to serve under him, and in June the Army impeached him, and ten other M.P.s, on charges which included the planning of another war. Massey, and Poyntz who had commanded the forces raised in London to oppose the Army, escaped to Holland. Massey returned after Pride's Purge, but was arrested that December. Escaping once more to Holland, he subsequently took service under Charles II and in 1650 accompanied him to Scotland, fought there, and preceded him into England where he was painfully wounded at Upton Bridge, serving as Lt-General. After Worcester he followed Charles in his flight as far as Droitwich, but then took refuge with Lady Stamford at Broadgate. He was moved, when sufficiently recovered, to the Tower for trial but once again managed to escape to Holland. He became a member of the Great Trust, successor to the Sealed Knot, and was the chief organizer of the Gloucester rising planned for 1659. Betrayed, he was taken, but escaped from his guards in the rainy dusk. Returning from abroad in June, he sat in the Convention Parliament for London, and later for Gloucester until his death, unmarried, in 1674 or 1675. He was knighted in 1660.

Massey's sanguine complexion matched his temperament, whether he was in prison or commanding in the field. As a staunch Presbyterian his opposition to Charles I had been on religious rather than on political grounds, and he found the rule of the sword more intolerable than that of the monarchy.

PRINCE MAURICE
(1621-1652)

He understood very little more of the war than to fight very stoutly when there was occasion.

CLARENDON

PRINCE MAURICE, the fourth son of Frederick V, Elector Palatine of the Rhine, and Elizabeth, daughter of King James I, was throughout his brief life the faithful friend and ally of his brother Prince Rupert. He was nevertheless an intrepid leader with substantial achievements to his credit. Unquestionably Clarendon was right in asserting that he knew nothing of the causes of the War – and indeed he cared less. A man of simple loyalties, it was sufficient for him that his beloved brother had thrown in his lot with the King, his uncle.

Maurice was born at the Castle of Cüstrin, Brandenburg, 6 January 1621 when his mother, the Winter Queen, was in flight after the Battle of The White Mountain, outside Prague. He was brought up in Brandenburg and at Leyden in Holland, and in 1637 went with his brother Rupert to learn the art of war under the Prince of Orange. They distinguished themselves at the Siege of Breda. Thereafter he pursued his studies in Paris. In 1640-1 he served a campaign under Banèr, being present at the Siege of Amberg (January 1641).

Maurice accompanied Rupert to England in August 1642 and raised a regiment of horse which, according to Richard Atkyns, one of its captains, 'was accounted the most active regiment in the army, and most commonly placed in the out quarters.' The Prince fought at Powick Bridge, where he was slightly wounded in the head, at Edgehill, and at the storming of Cirencester. He was then given an independent commission (2 March 1643) to defend Gloucestershire, which was threatened by the conquering progress of Sir William Waller.

After a minor success at Little Dean (11 April), he inflicted a sharp defeat upon Waller at Ripple (13 April), handling his army with real skill. He was then summoned to the unsuccessful attempt to relieve Reading. Soon after he went into the West as Lieutenant-General to the Marquess of Hertford. He received two shrewd hurts in his head and was briefly taken prisoner in the skirmish at

Chewton Mendip (10 June 1643), and played a distinguished part at Lansdown and Roundway Down.

After assisting his brother in the capture of Bristol, Maurice and the Earl of Carnarvon were sent to reduce Dorset and Devon. They took Dorchester (4 August) but then, unhappily, fell out, a quarrel due in part to pillaging by Maurice's ill-paid tropos. The Prince was sent into Devonshire and captured Exeter (4 September) an important success, and Dartmouth (6 October). He might have taken Plymouth but he fell ill of a slow fever, 'with great dejection of strength'.

In 1644 he laid siege to Lyme, but was successfully resisted by Blake. His forces, nevertheless, played an important part in the capture of Essex's army in the Lostwithiel campaign. At Second Newbury, however, his men were driven from the fortified village of Speen, a failure which jeopardized the whole Royalist position.

In December 1644 Maurice was given command of Worcestershire, Shropshire, Herefordshire, and Monmouthshire, with his Headquarters at Worcester, a charge which he found fraught with difficulties. Money was short and the soldiers prone to desertion. He was with the King at the storming of Leicester (30 May), at Naseby, and at the relief of Hereford in September.

When, after Bristol, Rupert was disgraced, Maurice stuck

147

by him, but without forfeiting the King's goodwill, and after the surrender of Oxford he went abroad with his brother. He served in the French army in Flanders, and then in 1648 joined Rupert in his seafaring adventures, serving as his vice-admiral. He was lost in a storm off the Anagadas when, on 14 September 1652, his flagship, the *Defiance*, foundered.

Overshadowed, throughout his brief career, by a brilliant brother, Maurice has been much underrated. He was a brave and handsome prince, with a number of solid military exploits to his credit.

SIR JOHN MELDRUM
(1585-1645)

JOHN MELDRUM, a professional Scottish soldier, was a captain as early as 1611 and on his return to England from the Low Countries in 1622 was knighted for his services. He went with the expedition to relieve La Rochelle in 1627-8 and later served as a colonel under Gustavus Adolphus. He had also served in Ireland, settling the province of Ulster, for which James I granted him lands in Fermanagh, and he is described as an agent to Lord Balfour of Burley who had extensive grants there. Another of his ventures was the

148

purchase of a half share in a patent for maintaining a lighthouse at Winterton Ness, Norfolk, which brought him in 1d on every passing ship. Complaints were raised against this in the Parliament of 1624 but James I refused to abolish it. Later on Meldrum bought a similar patent for erecting lighthouses on the N. and S. Forelands. The Royalists said that he adopted the Parliamentarian cause in order to preserve these lucrative patents. But when Charles I summoned him from Hull to York in June 1642 he replied that he 'had served him and his father 36 years, got nothing, and had spent £2000.'[1]

Meldrum's first duty for Parliament was to take reinforcements to Hotham in July during the first Siege of Hull where, in one sally, he drove the Royalist horse and foot back to Beverley, inflicting severe casualties. He was with Waller at the reduction of Portsmouth, and at Edgehill commanded a brigade of foot on the right which stood firm against the pick of the Royalist infantry. Next year with Essex he took part in the capture of Reading. In October he was sent with 400 men to reinforce once more the garrison of Hull, then undergoing its second siege, and, with Lambert and Rainsborough, led a sally in force in which he was wounded. But they drove the Royalists from their works, captured their guns (including those great guns Gog and Magog), and brought the siege to an end. Soon after this Meldrum and Sir Thomas Fairfax crossed the Humber, retook Gainsborough, and drove the enemy out of the Isle of Axholme. On 29 February 1644 he laid siege to Newark, stormed Muskham Bridge, and completely invested the town. But three weeks later Rupert, by a swift moonlight march, surprised him. After a fierce cavalry action, Meldrum found himself hemmed in and, short of provisions, had to surrender. When he marched out he left behind more than 3000 muskets, 11 brass cannon, 2 mortars, and a 32-pounder basilisk from Hull, 4 yards long, known as 'Sweet Lips'. In his next more successful action he assisted Fairfax at Selby where they defeated and captured Belasyse. Sent to oppose Rupert's invasion of Lancashire, he secured Manchester, but the Prince took Stockport, Bolton, and Liverpool. After Marston Moor, with Brereton, he defeated Lord Byron at Montgomery Castle and retook Liverpool. In February 1645 he laid siege to Scarborough, held by Sir Hugh Cholmley.

They kept up an acrimonious correspondence which perhaps lightened the tedium of the siege. Cholmley, reverting to the old joke about lighthouses, writes 'I do not please myself in raylings and personall recriminations, nothinge else being suteable to those I receive from you . . . all men knowinge what lights you study to preserve which, not like seamarks have directed but like *ignis* (sic) *fatui* have mislead you out of the way of obedience.' To which Meldrum, stung by this reference to his spiritual lights, retorts 'If you have not a better reply to that part of my letter pressing that a reformation doth dazzle your eyesight, than to fall very impertinently upon my lights I must answer you that such a poor and weak repartee doth argue some defect which I shall forbear to express . . . If you think yourself to be in a condition rather to give the law than to take it the issue will bear witness which of us have been most out of square.'² But the lights were soon to go out for him. He was mortally wounded resisting a sally from the castle, and died 21 July before it capitulated.

NOTES
1 *An Extract of Severall Letters sent from York and Hull*, dated 22 June 1642.
2 H.M.C. Xth *Report*, Appendix VI, pp. 155-7. Cholmley had referred to the 'dazeling lights of Reformation.'

JAMES GRAHAM, 5th EARL and
1st MARQUESS OF MONTROSE
(1612-1650)

He either fears his fate too much,
Or his deserts are small,
That puts it not unto the touch,
To win or lose it all.

JAMES GRAHAM lived true to his bold words. The son of the 4th Earl of Montrose and Margaret, daughter of the 1st Earl of Gowrie, he studied first at Glasgow and then at St. Andrews. In 1626 he succeeded to the earldom, and four years later married Magdalene, daughter of Lord Carnegie. From 1633 to 1636 he travelled on the Continent. Back in Scotland, he joined the Covenanters, and was sent in 1639 to Aberdeen where he took the anti-Covenanting Earl of Huntly prisoner. The Parliament which met in Edinburgh next year was dominated by the Presbyterian clergy and the Lords of the Articles, led by Argyll and Hamilton. To check the power of these ambitious lords, Montrose and his friends drew up the Cumbernauld Bond in which they expressed their loyalty not only to the Covenant but also to the Crown. With his regiment he then joined the Covenanting army at Coldstream and was the first to cross the Tweed. After the armistice in October he began to correspond with the King. But in June 1641 a letter to him from Charles was intercepted, and Argyll had him arrested and sent to Edinburgh Castle. When the King arrived in August Montrose appealed, in vain, for an open trial and was not released till November when Charles had gone. At York in 1643 the Queen encouraged him to lead a Royalist rising in North Scotland, aided by an Irish force under Antrim. But the King, when approached at the Siege of Gloucester, would not listen, trusting Hamilton's promise to keep the Scots neutral till the winter. However, by December, when Hamilton arrived in Oxford, the Scottish Alliance with Parliament had materialized; so he was arrested, and in February 1644 Montrose was appointed Lt-General of the Royalist forces in Scotland, and in May created a Marquess. In August, disguised as a groom and with only two companions, he crossed the Border and raised the Royal Standard near Blair Castle.

In the next twelve months, with an army of less than 4000 foot and 200 horse, he won six battles against the Covenanters: Tippermuir and Aberdeen in 1644, Inverlochy, Auldearn, Alford, and Kilsyth in 1645. After Kilsyth he entered Glasgow where, commissioned as Lt-Governor, he summoned a Parliament. The King now ordered him to march south. But the Macdonalds and Gordons deserted him, and the Lowlanders refused to rise. Left with only his Irish troops, he doubled back, but on 13 September was surprised and defeated at Philiphaugh by Leslie and his cavalry, come up from England after Naseby. But Montrose did not give up until July 1646 when the King, then a prisoner, ordered him to disband his army. He escaped in a small boat to Bergen and in 1647 visited the Queen in Paris. In 1649 he offered his services to Charles II and, as his Lt-Governor, raised men and money in Denmark and Sweden and sailed for the Orkneys in December with 1200 men, most of whom were lost by shipwreck. Next year he crossed to the mainland, but was defeated by Leslie at Invercarron. Betrayed by Macleod of Assynt, he was brought to Edinburgh. At his trial he defiantly proclaimed his loyalty to King and Covenant and said he was 'prouder to have his head set up on the place it was appointed to be, than he could have been to have had his picture hung in the King's bedchamber', and 'he heartily wished he had flesh enough to be sent to every city in Christendom, as a testimony of the cause for which he suffered.'[1] The barbarous sentence of hanging, drawing, and quartering was carried out in the Grassmarket on 25 May 1650. As poet, warrior, statesman, and devoted Royal servant, Montrose's name shines bright in the annals of Civil War history in which he showed himself one of the best commanders of raiding forces that our country has ever produced.

NOTES
[1] Clarendon, Bk. XII, § 139.

SIR PHILIP MUSGRAVE, BART.
(1607-1678)

*. . . A gentleman of a noble extraction, and ample fortune in Cumber-
land and Westmoreland, lived to engage himself again in the same
service, and with the same affection, and, after very great sufferings,
to see the King restored.*   CLARENDON

SIR PHILIP, the son of Sir Richard Musgrave, Bart., K.B., and
Frances, daughter of Philip, Lord Wharton, came of one of the
oldest families in the North. His estates were at Hartley in Westmorland and Edenhall in Cumberland. His father, the first
baronet, died in 1615 and thereafter Sir Philip lived for a time with
his grandfather and guardian, Lord Wharton, and later at the
Yorkshire home of Judge Hutton, one of whose daughters he
married in 1625. By that time he had studied both at Trinity
College, Oxford, whence he matriculated in 1624, and at Peterhouse, Cambridge. We are told that in his youth his health was
poor, that he was of a somewhat melancholy disposition, and little
inclined to an active life. However that may be, he assumed the
usual responsibilities of his rank, was a J.P. in both Cumberland
and Westmorland, a commissioner of oyer and terminer, and a
D.L. In 1639 he became colonel of a regiment of foot. In addition
he improved his estates which, during his minority, were said to
be much disordered, and when in 1640 he became M.P. for Westmorland he was among the wealthier members of the Long
Parliament. When war broke out in 1642, Musgrave was made
Governor of Carlisle, and raised regiments both of horse and foot.
When, on 27 October 1642, Royalist Commissioners for Cumberland and Westmorland met at Barnard Castle, Musgrave was
among them. They engaged to send 150 dragoons and 150 foot
to reinforce the Yorkshire Cavaliers. On 15 March 1643, for his
active Royalism, he was disabled from sitting in Parliament. He
is said to have fought at Marston Moor. Be that as it may, it seems
likely that a contingent from his garrison was present. After the
fall of York Sir Thomas Glemham came to Carlisle. To him at
least as much as to Musgrave must go the credit for the dogged
Royalist defence of that city. When, on 28 June 1645, the place
eventually surrendered, Glemham and Musgrave with the survivors of their garrisons joined the remnants of the King's army.

153

Musgrave was with the cavalry routed by Poyntz at Rowton Heath, outside Chester (24 September 1645), and was captured.

He remained an active Royalist and played a major part in the events leading up to the Second Civil War, for about the beginning of May 1648 he succeeded in surprising Carlisle. The Duke of Hamilton marched south through Carlisle to meet disaster at Preston (17 August 1648), leaving Sir George Monro to cooperate with Musgrave. Monro retreated into Scotland leaving Sir Philip in the lurch. Carlisle fell to Cromwell early in October, and Musgrave, who had stationed himself at Appleby, was compelled to quit the place soon after (9 October). He was nevertheless able to escape abroad. He was proscribed by Parliament on 24 March 1649 and his estates were sequestered. He accompanied Charles II to Scotland in 1650, but was one of the English Cavaliers banished by Argyll and his Committee. He joined the Earl of Derby in the Isle of Man and was there when it surrendered in November 1651. According to Charles Dalton, he fought at Worcester.[1] He was, however, permitted to reside in England but, continuing in the Royalist cause, was arrested in 1653 and imprisoned. At the Restoration his loyalty was rewarded with the Governorship of Carlisle. He was once again member for Westmorland in the

Cavalier Parliament. On 2 5 March 1650 a warrant had been granted creating him a peer but the patent was never issued. He died
7 February 1678 and is buried at Edenhall. Much of his correspondence has survived.[2]

NOTES

[1] C. Dalton, *English Army Lists and Commission Registers, 1661-1714*, Vol. I (1892),
p. 15.
[2] It is much to be hoped that Mr Rex Taylor will one day introduce it to a wider
public.

WILLIAM CAVENDISH, DUKE OF NEWCASTLE
(1592-1676)

'HIS EDGE HAD too much of the razor in it, for he had a tincture of a
romantic spirit, and had the misfortune to have somewhat of the
poet in him.'[1] So wrote Sir Philip Warwick of William Cavendish,
son of Charles Cavendish and Katherine, Lady Ogle. He was
educated at St. John's College, Cambridge, and in 1610 was
created a K.B. In 1618 he became Earl, in 1643 Marquess, and in
1665 Duke, of Newcastle. In 1618 he had married Elizabeth,
daughter of William Basset of Blore, Staffordshire, and the wealthy
widow of the Hon. Henry Howard. From 1638 to 1641 he was
Governor to Charles, Prince of Wales and, among other things,
turned him into a fine horseman.

On the outbreak of war Newcastle was appointed Governor
of Hull and Officer Commanding the four Northern counties. He
secured Newcastle for the King, set up his winter Headquarters in
York and, in 1643, met the Queen on her landing at Bridlington
with arms and ammunition from the Continent In June he expelled
Fairfax from the West Riding by the Battle of Adwalton Moor and
the capture of Howley House and Bradford. In September he laid
siege to Hull but was flooded out next month and had to raise the
siege, whimsically remarking that although his army was often
called the Popish Army it was clear that it did not trust in its good
works. Early in 1644 he marched north to deal with the invading
Scots, and when Belasyse, his second-in-command, was defeated
and captured at Selby, he had to return to hold York which, in

April, was besieged. Rupert relieved York on 1 July, but offended Newcastle by ordering him to be ready to march against the retreating enemy by 4 a.m. next morning. Newcastle, however, who had endured a gruelling siege, did not join him on Marston Moor till the afternoon, and advised against fighting that day. When, however, the battle did begin he tried to halt the fugitives on the right, and then led a troop of gentlemen volunteers in a gallant but forlorn charge, himself killing three of the enemy. After the Royalist defeat he returned to York but, 'transported with passion and despair'[2] at the way his army so painfully raised had been thrown away and dreading the laughter of the Court, he rode off to Scarborough and sailed, with some of his staff, to Holland.

Next year in Paris (his first wife having died in 1643) he married Margaret Lucas, sister to Sir Charles Lucas and a learned and eccentric lady. By 1650 he was advising Charles II to land in Scotland and raise an army there and was himself negotiating with the Elector of Brandenburg and the King of Denmark for a foreign invasion, until the Royalist defeat at Worcester ended these plans. Whilst living in Antwerp he set up a 'riding-house' which became famous, and published a book in French entitled *Le Méthode et Invention Nouvelle de dresser les Chevaux.* Charles II visited him there and delighted him with his horsemanship. At the Restoration he returned to England and started to restore his ruined estates and two houses, at Welbeck and Bolsover. In 1667 he published a companion volume, in English, to his first book on equitation. These, together with the plays and poetry he wrote, his love of music, and his swordsmanship, reveal a rich variety of interests. 'He liked the pomp and absolute authority of a general well', wrote Clarendon, but not the 'substantial part, and fatigue.'[3] He has been criticized for taking more than six months, with superior forces, to expel the Fairfaxes from the West Riding, but he was handicapped by the presence in Yorkshire of the Queen, for whose safety he was responsible. Had he co-operated more readily with Rupert before Marston Moor, and not fled overseas after the battle, the North might not have been irretrievably lost. Yet, as Clarendon says, he reverenced the King, beggared himself in his service, and set a fine example in the field of personal bravery.[4] He died on Christmas Day 1676 and was buried in St. Michael's Chapel,

Westminster Abbey. The too-flattering life of him which his wife wrote and published in 1667 of which Pepys said 'it showed him but an ass to suffer her to write it',[5] is a caricature of this 'gentleman of grandeur, generosity, loyalty and steady and forward courage.'[6]

NOTES

[1] Sir Philip Warwick, *Memoirs of the Reign of King Charles the First*, p. 258.
[2] Clarendon, Bk. VIII, § 87.
[3] Clarendon, Ibid., § 85.
[4] Clarendon, Ibid., § 83.
[5] Pepys, *Diary*, 18 March 1668.
[6] Warwick, *op. cit, loc. cit.*

SIR EDWARD NICHOLAS, BART.
(1593-1669)

THOSE WHO TAUGHT Edward Nicholas at Salisbury Grammar School, Winchester, Queen's College, Oxford, and the Inner Temple would have been gratified as they watched his progress, becoming Buckingham's secretary, M.P. for Winchelsea (1621 and 1624) and Dover (1627), secretary for the Commissioners of the Admiralty (1625), clerk of the Council in Ordinary (1627) and clerk to the Council of War (1640). So would his parents, John Nicholas of Winterbourne Earls, Wiltshire, and Susan, daughter of William Hunton, of East Knoyle in the same county. But higher honours and greater responsibilities lay ahead. When the King went to Scotland in 1641 Nicholas was left in London to forward intelligence, and implored the King to be conciliatory with the Scots, urging him to hasten his return before Pym's Grand Remonstrance got through the Commons. Sensing the King's growing unpopularity, he respectfully advised him to smile and 'speak a few good words'[1] to those who welcomed him back to London. The King, on his return, made him Secretary of State, in place of Sir Harry Vane, and a Privy Councillor.

In 1642 Nicholas accompanied the King to York, and ultimately to Oxford, where he set up his headquarters in Pembroke College. On him fell the business side of the peace negotiations at Uxbridge. When Oxford was besieged in May 1645 he

157

wrote to warn the King that, short of food, it could not hold out for long ; and early next month he reported the Council's condemnation of Rupert's plan to march north and join Montrose, and its own proposal that he should attack the Eastern Association. To this the King retorted that 'it were a strange thing if my marching army – especially I being at the head of them – should be governed by my sitting Council at Oxford' and that Nicholas must take care that 'the like of this be not done hereafter.'[2] When Rupert came to Oxford in September, after surrendering Bristol, it was Nicholas's painful duty to arrest him, and to forward the Prince's unhappy letter to the King, to which he added a note that, despite mischievous rumours that he had been handsomely bribed for betraying Bristol, he had barely £50 in the world. In March 1646 the King, back in Oxford, ordered Nicholas to try to persuade the Independents to join him in expelling the Scots ; but next month to tell Montreuil that he was ready to take refuge with the Scottish Army at Newark, on suitable conditions. It was Nicholas who, with Ashburnham, prepared him to carry out this desperate plan, although he thought that the King should stay in Oxford and perish honourably. When Oxford surrendered in June Nicholas treated for terms, and was then allowed to go abroad with his wife and family. They settled in Caen.

Nicholas himself, with Charles II in Jersey in 1649, opposed his going to Ireland, lest he capitulated to the Catholics ; and next year, at Breda, his going to Scotland and surrendering to Presbyterian demands. For this he was excluded from further negotiation with the Scottish Commissioners. His honesty and dislike of intrigue had made him hated by the Queen, who resented his efforts to stop her trying to convert the Duke of Gloucester to Catholicism and thereby make an ally of the Pope and, naturally enough, his advice to the impecunious Charles to sell her jewels. Nevertheless, Charles after Worcester summoned Nicholas to Paris, but he could not afford to leave The Hague and had, indeed, sent his wife to England to compound for his estates. Next year (1653) Charles gave him a baronetcy, telling him to sell the title, but there were no bidders. In October 1654 he accompanied Charles to Cologne, and was made Secretary of State. At the Restoration, however, he was too ill to fill this post, and too poor to accept the barony offered him. So he retired to the manor of West Horsley, Surrey, and began to collect pictures. He died 1 September 1669 and was buried in West Horsley church where his wife, Jane, daughter of Henry Jaye of Holverston, Norfolk, whom he had married in 1622 and who lived to be 89, was later buried. The Royal cause had no more 'honest, painstaking, faithful, servant'[3] than Edward Nicholas.

NOTES
[1] *Nicholas Papers*, Vol. I, p. 127: Evelyn, *Memoirs*, Bohn edn., Vol. IV (1879), p. 150.
[2] The King to Nicholas, 11 June.
[3] C. V. Wedgwood, *The King's Peace* (1955), p. 308.

SPENCER COMPTON, 2nd EARL OF NORTHAMPTON
(1601-1643)

I scorn to take quarter from such base rogues as you are.

THE EARL'S LAST WORDS AT HOPTON HEATH, 19 MARCH 1643.

SPENCER COMPTON was born in May 1601. He spent some time at St. John's College, Cambridge, and about 1621 married Mary, daughter of Sir Francis Beaumont. He represented Ludlow in the Parliament of 1621, and next year became Master of the Robes to Prince Charles, and later to him as King. In 1623 he accompanied him when he went to Spain to seek a bride. In 1630 he succeeded to his father's title, and was Lord Lieutenant of Warwickshire until his death.

Northampton was a soldier of experience before the Civil War for he served not only in the two Scots Wars but on the Continent. He was at the famous Siege of Breda (1637) as a volunteer in Colonel George Goring's company in the Dutch service. He was also at the Battle of Vlotho (1638) with the Elector Palatine, when Prince Rupert was taken prisoner. An ardent Royalist, he joined King Charles at York and, besides promising him 40 horse, he executed the Commission Array in Warwickshire in July 1642. In addition he was commissioned to raise a troop of cavalry and a regiment of foot. Northampton had an early success when he carried off the guns which Lord Brooke intended to defend Banbury Castle (8 August), but met with a setback in an action at Southam where his opponents were Colonel John Hampden and Colonel Thomas Ballard (23 August). With his troop – 'one hundred gentlemen', according to Sir Richard Bulstrode who was one of them – he took part in Prince Rupert's first significant victory at Powick Bridge (23 September). At Edgehill he and several of his sons served in Prince Charles's Regiment of Horse on the Royalist right, under Rupert. Their charge met with little opposition, but Northampton and his gallant sons had made their mark in the Royalist Army. In November the troop of horse was expanded into a regiment, which was commanded by his eldest son, James, with Charles, the second son, as lieutenant-colonel. William, the third son, became Governor of the recently captured castle at Banbury, which became the family's main base during the rest of the War.

PLATE 65   Prince Maurice   *William Dobson*

PLATE 66   Sir John Meldrum

PLATE 67   James Graham, 5th Earl and 1st Marquess of Montrose
after Gerard van Honthorst

PLATE 68   William Cavendish, Duke of Newcastle   *Sir Anthony van Dyck*

PLATE 69   Sir Edward Nicholas, 1662   *Sir Peter Lely*

PLATE 70   Spencer Compton, 2nd Earl of Northampton
Henry Paert after Cornelius Johnson and Sir Anthony van Dyck

PLATE 71   George Goring, Earl of Norwich   *Samuel de Wilde*

PLATE 72   James Butler 12th Earl and 1st Duke of Ormonde   *after Sir Peter Lely*

Early in March the Earl led a column, mostly cavalry, to the relief of Lichfield Close but, coming too late, turned aside to Stafford. Here he joined forces with Henry Hastings and together they defeated Sir John Gell and Sir William Brereton on the 19th in the hard-fought Battle of Hopton Heath. The Roundhead cavalry were driven from the field, eight guns were taken, and their foot compelled to make off after suffering heavy casualties. But in the second charge Northampton's horse came down, and he was hemmed in. He is said to have killed a colonel before someone knocked off his helmet with a halberd and, scorning quarter, he was slain.

'He was', writes Clarendon, 'a person of great courage, and honour, and fidelity, and not well known till his evening . . . . All distresses he bore like a common man, and all wants and hardnesses as if he had never known plenty or ease ; most prodigal of his person to danger'. He would often say that 'if he outlived these wars he was certain never to have so noble a death.'[1] It was fortunate indeed for the Royal cause that he had bred six loyal sons of the same stamp.

NOTES
[1] Clarendon, Bk. VI, § 283.

GEORGE GORING, EARL OF NORWICH
(1583?-1663)

GEORGE GORING, described as one of King James I's 'three chief and masterfools',[1] was the son of George Goring of Hurstpierpoint and Ovingdean, Sussex, and Ann, daughter of Henry Denny of Waltham. He is said to have been a gentleman-pensioner at the Court of Queen Elizabeth, was educated at Sidney Sussex College, Cambridge, and then served in Flanders. Knighted in 1608, he became a gentleman of the privy chamber of Henry, Prince of Wales, and a popular member, and practical joker, of the Court. He followed Prince Charles to Spain in 1623 and later was engaged in negotiating his marriage with Henrietta Maria, whose Master of the Horse he became. In 1628 he was created Baron Goring, and over the next ten years, as 'the leader of the monopolists,' made a fortune. He became a Privy Councillor in 1639, but his period of prosperity ended when the Long Parliament abolished the tobacco monopoly. Yet in 1641 he still had an income of £26,000 which he began to expend freely in the King's cause. 'I had all from His Majesty', he said, 'and he hath all again.'[2]

Goring accompanied the Queen when in February 1642 she sailed to Holland to raise money, returning to surprise the younger Fairfax at Seacroft Moor. Later he went as ambassador to France to negotiate an alliance, and aid in money and arms. His letter announcing his success was intercepted and he was impeached for high treason, but rewarded by the King in 1644 with the title of Earl of Norwich. In 1647 he returned to England, ostensibly to compound but also commissioned to raise the Kentish Royalists, although, as Clarendon justly comments,[3] he was fitter to recruit men by his pleasant humour than to lead them. Nevertheless, his quarter-master, Carter, praised his courage, prudence, and energy, while admitting his inexperience. From Barham Down, where his forces had their rendezvous on 30 May 1648, he watched the hard-fought battle for Maidstone and then, bypassing Rochester, made for London hoping to gain an entry. When the City declined to rise, leaving his main force he crossed the Thames and rode to Chelmsford to meet the Essex Royalists. In his absence many of his men deserted, but the cavalry swam their horses over and took up positions at Stratford-atte-Bow where Norwich rejoined them. Four days later he, Sir Charles Lucas, and Lord Capel joined forces at Chelmsford and by a roundabout route made for Colchester, Lucas's home town. During the siege that began on 11 June Norwich was nominally in command but Lucas directed the defence, defeating Fairfax's first attacks. At the end of 11 weeks the defenders, and the inhabitants, who suffered most, were reduced to near starvation. Norwich refused to surrender while there was still hope of relief by Langdale and the 'Engagers' advancing from Scotland. But after their defeat at Preston, threatened with mutiny among his troops, he agreed to treat for terms. By these he, Capel, and other senior officers were granted quarter for their lives. Norwich was imprisoned in Windsor Castle to await the judgment of Parliament, which voted to banish him. But the Independents rescinded this vote and constituted a high court of justice which sentenced him, Holland, and Capel to death. Capel and Holland were executed, but Norwich was saved by the casting vote of the Speaker, Lenthall.

He went abroad and proved 'the ablest and faithfullest servant of the King.'[4] He tried to use Sexby and the Levellers to serve the Royal cause, and was instrumental in having Manning, the ex-Royalist captain turned Parliamentarian spy, arrested. At the Restoration he was appointed Captain of the King's Guard and a Privy Councillor, and was granted a pension of £2000. He died at Brentwood 1 January 1663 and was buried in St. John's Chapel, Westminster Abbey, where his wife, Mary, daughter of Edward Nevill, Lord Abergavenny, had been buried in 1648. They had two sons, George and Charles, and four daughters.

NOTES

[1] Sir Anthony Weldon, The Court and Character of King James, which is included in The Secret History of the Court of James I (1811), p. 399.
[2] C.S.P.D. 1644, p. 261.
[3] Clarendon, Bk. XI, § 55.
[4] Nicholas Papers, Vol. I, p. 254.

163

JAMES BUTLER, 12th EARL, 1st DUKE OF ORMONDE
(1610-1688)

'HE HAD EITHER no enemies or such who were ashamed to profess they were so ;'[1] thus writes Clarendon of this distinguished soldier-statesman. His father, Thomas, Viscount Thurles, was drowned when he was nine. His mother wanted him brought up a Catholic but James I, whose ward he was, disagreed and placed him at Lambeth with the Archbishop of Canterbury with whom he remained from 1624 to 1628. Next year he married Lady Elizabeth Preston, daughter of the Earl of Desmond, and in 1633 succeeded his grandfather. After a brush with Wentworth, the Lord Deputy, over the wearing of swords in the Irish Parliament of 1634 which Wentworth had forbidden but which Ormonde insisted upon,[2] threatening to leave his sword in the guts of the usher who demanded it, he became the Lord Deputy's most loyal supporter. When, in 1641, the Irish Rebellion broke out, he commanded the forces of the Protestant Dublin government and next year beat the Catholic rebels at Kilrush. His wife in the meantime, with her children and hundreds of fugitives whom she was relieving, were cut off in Kilkenny Castle. Charles I, who created Ormonde a Marquess in August 1644 and was in desperate need of reinforcements from Ireland, ordered him to conclude a truce. The so called 'Cessation' which followed in September enabled him to send 5000 troops to England where they joined Byron in Cheshire. In 1644 Ormonde became Lord Lieutenant of Ireland and sent more troops under the Earl of Antrim to help Montrose in Scotland. The 'Cessation' was unpopular with both sides but Ormonde had been negotiating a peace treaty until, in August 1645, he was confronted by a private treaty with the rebels which Glamorgan, the King's envoy, had arranged with the Papal Nuncio, Rinuccini, and signed in the King's name. This granted them all their demands for Roman Catholic supremacy in return for sending 10,000 troops to England. Parliament, hearing of this, was outraged, and when Glamorgan reached Dublin, Ormonde, to save the King's good name, arrested him. By March 1646 Ormonde had arranged further peace talks, with concessions to the rebels when the promised troops had been sent to England. But in July this Ormonde Treaty was rejected by the insatiable Rinuccini and Ormonde, knowing that the King was now a prisoner and fearing for the safety of the Protestant loyalists, appealed for help to the English Parliament. Surrendering Dublin to the Parliamentary Commissioners in September, he sailed in 1647 for England. Here he conferred with the King at Hampton Court, and went on to see the Queen in Paris, returning to Dublin in October 1648 with a new commission as Lord Lieutenant and with orders to obey only her until the King was free.

After Charles I's execution Ormonde took another new commission from Charles II and in August 1649 attacked Dublin, but was beaten at Rathmines. Cromwell's landing this same month, and his subsequent ruthless successes, forced Ormonde to leave Ireland (December 1650). From 1651 he was abroad in personal attendance on Charles II and several times crossed to England in disguise to discuss Royalist risings, narrowly escaping capture in London in a house-to-house chase in 1659. At the Restoration he was created a Duke and was appointed Lord High Steward of the Household and reappointed Lord Lieutenant of Ireland. As such he had the good sense to stop the King's grant of Phoenix Park to Lady Castlemaine. In 1667 he had to return to London to answer Buckingham's accusations of arbitrary acts committed by him in Ireland. He was dismissed from the Lord Lieutanancy in 1669 at the instigation of Buckingham, who was suspected of having hired a certain Captain Blood to assassinate him. The attempt took place one night in St. James's Street when he was dragged from his coach and carried off *en croupe* to be hanged at Tyburn, a delay which gave time for a rescue. His son, Lord Ossory, told Buckingham to his face in the Lords that he would pistol him if any further ill befell his father.

From 1671 to 1678 Ormonde, back in Ireland as Lord Lieutanant, proclaimed James II in Dublin and was High Steward at his coronation. But, broken by the death of his wife (who had borne him eight sons and two daughters), and the death of his son Ossory in 1680, he died 21 July 1688. Exceptionally strong (he once rode from Edinburgh to Ware, 360 miles, in three days), his handsome appearance and gracious manners mirrored an honesty rarely found in the corrupt Restoration Court. Clarendon praised especially his 'courage and conduct and almost miraculous success' against the Irish rebels.[3]

NOTES
[1] Clarendon, Bk. VI, § 313.
[2] He appeared, as ordered by the writ of summons, *cum gladio cinctus*.
[3] Clarendon, *loc. cit.*

COLONEL ROBERT OVERTON
(c. 1609-1668?)

ROBERT OVERTON, son of John Overton of Easington, Holderness, entered Gray's Inn in 1631, and later became a great friend of Milton, 'bound to me', as Milton wrote in *Defensio Secunda*, 'in a friendship of more than brotherly closeness ... both by the similarity of our tastes and the sweetness of your manners.' Overton, though no poet, was a writer of pamphlets with stirring titles such as *An Arrow against all Tyrants and Tyrannies shot from the Prison of Newgate into the Prerogative Bowels of the ... House of Lords.* As one of Lord Fairfax's colonels he fought at Marston Moor, reduced Sandal Castle in 1645, and in 1647 was made Governor of Hull where, as an ardent Fifth Monarchy man, he had a thick wall built across Trinity Church so that he and the garrison would not be disturbed by the Presbyterian services on the other side. In 1650 he joined Cromwell in Scotland and commanded a brigade at Dunbar, afterwards being appointed Governor of Edinburgh where he issued orders forbidding, among other things, soldiers 'to throw squibs amongst the market people' and citizens 'to empty chamber-pots and close-stools from their windows.'[1] At Inverkeithing he commanded the reserve, helped to complete the subjugation of Scottish Royalists, led the expedition which reduced Orkney and Shetland, and thereafter commanded all English forces in Western Scotland. On succeeding to an estate in Easington in 1653, he resumed the Governorship of Hull.

Overton had, as far back as February 1648, advocated the King's 'trial', saying that it would be a good thing if God disposses-sed him 'of three transitory kingdom to infeoff him in an eternal one.'[2] But now, although he hailed Cromwell's dissolution of the Long Parliament, he feared the establishment of a Protectorate and told Cromwell, in London, that if he exalted himself and not the good of the nation, 'he would not set one foot before the other to serve him.' To which Cromwell replied 'Thou wert a knave if thou wouldst.'[3] He returned to Hull, and then went on to take command in the north of Scotland. But he was a marked man. Even in 1649 Cromwell had pressed Colonel Hutchinson to be Governor of Hull in his stead, giving as his only reason 'We like him not,' which drew a stinging refusal from Hutchinson.[4] He was now

167

suspected of plotting to seize Monck, take over his army, and march on London. Although Monck did not believe this, he was ordered in December 1654 to send Overton up to London. Cromwell suspected, but never tried, him and he spent the next two years in the Tower and a third in Elizabeth Castle, Jersey, out of the reach of English judges and writs of *habeas corpus*. A petition from his sister, Grizell, to Richard Cromwell finally freed him in 1659 and he was examined by Parliament, where, weakened by years of imprisonment, he could hardly cross the bar of the House. His imprisonment was declared illegal and he became one of seven commissioners in whom the government of the Army was invested. He returned to Hull, but when Monck came south in 1660 he refused to open the gates to any but 'those who bore the image of Jesus Christ.'[5] Monck prudently left Hull alone, but from London ordered Overton to hand over to Colonel Fairfax and come to answer for an inflammatory letter, opposing a Restoration, which he had circulated among his officers. At the Restoration, although included in the Act of Indemnity, he was as a leader of the Fifth Monarchy men, considered too dangerous to be at large and was lodged in the Tower. A year later he was moved to Chepstow Castle, and then back to Jersey where he remained from 1664 to 1668. The date and place of his death are not known. In 1632 he had married Anne, daughter of Jeremy Gardiner of Stratford, Bow, Middlesex, who bore him two sons.

Overton disliked Cromwell but, although various 'unhandsome verses on the counterfeit effigy of a king with a copper nose' were found in his letter-case, he was above personal animosity. 'If I be called to seal the cause of God and my country with my blood', he had written in 1654,'He is able to support and save me, as the sun is to shine upon me.'[6]

NOTES
[1] C. H. Firth and Godfrey Davies, *The Regimental History of Cromwell's Army* (1940), p. 547.
[2] *Fairfax Correspondence*, Vol. III (1849), p. 11.
[3] R. F. D. Palgrave, *Oliver Cromwell the Protector* (1890), pp. 66-7.
[4] *Ibid.*, p. 86.
[5] *Yorkshire Archaeological Journal*, Vol. XXXIX (1958), p. 499.
[6] Palgrave, *op. cit.*, p. 86.

COLONEL JOHN PENRUDDOCK
(1619-1655)

JOHN PENRUDDOCK, one of the eighteen sufferers for the Royal cause whose portraits, engraved by Vertue, were grouped in a composite picture around that of Charles I,[1] was the eldest son of Sir John Penruddock of Compton Chamberlain, Wiltshire. Educated at Blandford School and Queen's College, Oxford, he entered Gray's Inn in 1636. Three years later he married Arundel, daughter of John Freke of Ewerne or Iwerne Courtenay and Melcombe, Dorset. One of his brothers had been killed, and one died, in the Civil War, and he became the main organizer of the Western Rising in 1655. In the previous December he had drawn up a statement of his debts incurred during and after the War, hoping that 'God will so bless me that I shall be able to go through this great trouble' and, if not, that 'my wife and children will be so just as to see that no man shall suffer a penny for me.'[2] The Rising was to be commanded by Sir Joseph Wagstaffe who had crossed from Flanders with Lord Rochester. The first plan was to march to Winchester where the judges of assize were in session, but the arrival there of Parliamentarian troops caused a switch to Salisbury whither the judges were moving. In the early hours of 12 March Penruddock and Wagstaffe entered Salisbury with about 200 men, opened the gaol, horsed some of the prisoners, and seized the sheriff and two judges, Rolles and Nicholas, whom Wagstaffe would have hanged but for Penruddock. The sheriff, who refused to proclaim Charles II, they carried off as a hostage in his night clothes to Blandford where Penruddock proclaimed the King. They moved on to near Yeovil, but their numbers, never more than 400, began to diminish and by now regular troops were closing in on all sides. At South Molton, where they were resting for the night of 14 March, a troop of horse under Captain Croke surprised them and after a night of bitter house-to-house fighting, Penruddock, to avoid further bloodshed, surrendered (Wagstaffe having in the meantime made his escape).

Penruddock understood that they had been promised security of life and estates, but this Croke later denied. The sixty prisoners were lodged in Exeter Gaol whence Penruddock wrote to his wife, asking her to plead with Cromwell for mercy, taking some of her seven children with her. The Protector allowed trial by jury, instead of by a high court of justice, and Penruddock was able to object to 22 of the jurors before 12 had been sworn in. His plea that his crime was not legally high treason and that he had surrendered on promise of life was overruled. Thirty-nine of the prisoners were sentenced to traitors' deaths but Penruddock's petition 'for more honourable deaths than our sentences hath condemned us unto' resulted in an order that he and Colonel Hugh Grove should be beheaded and the rest hanged only. When Mrs Penruddock heard the news she sat down late at night and wrote her husband 'one of the most moving letters of all its kind',[3] folded it in the three-cornered shape of a *billet-doux*, and sent it post-haste.

Two versions of his reply exist but both are of doubtful authenticity. He was beheaded on 16 May in the yard of Exeter Gaol, saying as he mounted the ladder that he hoped it would be a Jacob's Ladder with its feet on earth but its top in heaven. After kissing the axe he first tried his neck on the block and then asked the people to pray for him when he gave the sign. Grove's execution followed immediately, and the *Perfect Diurnall* of 21 May reported that 'they dyed very stoutly and very desperately vindicating their carriage and actions without any confession or contrition for sin at all.' Penruddock was buried at Compton Chamberlain under the family pew. One small consolation for his widow and family, had they known it then, was that the unpopular rule of the Major-Generals which resulted from these risings was a major factor in bringing about the Restoration.

NOTES

[1] Reproduced in Lord Birkenhead, *Strafford* (1938), p. 196: the original print is in the British Museum.

[2] *Wiltshire Archaeological and Natural History Magazine*, Vols. XIII, XIV, and XV (1872, 1874, and 1875).

[3] A. H. Woolrych, *Penruddock's Rising, 1655* (1955), p. 22.

COLONEL-GENERAL SYDENHAM POYNTZ
(1607-1665?)

SYDENHAM POYNTZ, the fourth son of John Poyntz and Anne Skinner ,was first apprenticed to a London tradesman but, deeming that 'little better than a dog's life and base',[1] he went abroad about 1626 and served in the Thirty Years War as a volunteer under Count Mansfeld, who died the same year. About this time Poyntz fell into the hands of the Turks and was bought as a slave by a lieutenant whom he names Bully Basha. The relation of his subsequent escapes, and recaptures, over the next six years reads like *The Arabian Nights* – in and out of seraglios, swimming the Danube, marched with 'a double bag full of filth, earth, and stones'[2] tied round his neck and waist, a year in the galleys,[3] 'the Bastinado', and his final escape, on a Barb which he was supposed to be exercizing, into Hungary where Franciscan friars befriended him and, by 'their wonderfull humility and charity', converted him to Catholicism (temporarily) and sent him on, 'like a souldier de cap a pied with a good horse under mee,'[4] to the wars. There he served, as a captain of horse, under the Lutheran John George, Duke of Saxony, and fought at Breitenfeld (1631). Thereafter he transferred his allegiance to the Emperor and served under Wallenstein.

He fought at Lützen (1632) where he had three horses shot under him, and at Wordlingen (1634).

After the Peace of Prague in 1636 Poyntz left Germany but did not, so far as is known, return to England until 1645. Here he was made Colonel-General of the Northern Association (27 May) and in August Governor of York. After Naseby he followed the King's Army and ultimately defeated it at Rowton Heath in September. Next month he laid siege to Belvoir Castle, held by Sir Gervase Lucas, but was unable to capture it, and withdrew to Nottingham. He then besieged Newark, fixing his Headquarters at East Stoke. By mid-April he had moved in to Farndon and successfully dammed the river Devon and that arm of the Trent which runs past Newark Castle in order to put the town mills out of action. It was at his Headquarters in Farndon that the commissioners met on 3 May to discuss terms for the surrender of Newark. For his services during the siege Parliament gave him £300. In the subsequent struggle for power between Parliament and the Army he sided with Parliament, for which he was roughly seized in his house by 'agitators' and sent to Reading, where Fairfax released him on parole. When the Army planned to march on London he and Massey organized its defence. But after this collapsed they both fled to Holland where they published a joint *Vindication* of their conduct, frankly acknowledging that they had 'held it safer wisdom to depart from the City and for a while from the Kingdom.'

In 1650 Poyntz accompanied Lord Willoughby of Parham to the West Indies and was Governor of St. Christoper till Willoughby surrendered Barbados to a Parliamentarian Fleet, when he retired to Virginia. In 1661 he was offered the Governorship of Antigua but there is no trace of his tenure. There is also no record of his death, although he was still alive in 1663, and he probably died in Virginia. He had three wives: first a rich merchant's daughter who was 'of an humble condition and very house-wifely' but who died in child-bed two years later; the second, whom he married in 1635, was 'Anne Eleanora de Count de Casy'[5] who was better born but lived above their means and, while he was away at the wars, was killed with her child when French troopers burned her house and the whole village. His third wife was English. Though his autobiographical *A True Relation of the German*

Warres . . . 1624-36 abounds in chronological and geographical inaccuracies, when the author writes as an eye-witness, and is not repeating hearsay, it is an invaluable record of those sparsely recorded wars. It is also a graphic self-portrait of a typical mercenary soldier of his day.

NOTES

[1] *The Relation of Sydenham Poyntz 1624-36*, ed. the Revd. A. T. S. Goodrick, Camden Society, Third Series, Vol. XIV (1908), p. 45.

[2] *Ibid.*, p. 51.

[3] *Ibid.*, p. 53.

[4] *Ibid.*, p. 54-5.

[5] Sir John Maclean, *Memoirs of the Family of Poyntz* (privately printed, 1884-6), p. 175

COLONEL THOMAS PRIDE
(c. 1605-1658)

Here comes strong beere, the Citizens to quell,
A Dray-man boyl'd up to a Colonell,
But yet for all his militarie Art
At Nazeby fight he let a Brewer's — .[1]

THOMAS PRIDE was born probably at Ashcott, near Glastonbury, and is said to have been left as a foundling in the parish of St. Bride's from which he took his name. The Royalist pamphleteers, as in the lines quoted above, never let him forget the story that he had once been a brewer's drayman. Nevertheless he served as a major in Essex's Cornish campaign of 1644 ; and at Naseby, in the absence of his colonel, Edward Harley, who had been wounded, commanded a New Model regiment of foot and distinguished himself ; as he did also at the storming of Bristol and capture of Dartmouth. In the struggle for power between the Army and Parliament which wished to disband it after the War, he actively supported the Army, and in March 1647 was accused of securing, for the soldiers' petition, 1100 signatures from his regiment by threatening to cashier any who refused. Harley, his colonel, as M.P. for Herefordshire reported this to the House, and Pride was summoned to the bar, where he denied the charge. With others he now

173

began to prepare the Army's impeachment of the Eleven M.P.s among them Harley, and Fairfax gave him the command of Harley's Regiment. Next year, under Cromwell, he fought Hamilton at Preston, and on 2 December entered London with the Army. Four days later came the event for which he is best known, Pride's Purge. Aided by Lord Grey of Groby, who stood beside him to identify them, he purged the House of 90 M.P.s and arrested more than 40, including his old colonel, Harley. When asked by what authority he acted, he pointed to the swords and muskets of his troops. As one of those nominated to 'try' the King, he attended every meeting but one, and set his signature to the death warrant, 'so strangely written that it is scarce legible'. Throughout 1649 his regiment remained in London to guard Parliament, and in December he was elected to the Common Council. Next year he went to Scotland with Cromwell, commanded a brigade at Dunbar, and, in 1651, fought at Worcester. For his services he was rewarded with a grant of lands in Scotland worth £500 a year. But when his regiment returned there in 1654 he was detained in England, possibly because he had contracted to victual the Navy. At this time he bought Nonesuch Park and House and became High Sheriff for Surrey. In January 1656 Cromwell knighted him with, according to Ludlow, a faggot stick. As one of the commissioners for securing the peace in London he rigorously suppressed cock-fighting and bear-baiting and had all the bears killed, which brought this riposte:

'The crime of the bears was they were cavaliers
And had formerly fought for the King.'[2]

Pride strongly opposed the offer of the crown to Cromwell, and concerted the Army petition which caused him to refuse it. Nevertheless he accepted from Oliver a seat in the Lords. So it was said 'He hath now changed his principles and his mind with the times ... and the lawyers need have no fear now that he would hang up their gowns alongside of the captive Scottish colours in Westminster Hall as he had once threatened.'[3] In May 1658 he was one of the forty commissioners nominated by Cromwell to sit on a high court of justice under John Lisle to try three Royalist plotters – Slingsby, Hewitt, and Mordaunt. Slingsby and Hewitt were sentenced to traitors' deaths, but Mordaunt was acquitted by the casting vote of the president in the timely absence of Pride, determined to condemn but struck down with a sudden attack of the stone. Four months later, 23 October, he died at Nonesuch, where he was buried. In his last words he bewailed 'the most sad and deplorable condition' of the three nations. He had married Elizabeth, natural daughter of Thomas Monck, George Monck's brother, and had one son, Thomas, who served in his regiment, and two daughters. At the Restoration he was attainted and his body ordered to be exhumed. But this mean sentence was never carried out.

NOTES

[1] *A Case for the City-Spectacles* (1647): Thomason Tracts, E. 422-(7).
[2] *The Rump* (1662), p. 299.
[3] *Harleian Miscellany* Vol. III, p. 481.

JOHN PYM
(1584-1643)

DUBBED 'KING PYM' by the Royalists, John was the son of Alexander Pym of Brymore, near Bridgwater, and was educated at Pembroke College, Oxford. He was Receiver-General for Wiltshire, Hampshire, and Gloucestershire from about 1607 till 1636. In 1614 he married Anne Hooker (Hooke?) who died in 1620, having borne him two sons, one of whom received a baronetcy from Richard Cromwell which Charles II confirmed. Pym was M.P. for Calne in 1614, 1621, and 1624, and for Tavistock in 1625, 1626, 1628, and 1640. He was one of the managers of Buckingham's impeachment in 1626, supported the Petition of Right in 1628, and opposed the imposition of Tonnage and Poundage. For some time thereafter he contemplated emigrating to America where, in 1630, the Puritan company for the plantation of Providence Island in the West Indies, of which he was secretary, had been formed. In the Short Parliament in 1640 he drew up a petition demanding the trial of the King's 'evil counsellors', chief of whom was in his view the Earl of Strafford, and in November in the Long Parliament he headed the delegation which laid his impeachment before the House of Lords. Strafford was arrested and Pym proceeded to collect evidence against him. Next he moved the impeachment of Archbishop Laud, who was sent to the Tower. Strafford, on trial in March 1641, defended himself so successfully that Pym was forced to drop the impeachment and substitute a Bill of Attainder, confronting the House with Vane's copy of the note, minuted at a Council meeting, of Strafford's offer to bring his Irish army over 'to reduce this kingdom' (which Pym insidiously interpreted as England) and with details of the Army Plot to seize the Tower. The Bill was passed by a majority of 145 and Strafford was executed on 12 May. Pym now supported the Root and Branch Bill, primarily to please the Scots, and in November took the lead in preparing the Grand Remonstrance which, among other items, condemned the King's control of the army especially in connexion with the tardy suppression of the Irish rebellion which, Pym hinted had the Queen's approval. Fearing that Parliament intended to impeach her, Charles offered Pym the Chancellorship of the Exchequer, an offer which he declined. He was now warned by Essex of the King's plan to arrest him and four other M.P.s, but 'the birds had flown' when Charles entered the House in January 1642, and the City refused to surrender them. They made a triumphal reappearance once the Royal Family had moved to Hampton Court.

Seeing that war was now inevitable, Pym began to create a middle group in Parliament, playing off the peace party against the warmongers, while at the same time mobilizing financial support for the War. To Royalists he was 'the promotor of the present rebellion and the director of the whole machine.'[1] During the peace negotiations with the King at Oxford in the winter of 1642-3 he formed a Committee of Assessment, Sequestration, and Compounding for Royalist estates which fixed the weekly pay to be rendered by each county; and issued the Excise Ordinances imposing a tax on tobacco, ale, and beer. This regular revenue, together with Pym's influence in the City, with its great wealth, laid the foundations of Parliament's military power. It was thanks to the City that Essex, backed by Pym when all were applauding Waller, was able to march out of London with a new army to

PLATE 73   Colonel John Penruddock

PLATE 74   Col. Gen. Sydenham Pointz

PLATE 75   Colonel Pride   *Athow*

PLATE 76   John Pym   *Samuel Cooper*

PLATE 77   Colonel Thomas Rainsborough   *William Gardiner*

PLATE 78   James Stuart, 4th Duke of Lennox and 1st Duke of Richmond
attributed to Theodore Russel

PLATE 79   Henry Wilmot, 1st Earl of Rochester   *Sir Peter Lely*

PLATE 80   Prince Rupert c. 1644   *William Dobson*

relieve Gloucester in September. Pym also realized that Parliament would never win the War without the help of the Scots. Negotiations begun in Edinburgh were concluded in November 1643 with the Scots agreeing, on condition that Parliament took the Covenant and paid their army, to provide 18,000 foot, 2000 horse, and a train of artillery. The Scottish Alliance crowned Pym's tireless work for the Parliamentarian cause. Within a fortnight of the first instalment of pay reaching Scotland he died of cancer (8 December) and was buried in Westminster Abbey. Although he has been called crafty, devious, and unscrupulous, his policy had ensured the final victory for Parliament, and the ultimate evolution of a limited monarchy for which he, no republican, would have wished.

NOTES
[1] *Calendar of State Papers, Venetian*, 1643-7, p. 53.

COLONEL THOMAS RAINSBOROUGH
(1610?-1648)

HE WAS THE son of a distinguished sailor, Captain William Rainsborough, and was 'brought up to the sea'. In 1642 as Vice-Admiral he was guarding the Irish Sea and next year was ordered to Hull, then undergoing its second siege. He landed his crew and took part in the sally in October 1643 which caused Newcastle to raise the siege. In 1644 he besieged Crowland Abbey, surrounded by flood water, and, with ordnance mounted on long-boats, starved it out. In the New Model Army he commanded a regiment of foot, but without the New England lt-colonel, major, and captain of his previous one.[1] He fought at Naseby (14 June 1645) on the right of the second line of foot, took Bridgwater (July) and Sherborne Castle (August). It was his capture of Prior's Hill Fort that, after three hours of bloody fighting, rendered Bristol untenable (September). A fortnight later he besieged Berkeley Castle and forced Lucas to surrender on favourable terms. The terms were not so favourable the next time they met. During the siege of Woodstock Manor Charles I, negotiating its terms of surrender, offered to place himself under Rainsborough's protection. But without waiting for Rainsborough's reply, he left Oxford in disguise in April 1646.

After becoming Governor of Worcester, and of Raglan, Rainsborough was elected M.P. for Droitwich. He opposed any further dealings with the King, and proposed an expedition to Jersey to capture the Prince of Wales. But his troops mutinied and marched away from the coast towards Oxford, with Rainsborough's alleged connivance, to prevent Parliament from seizing the artillery there. They then assembled with the rest of the Army on Thriplow Heath, near Cambridge, to hear Parliament's terms for their disbandment. Rainsborough, with other Commissioners, was sent to obtain the support of the King, then at Woburn, for the Army's plan to overthrow Parliament. But when Charles bluntly told them that they could do nothing without him, Rainsborough abruptly left the conference, and his report of the King's words led to the arrest of Lauderdale, who had come to conclude with the King the Scottish invasion plans. When the Army entered London on 6 August 1647 Rainsborough's Regiment, in battle formation, brought up the rear of the triumphal march. In the Putney debates that followed, Lilburne's revolutionary *Agreement of the People*, backed by Rainsborough, was opposed by Cromwell. So Rainsborough proposed a rendezvous for the whole Army, hoping for a Levellers' majority there. In the meantime he planned to seize the King, then at Hampton Court. This scheme miscarried when Whalley, responsible for the King's safety, was alerted by Cromwell and allowed Charles to escape. At the rendezvous on Corkbush Field, Ware, in November two Leveller regiments wore copies of the *Agreement* in their hats, and Rainsborough tried to give Fairfax a copy, but was waved aside. But fears of a Royalist revival united the Army, and Rainsborough went to sea in January 1648 as Vice-Admiral in order to prevent help coming from abroad. When the Navy mutinied in May he was replaced by Warwick, and joined Fairfax at the siege of Colchester. By destroying the water-mill he cut off the last food supply, and ordered the five hundred women dying of starvation, whom the Royalists sent out to beg for food for themselves, to be stripped naked and driven back. On the surrender of Colchester in August he presided over the execution of Lucas and Lisle. Next month he was sent to relieve Sir Henry Cholmley, then leisurely besieging Pontefract. But Cholmley refused to hand over to 'a bare Colonel of Foot'. So Rainsborough retired to Doncaster where, on 29 October, a party of Pontefract Cavaliers tried to seize and exchange him for Langdale, imprisoned in Nottingham Castle and in danger of suffering the same fate as Lucas and Lisle. Dragged out of bed and into the courtyard, he refused to mount a horse and, after pulling one sword out of his body, was finally killed. Had he lived he would have been a serious rival to Cromwell to whom he once said at Putney 'One of us must not live'. The line of coaches and regiments of cavalry that formed the imposing funeral procession of this uncompromising Leveller at Wapping must have seemed to some spectators at variance with his creed.

NOTES

[1] Lt-Colonel Israel Stoughton, Major Nehemiah Bourne, and Captain John Leverett (H. R. Williamson, *Four Stuart Portraits* (1949), p. 110.

JAMES STUART, 4th DUKE OF LENNOX and 1st DUKE OF RICHMOND
(1612-1655)

JAMES STUART, the son of Esmé, 3rd Duke of Lennox, and Katherine, daughter of Lord Clifton of Leighton Bromswold (George Herbert's parish), was nearest in blood to the King, except for the descendants of James I who, by Scottish law, became his tutor and guardian on his father's death in 1624. The King sent him to Cambridge, and then on to France, Italy, and Spain where he was created a Grandee. On his return in about 1632 Charles I made him a Privy Councillor and in 1633 he accompanied the King to Scotland for the coronation, and sold to him at a reduced price some of the land confiscated from the Church, for a bishopric of Edinburgh which the King was endowing. Soon after his marriage in 1637 to Mary, daughter of the King's murdered favourite, Buckingham (which Laud solemnized, noting in his diary 'the day Rainy, the King present'), he attended his mother's funeral in Edinburgh, and was asked by the Council, already alarmed at the increasing power of the bishops, to dissuade the King from introducing the new Prayer Book.[1] But Charles was adamant though Lennox, as Clarendon observed, was the only member of his intriguing Council whom he could trust. Although this obstinacy resulted in the First Scots War and the King had to call on his friends for loans, Lennox, whilst others were making excuses, promtly lent him £20,000, remarking that 'he had re-ceived great bounties from the King' and so 'sacrificed all he had to his service.'[2] In 1640 he was made Warden of the Cinque Ports and in 1641 created Duke of Richmond.

On the outbreak of the Civil War Richmond summoned three of his brothers to the Royal Standard. Two months later the eldest, Lord George Stuart, Seigneur d'Aubigny, was mortally wounded at Edgehill. Thereafter Richmond remained with the King, and was one of his Commissioners for the peace negotiations in the winter of 1644-5 at Uxbridge whose failure disappointed him keenly. After Naseby Rupert wrote urging him to persuade the King not to march north but to save the kingdom by making peace. The King, to whom he showed the letter, replied that he would die first. But Richmond, a staunch supporter of Rupert, clearly saw the sense of his advice, for when the King left Oxford for the West in August 1645, he stayed behind, declining to follow him any further. He had already lost the second of his soldier brothers, Lord John, mortally wounded at Cheriton (March 1644) but when the youngest, Lord Bernard, was killed at Rowton Heath (September 1645) and buried with the other two in Christ Church, Oxford, he had no heart left for further resistance. In May 1646 he surrendered to Parliament. Next year he met Charles at Hatfield in June, and again in October at Hampton Court. He was allowed to attend him, with Lindsey, Hertford, and Southampton, at Carisbrooke and was one of the Royal Commissioners for the Treaty of Newport. He and Lindsey urged the King to escape when troops arrived to remove him to Hurst Castle, demonstrating how easy this would be by donning a soldier's cloak and walking past the sentinels with the guard commander, who was well-disposed. But Charles would not break his parole. During his 'trial' these four noblemen offered their lives and estates to guarantee any terms on which the Army and Parliament would set free their master and recognize him as King, but their offer was not considered. On his way to the scaffold Charles told Colonel Tomlinson, who walked beside him, that he hoped Richmond would see to his burial. This was permitted and Richmond was granted £500 for the purpose. He died in 1655, 'without the comfort of seeing the resurrection of the Crown,'[3] and was buried in Westminster Abbey. He left one son, Esmé, who died young, and one daughter, Mary. The thing he most regretted was having advised the King to entrust Scottish affairs to 'Duke Hamilton, his enemy, rather than to the Marquess of Huntly, his friend.'[4] In an age when few men could tell who were their friends, Richmond, regardless not only of his interests but also perhaps of his instincts, committed himself to the Royal cause.

NOTES

[1] Lady Elizabeth Cust, *James Stuart, Duke of Lenox and Richmond, Archaeologia Cantiana*, Vol. XII (1878), pp. 75-6.
[2] Clarendon, Bk. VI, § 384; Duncan Stewart, *A Short Historical and Genealogical Account of the Royal Family of Scotland* (1739), p. 157.
[3] Clarendon, *loc. cit.*
[4] Lloyd, p. 335.

HENRY WILMOT, 1st EARL OF ROCHESTER
(1613-1658)

WILMOT WAS IN great place and lived through great events; he fathered a rake, but he was no great person on his own account. The son of Charles, 1st Viscount Wilmot, he served in the Dutch Wars in 1635 as a captain of horse, and was wounded at the Siege of Breda (1637). In the Second Scots War of 1640 he was Commissary-General of Horse and fought at Newburn where he was captured. He sat for Tamworth in the Long Parliament and was deeply implicated in the Army Plot of 1641 to seize the Tower, but was himself imprisoned there. Next year he joined the King and raised a regiment of horse. Commanding the left wing at Edgehill, he delivered a cavalry charge which, like Rupert's on the right wing, swept on too far. But, unlike Rupert, he was opposed by a single regiment only. In December, with Digby, he stormed Marlborough thus cutting Parliament off from the Wiltshire wool and cloth trade. In June 1643 he was created Baron Wilmot of Adderbury, and inflicted a crushing defeat on Waller at Roundway Down on 13 July. When the King sent those 'peremptory commands' on 14 June 1644 to Rupert, Wilmot, who hated the Prince, interpolated three words after the King's 'then' – 'But if York be relieved and you beat the rebels, then [but not otherwise], I may possibly make a shift... to spin out time'[1] – which may have induced Rupert to fight when he did. In the meantime Wilmot was twice wounded and temporarily captured in the Royalist victory of Cropredy Bridge (29 June). But in August his intrigues with Essex, whose army he was surrounding in Lostwithiel, on the basis of deposing the King in favour of the Prince of Wales, were discovered. Charles arrested him at the head of his troops and replaced him by Goring, a much better officer. He was later allowed to retire to France.

In 1650 Wilmot accompanied Charles II to Scotland, and next year fought at Worcester. After the battle he took refuge in Moseley Hall where Charles, hiding in Boscobel eight miles off, joined him. In their subsequent adventures they covered more than three hundred miles. Near Charmouth Wilmot's horse cast a shoe and the blacksmith's suspicions were aroused by his appearance (for, unlike his royal master, he disdained any disguise) and by the fact that the three other shoes were of Midland design, and not West Country, where he said he had come from. The blacksmith alerted the troops, but the fugitives escaped, and three weeks later boarded a brig at Shoreham and landed at Fécamp the next morning, 16 October. In France Wilmot became one of a committee of four to advise Charles, and was created Earl of Rochester in 1652. They kept in close touch with Royalist plotters in England, and in February 1655 Rochester, appointed Field-Marshal-General, reached London and secretly met the agents for the regional risings being planned in the shop of an Aldgate tailor who described him as a fat, round-faced, clean-shaven man in a yellow periwig. Encouraged by the agents' reports, Wilmot rode up to Yorkshire to command the Northern Rising, to the dismay of the Northerners who had asked for Langdale. A bare tenth of those who had promised to turn out on Marston Moor did so on the night of 8 March, and the small assembly broke up in panic. After mutual recriminations Rochester, this time in disguise, 'departed very unwillingly from all places where there was good eating and drinking',[2] and made for London where he hid for some time before crossing to The Hague in June. Three years later he died at Sluys 19 February 1656 and was buried by Hopton at Helvoetsluys. At the Restoration his remains are said to have been reinterred at Spelsbury, Oxfordshire. He married first, about 1644, Frances, daughter of Sir George Horton of Clunston, Devon; and secondly, Anne, widow of Sir Francis Lee and daughter of Sir John St. John. His second son, John, the poet and libertine, succeeded to the title.

Clarendon called him 'a man of a haughty and ambitious nature, of a pleasant wit, and an ill understanding'[3] which prevented him from concentrating on more than one thing at a time. But his 'excessive good-fellowship', which made him popular with the troops, would also have made him a good, if risky, companion for a hunted man.

NOTES
[1] *Marston Moor*, p. 87.
[2] Clarendon, Bk. XIV, § 135.
[3] *Ibid.*, Bk. VIII, § 30.

PRINCE RUPERT,
COUNT PALATINE OF THE RHINE,
DUKE OF BAVARIA, EARL OF HOLDERNESS,
DUKE OF CUMBERLAND
(1619-1682)

PRINCE RUPERT, the third son of Frederick V, Elector Palatine, and Elizabeth, King Charles's sister, spent his childhood in exile with them in Holland, after the evacuation from Bohemia where he was born. When he was sixteen he visited England and became a popular figure at his uncle's Court. Campaigning in Westphalia for the recovery of the Palatinate in 1638, he was captured at Vlotho. Released three years later, he joined the King at Nottingham in August 1642. He was made General of Horse (exempt from all orders except from the King himself) and as such revolutionized cavalry tactics by charging at full gallop with the sword and reserving the pistol for the pursuit. In September 1642 at Powick Bridge he routed a superior force of Essex's cavalry, and next month at Edgehill, commanding the right wing, swept his opponents off the field. In November he covered the Royalist retreat from Brentford and on 2 February 1643 captured Cirencester. In June, after raiding Essex's quarters near Thame, he defeated the pursuing cavalry at Chalgrove Field, where John Hampden was mortally wounded. He captured Bristol in July and in August was at Gloucester which was besieged by the King. In September Essex relieved it, but returning to London was delayed at Aldbourne Chase by Rupert who then beat him to Newbury by two hours. Despite Rupert's advice to wait for ammunition supplies from Oxford, the Royalists attacked but failed to stop Essex from marching on. In March 1644 Rupert relieved the Siege of Newark, and in June captured Liverpool, thus obtaining a port for Ireland. He now received an urgent order from the King to relieve Newcastle, besieged in York, and to beat the Scots who had joined the siege. He outmanoeuvred the besieging armies, pursued them, and ordered Newcastle to follow. But Newcastle arrived so late on Marston Moor that Rupert unwillingly agreed not to attack that evening. Cromwell, seizing his opportunity, surprised Rupert's horse and by midnight the battle that lost the North for the King was over. Nearly 3000 Royalist dead were left on the field. One other casualty, hailed with delight by the enemy, was Rupert's faithful companion since Vlotho days, his poodle, Boye, who had slipped his collar. Next day Rupert, with the remains of his cavalry, retired to the North-West. In November he was made Commander in-Chief of the Army, and in May 1645 captured Leicester. He urged the King to continue north and join Montrose in Scotland.

But Digby's and Ashburnham's counsel to turn and fight Fairfax prevailed, and the result was the disastrous Royalist defeat of Naseby on 14 June. In September Rupert, to save useless slaughter, surrendered Bristol, blockaded both by sea and land. The King, hearing this, wrote a furious letter ending 'My conclusion is, to desire you to seek your subsistence . . . somewhere beyond seas, to which end I send you herewith a pass.'[1] But Rupert, rightly suspecting Digby's hand in this, followed his uncle to Newark and demanded a court-martial. He was unanimously acquitted, but the King, displeased, removed Rupert's friend Willys from the Governorship of Newark. This led to an angry scene between the King and Willys's friends, and the so-called 'mutiny' of the cavalry, led by Rupert. In December, however, they were reconciled at Oxford. Had the King listened more to his loyal nephew in councils of war, 'rough and passionate' though he often was, and less to those courtier-soldiers who were jealous of him, the Royalist cause might have been saved.

From 1646 to 1648 Rupert served in the French Army, and then in command of the Royalist Fleet, harrying Parliamentarian shipping on the high seas, from Spain to the West Indies where his brother Maurice was drowned. In 1660 he returned to England and in 1665, as Admiral of the White, fought the Dutch in the Battle of Solebay. As a founder of the Hudson Bay Company he gave his name to Rupert's Land. Other interests were North African trade, scientific experiment, and the Royal Society. In 1673 he succeeded the Duke of York as Admiral of the Fleet and again fought the Dutch, off the Texel. He died 29 November 1682 and was buried in Henry VII's Chapel, Westminster Abbey, leaving a natural son Dudley by Francesca, daughter of Sir Henry Bard, Viscount Bellamont, who was killed in 1686 before Buda, and, by the actress Margaret Hughes, a natural daughter Ruperta.[2]

NOTES
[1] Clarendon, Bk. IX, § 90.
[2] Portraits of her (resembling her father) by Wissing and Kneller survive, as do her descendants.

186

EDWARD MONTAGU, 1st EARL OF SANDWICH
(1625-1672)

WHEN EDWARD MONTAGU, the son of Sir Sidney Montagu of Hinchingbrooke and Paulina Pepys, appointed his first cousin once removed as his secretary he unwittingly immortalized the name of Pepys. He had previously joined the Parliamentarian cause and married Jemima, the 17-years-old daughter of John Crew, in 1642. Next year he raised a regiment of foot in Cambridgeshire, and in 1644 took part in the storming of Lincoln and the Battle of Marston Moor. He commanded a New Model regiment at Naseby where he did well, as also at the storming of Bristol. After this he was M.P. for Huntingdonshire but took no part in public affairs until 1653 when he reappears as a member of the Council of State. He became a Commissioner of the Treasury in 1654 and, although he had no sea experience, conjoint general at sea with Blake two years later. In the Spanish War he carried back to London the treasure, worth £600,000, captured from West Indiamen off Cadiz. He attended Cromwell's second installation as Protector in 1657, having earlier urged him to accept the crown, and in December was made a Lord and given a regiment of horse. On the Protector's death he loyally supported Richard and assumed command of the Fleet sent to the Sound to arrange peace between Denmark and Sweden. When Richard fell, uncertain of his own future, Montagu listened to suggestions from Charles II that he should bring the Fleet back to England and co-operate with Booth's imminent rising. This he did, and on reaching England reported to Parliament. But by then Booth's Rising had already failed, so he prudently resigned his command and retired to Hinchingbrooke.

In 1660 Montagu was reappointed General of the Fleet with Monck, and in April received Charles II's Declaration to the Fleet which Pepys carried round from ship to ship. Pepys goes on to tell how the King kissed Montagu when they first met and invested him with the Garter on board the *Naseby*, and also created him Viscount Hinchingbrooke and Earl of Sandwich. In June he took the Mediterranean Fleet to receive Tangier as part of Catherine of Braganza's dowry, and then to Lisbon to collect the remaining £300,000 of the dowry and the Queen herself. He was later blamed by the King for having brought only half the money, and by the Queen for the false account which he gave of her husband's 'good nature and virtues'. In 1665 he beat the Dutch off Lowestoft, and later captured nine Dutch East Indiamen laden with rich cargoes, part of which he ill-advisedly allowed to be distributed among his captains, helping himself to £5000 worth. For this he was deprived of his command and threatened with impeachment until Clarendon arranged for his appointment, as ambassador-extraordinary, to Spain where he concluded a most satisfactory treaty. He became President of the Council of Trade and Plantations in 1670, and two years later was second-in-command to the Duke of York whose Fleet was at anchor in Solebay. With an east wind blowing, he advised the Duke to put to sea, but no notice was taken till the Dutch Fleet appeared. Hurriedly putting to sea, with half the crews left behind, Montagu led the Blue squadron out and beat off repeated attacks until his ship caught fire. Although urged to leave it he refused, and later it blew up (28 May 1672). His body was recovered off Harwich and buried in Henry VII's Chapel, Westminster Abbey. Among his writings were contributions to *Philosophical Transactions*. He had four daughters and six sons, the eldest, Edward, who succeeded to the title, being 'the child' in Pepys's *Diary*. Family connections and the friendship of Cromwell undoubtedly helped his preferment, which was accelerated when he changed sides at the Restoration. But he was courageous, honest, and tolerant both in religion and politics.

WILLIAM FIENNES, 1st VISCOUNT SAYE AND SELE
(1582-1662)
Old Subtlety.

'A MAN OF A CLOSE and reserved nature . . . of great parts and of the highest ambition'[1] . . . 'who had the deepest hand in the original contrivance of all the calamities which befell this unhappy kingdom.'[2] Thus Clarendon, no admirer of this Puritan peer.

Born in 1582, the son of Richard Fiennes, 1st Baron Saye and Sele, and Constance, daughter of Sir Richard Kingsmill, he entered New College, Oxford, in 1596, became a Fellow in 1600, and succeeded his father in 1613. Next year he opposed James I's efforts to raise money by benevolences and, in consequence, was sent to the Tower for six months. He owed his viscountcy (1624) to Buckingham, but during the eleven years when Charles I called no Parliament, he devoted his energies, with Brooke, Warwick, and Hampden, to the Providence Company which controlled the Caribbean settlements where Puritans practised their religion and preyed on Spanish traders, both of which activities were displeasing to an Anglican King who also favoured Spain. From the New England Company Saye obtained in 1632 a patent for land on the Connecticut River, whose name was changed to Saybrook, and sent over a shipload of colonists. His house, Broughton Castle, twenty miles north of Oxford, was the rendezvous of all the chief malcontents. He headed the resistance to Ship Money in Oxfordshire and Gloucestershire and refused to recognize the judgment against Hampden. At the time of the First Scots War he and Brooke reluctantly followed King Charles, but refused to take the oath of loyalty and obedience demanded of all peers, and were put under arrest. On being released, Saye took his troops home with him. Before the Second Scots War the rooms of the Puritan peers were searched for evidence of correspondence with the Scots and he and six others were sent to the Tower. The King tried in vain to woo him from the malcontent party by making him a Privy Councillor and Master of the Court of Wards. Next year (1642) Parliament made him Lord Lieutenant of Oxfordshire, Gloucestershire, and Cheshire, as well as a member of the Committee of Safety.

Saye raised a regiment of foot (Bluecoats) for Parliament in North Oxfordshire, but handed it over to Sir John Meldrum before

Edgehill. Four days after the battle Banbury, which Saye had garrisoned, surrendered to the King without offering any resistance. In February 1644 Saye introduced in Parliament the first ordinance for the establishment of the Committee of Both Kingdoms (England and Scotland), and was influential in bringing about the Self-Denying Ordinance (1645). When Parliament abolished the Court of Wards he received £10,000 in compensation. But in December 1647 he signed the 'Engagement', a compact with the Scots made at Carisbrooke, Isle of Wight, by which the King (then a prisoner there) engaged to support the Covenant and Presbyterian party against the sects in a free Parliament. Saye had no thought of doing away with the monarchy for he 'was as proud of his quality, and of being distinguished from other men by his title' as any man alive,[1] and 'well foresaw what would become of his peerage if the treaty proved ineffectual' and the Army took over and made 'their own model of the government.'[3] So later, after the defeat of the Scots at Preston (17 August 1648), as a Commissioner for the Treaty of Newport in November he urged the King 'with more passion than was natural to his constitution,'[4] to agree with Parliament. Although no treaty materialized his peerage survived.

Saye is said to have retired to Lundy, but he resumed his seat in the Lords in the Convention Parliament of 1660. On 10 July 1661 he wrote to the Governor of Massachusetts promising to use his influence with Charles II to advance the colony's interest, concluding 'I was loth to omit writing because it may be my last, my glass being almost run, and I returning home.' He died 14 April 1662 and was buried in Broughton church beside his wife, Elizabeth, daughter of John Temple of Stowe. Their second son was Nathaniel whose boldness in battle matched his father's cunning in council, a trait which had earned the latter the nickname of 'Old Sublety'.

NOTES

1 Clarendon, Bk. III, § 26.
2 Ibid., Bk. VI, § 409.
3 Ibid., Bk. XI, § 155.
4 Ibid., Bk. XI, § 160.

MAJOR-GENERAL PHILIP SKIPPON
(d. 1660)

PHILIP, THE SON of Luke and Anne Skippon, came from West Lexham in Norfolk. He began his military life as a pikeman and served under Vere in the Palatinate. In 1622 he married Maria Comes at Frankenthal in Germany. He was at the Siege of Breda in 1625, where he was wounded, as well as at the Sieges of Bois-le-Duc and Maastricht in 1629. When ten years later he returned to England 'the Martiall-spirited Sparkes of the famous Artillery Gardens'[1] chose him as their *Gimnasiarchus* to instruct them in military discipline. After the King's attempted arrest of the Five Members he was appointed to command the London Trained Bands and, by order of Parliament, blockaded the Tower until the King removed Byron, the Royalist Lieutenant. After Edgehill he encouraged the City Trained Bands, company by company, as they marched out to Turnham Green to face the Royal Army, and caused the King to withdraw. He took a prominent part in the Siege of Reading in 1643, and the relief of Gloucester. At First Newbury he commanded Essex's left wing, and next year covered his retreat towards Fowey. When the Earl escaped by sea Skippon was left with orders to make the best possible terms of surrender. At a Council of War he was for fighting his way out, but got no support. His army was allowed to march away with its colours, but had to abandon all arms and ammunition. Next month at Second Newbury Skippon commanded the foot in a 13-miles circuitous march to take the Royalists in the rear. His attack, launched late in the afternoon, took Speen, but Manchester's frontal attack went in too late and the Royalists slipped away under cover of darkness, leaving behind six of the guns they had captured in Cornwall.

With the formation of the New Model Army in 1645 Skippon became Major-General under Fairfax, and persuaded many of Essex's old soldiers to re-enlist. He promised regular pay and that justice would be done to all claims. Some sergeants and corporals even agreed to enlist as privates. At Naseby Skippon commanded the foot in the centre, and was wounded early on by a bullet which drove part of his armour into his left side. But he refused to quit the field. He was carried to London in a litter, but at Islington 'a great Mastiff-Dog' ran out and savaged one of the horses. The dog had to be killed with a sword, but not before the litter had been almost overturned. Skippon recovered, and next year became Governor of Newark, and commanded the convoy which carried Parliament's £200,000 to the Scots at Newcastle in exchange for the King. In April 1647 he was appointed, much against his will, to command all forces in Ireland. But many regiments, their pay in arrears, were unwilling to serve there unless under their old generals. So Skippon, Cromwell, Ireton, and Fleetwood were sent as Parliamentary Commissioners, to talk in Saffron Walden church to the disgruntled officers who said that they must first consult their men. In June the Army, drawn up on Thriplow Heath, near Cambridge, confronted the Commissioners and vociferously rejected the new terms which Skippon read out. Two months later the Army marched into London.

In the Second Civil War Skippon in April 1648, with his Trained Bands, prevented the Kentish Royalists from entering the City but, after Cromwell's victory at Preston, pleaded for treating with the King. So it was cruelly unjust that scandalmongers associated him with the alleged Rolfe plot to kill the King at Carisbrooke merely because he had a son-in-law named Rolfe. Though nominated as one of the King's judges, he never attended the 'trial'.

PLATE 81　　Prince Rupert 1642　　　　　　　*Gerard van Honthorst*

PLATE 82   Edward Montague, 1st Earl of Sandwich

ISCOUNT SAY AND SELE.
VAN SOMER . PINX.

PLATE 83   William Fiennes, 1st Viscount Saye and Sele

PLATE 84   Maj. Gen. Philip Skippon

PLATE 85   Colonel Sir Henry Slingsby

PLATE 86   Sir Philip Stapylton   *Bulfinch*

PLATE 87   Maj. Gen. Sir Thomas Tyldesley

PLATE 88   Sir Henry Vane   *after Michiel Jansz van Miereveldt*

When Cromwell was fighting his Scottish campaign in 1650 Skippon commanded all forces in and around London, a district he later supervized during the unpopular rule of the Major-Generals. He was M.P. for Kings Lynn in 1654 and 1656 and acquired property, including the Bishop's Palace, in Norwich. He died early in March 1660, leaving by his first wife one son, Philip, later knighted; and by his second wife, Katherine Phillips, three daughters. He was author of *The Christian Centurion's Observations* (1645) and other practical works of devotion, 'with rude verses interspersed', written for fellow soldiers whose constant friend he was. A plain, blunt man, an efficient and honest soldier, he was respected for his courage and integrity.

NOTES
1 John Vicars, *England's Worthies* (1647), p. 50.

COLONEL SIR HENRY SLINGSBY
(1602-1658)

THIS SECOND SON, of a family of fourteen, of Sir Henry Slingsby of Scriven and Frances Vavasour, daughter of William Vavasour of Weston, Yorkshire, went up to Queens' College, Cambridge, in 1618. In 1631 he married Barbara Belasyse, daughter of the 1st Viscount Fauconberg of Newburgh Priory, and two years later they entertained Charles I at their home, Redhouse, near York, on his way to Scotland. Created a baronet this same year, he took part in both Scots Wars and found soldiering — as many of his contemporaries had already found it, serving in the Low Countries — 'a commendable way of breeding for a young Gentleman . . . for as idleness is the nurse of all evil . . . this employment of a soulgier's is the contrary unto it', requiring work, watchfulness, and obedience 'without reply', not caring 'how hard he lyeth, nor how meanly he fareth', and learning to be 'not over fond of this life, but willing to resign it'.[1]

As M.P. for Knaresborough Slingsby was one of the 59 'Straffordians' who opposed Strafford's attainder in 1641, the year also in which his wife died, leaving him with three young children. Next year he was commissioned to command the Trained Bands of York, and shortly afterwards to raise his own regiment of foot. With this he joined Newcastle at Bridlington, and took part in the Siege of Hull. In the summer of 1644 his regiment was one of those garrisoning York, but throughout the siege he could get no word of his children, only six miles off at Redhouse. He fought at Marston Moor, and after the surrender of York, marched with some of the garrison into Lancashire. After months of skirmishing around Barrow they began a hazardous march to Oxford, mostly by night. Attacked near Daventry, they lost two thirds of their small force, and Slingsby himself only escaped, when his horse tired, by jumping up behind Lord St Pol. Reaching Oxford by Christmas, he lodged with the Master of the Royal Mint (Sir William Parkhurst) who struck three medals,[2] for his children, to commemorate this eventful march. Next year he was with the Northern Horse at the capture of Leicester, and with them again on the left wing at Naseby. He remained with the Royal Army on those subsequent marches which ended at Newark, marvelling at the equanimity of the King whom 'no peril could move to astonishment . . . neither was he exalted in prosperity nor dejected in adversity.'[3] He was in Newark through the siege until its surrender by the Governor, his brother-in-law Belasyse, on 8 May 1646, and then rode north with the Scots Army till they reached Topcliffe where the King commanded him to return home. But because he refused to compound, troops were sent from York to arrest him, and for some time he had to hide in a secret room at Redhouse where he completed his Diary.

Slingsby was one of the leaders of the ill-fated Northern Rising of 1655 on Marston Moor, and soon afterwards was seized in his own garden and imprisoned, first in York and then in Hull. Here he tried to persuade two of the officers to betray the castle. Learning of his activities, Cromwell ordered the Governor to 'trepan' him. No sooner had he given a commission, signed by Charles II, to the second-in-command than he was sent up by sea to the Tower. On 25 May 1658 he was tried in Westminster Hall by John Lisle and sentenced to a traitor's death. Cromwell, entreated by his daughter Mary, who had married Slingsby's nephew, the 2nd Viscount Fauconberg, mitigated the sentence to beheading. While in the Tower Slingsby wrote *A Father's Legacy to his Sons*,[4] beseeching them not to mourn his death which he hoped was 'without touch of dishonour.'[5] On 8 June he was beheaded on Tower Hill, taking with him to the scaffold a copy of Augustine's *Meditations* given to him by his Queens' College friend Arthur Capel, beheaded nine years before. He was buried in the Slingsby Chapel in Knaresborough church, survived by two sons, Thomas and Henry, and one daughter, Barbara. There was no more loyal Cavalier than Slingsby, nor one who, in his puritanical manner of life, less typified the conventional idea of the men who supported King Charles I.

NOTES
[1] Slingsby, pp. 38-9.
[2] Two medals are in the British Museum, the third in the library of Oriel College, Oxford.
[3] Slingsby, p. 169.
[4] Published in York c. 1700.
[5] Slingsby, p. 218. Geoffrey Ridsdill Smith, *op. cit.*, p. 158.

SIR PHILIP STAPYLTON
(1603-1647)

PHILIP STAPYLTON, 'of a thin body and weak constitution, but full of spirit,' as his friend Denzil Holles described him, was the second son of Sir Henry Stapylton of Wighill, Yorkshire, and Mary, daughter of Sir John Foster of Bamborough. In 1617 he went up to Queens' College, Cambridge, with his elder brother, Robert, and ten years later married the widow of John Gee and eldest daughter of Sir John Hotham. He was knighted in 1630 and bought the estate of Warter Priory on the edge of the Yorkshire Wolds, where 'he spent his time in those delights which horses and dogs administer.'[1] His wife died, leaving him with five children, and in 1638 he married Barbara (daughter of Henry Lennard, 1st Lord Dacre) who became a client of William Lilly, the astrologer, and frequently consulted him over domestic problems, as well she might with five step-children and five of her own.[2]

Sir Philip was M.P. for the Yorkshire constituencies of

Hedon in the Short Parliament and Boroughbridge in the Long Parliament (1640) where he joined his relatives, Hotham and Holles, in the prosecution of Strafford for his activities as President of the Council of the North and relentless extracter of Ship Money. But 'he quickly outgrew his friends and countrymen in the confidence of those who governed, and so joined him with Mr Hambden in this their first employment . . . to so great a master.'[3] With Hampden he was one of the four Commissioners sent with the King to Scotland in 1641.

Stapylton became Captain of Essex's Lifeguard of Cuirassiers, and at Edgehill commanded, with Balfour, the horse on the right. In two charges he broke the best of the Royalist infantry. In January next year (1643) he intervened to have the President of his old college, Queens', a prisoner in London with other Royalist Heads of Colleges, transferred to more comfortable lodgings. He was with Essex's army at Thame in the spring, but his regiment was not engaged on Chalgrove Field. It did well at the relief of Gloucester, and also at First Newbury where at one moment Stapylton is said to have ridden up to Rupert and fired in his face, but the pistol misfired. He commanded the right wing of the Parliamentarian horse and sustained three charges before being driven off the field. Next year he was in Essex's Western campaign but was sent to Tavistock to plead for reinforcements. After Essex had had to surrender at Lostwithiel he wrote Stapylton a despairing letter on the way his army had been neglected by Parliament, and his own wish to be brought to trial. Stapylton was able to represent these views to the House. With Holles he now led the Presbyterian peace party opposed to the Independents in Parliament, and on 11 December they met the Scottish Commissioners at Essex House to discuss the impeachment of Cromwell as an 'incendiary' who would destroy the Scottish Alliance. But not enough evidence was forthcoming, unlike that uncovered this same month to have the Hothams, the father and brother of Stapylton's first wife, condemned to death.

Two months later the Self-Denying Ordinance deprived Stapylton of his military command. In February 1647 he was put on the commission for disbanding the Army. At the presentation of the first Army petition of protest next month a violent altercation broke out and Stapylton seized a Major Tulidah by the throat and dragged him to the door. Tulidah was imprisoned for a month, and Stapylton was denounced by the Army for seeking to deny the right of petitioning. In June the Army impeached eleven M.P.s, among them Stapylton, and when it marched into London in August he and four others seized a pink at Margate and sailed for Calais. Stapylton was 'feaverish with the Flux' when he left and died 18 August, the day after reaching Calais, in the *Three Silver Lyons*. Suspected of having died of the Plague (for which the inhabitants demanded £250 damages), he was immediately buried in the Protestant burying-ground. He had instructed his man 'to commend him to his wife, and not to forget his children',[4] all of whom he remembered in his will. Bailie called him the second gentleman after Holles 'for all gallantrie in England.'[5] This, with native tenacity, he constantly exhibited, both in the field and in Parliament.

NOTES
[1] Clarendon, Bk. IV, § 19.
[2] *Yorkshire Archaeological Journal*, Vol. VIII (1883-4), p. 464. Lilly's horoscope of one of Stapylton's daughters-in-law appears in diagrammatic form on p. 463.
[3] Clarendon, *loc. cit.*, p. 458.
[4] *Yorkshire Archaeological Journal*, *lic. cit.*, p. 458.
[5] Robert Baillie, *Letters and Journals, 1637-62*, ed. D. Laing, Vol. III (1842), p. 19.

MAJOR-GENERAL SIR THOMAS TYLDESLEY
(1596-1651)

Sir Thomas Til(de)sley was a gentleman of a good family and a good fortune, who had raised men at his own charge at the beginning of the war, and had served in the command of them till the very end of it with great courage; and refusing to make any composition, after the murder of the King he found means to transport himself into Ireland to the marquis of Ormonde; with whom he stayed till he was, with the rest of the English officers, dismissed, to satisfy the barbarous jealousy of the Irish, and then got over into Scotland a little before the King (Charles II) marched from thence (1651) and was desired by the earl of Darby to remain with him.

CLARENDON

TYLDESLEY WAS THE elder son of Edward Tyldesley of Morley's Hall, Astley, Lancashire. The family were Roman Catholics. In 1634 he married Frances, daughter of Ralph Standish of Standish Hall which was later to become a centre of Jacobite plotting. He fought in the German wars and is said to have come home in 1642, when war between King and Parliament seemed inevitable, to serve Lord Strange, later Earl of Derby. Certainly he was with him at his abortive Siege of Manchester in September 1642. He fought at Edgehill as a lieutenant-colonel, but in what regiment does not appear. By March 1643 he was back in his own country, taking part in the capture of Lancaster on the 18th. He greatly distinguished himself when, on 2 July 1643, the Queen's army took Burton-on-Trent. He was knighted for storming the town over a bridge of 36 arches — no mean feat! By this time he was a colonel and had raised regiments both of horse and foot. In 1644 his foot regiment was with Rupert when, on 28 May, he stormed Bolton. Whilst the Prince was in Lancashire the Earl of Derby and Sir Thomas brought in great numbers of horse and foot but they were for the most part unarmed. These levies fought at Marston Moor where Tyldesley's Regiment of Foot fought in two bodies in the front line of the Royalist centre, being evidently one of the strongest units present. One of his soldiers, John Hilton of Wheelton, suffered no less than 18 wounds on that fatal day.[1] In the battle Tyldesley himself probably led his Regiment of Horse, which formed two of the six bodies comprising Lord Molyneux's Brigade

198

of 800 horse, the second line of the Royalist right, under Lord Byron. Sir Thomas survived the disaster and a Parliamentarian *Diurnall* reports him as 'either kild or fled privately' when, on 20 August 1644, a Royalist force was routed at Ormskirk.[2] Tyldesley was with Byron in the fight at Montgomery Castle on 18 September and was captured. He languished in prison for many months. On 25 July 1645 Charles Gerard and Sir Lewis Kirke, the Governor of Bridgnorth, were both, separately, instructed to arrange his exchange. He was then in Eccleshall Castle.[3] It seems, however, that he was not exchanged, but that he escaped from the Roundhead garrison at Stafford.[4] He was made Governor of Lichfield Close, where he held out until July 1646.

During the Second Civil War Tyldesley was with his old leader, Derby, when he came over from the Isle of Man. He was killed when Colonel Robert Lilburne overcame the Earl at Wigan Lane on 25 August 1651. His cornet, Alexander Rigby, erected a monument where he fell, half a mile from Wigan, as 'an High act of gratitude which conveys the memory' of this diehard Cavalier. The inscription goes on to say that he 'followed the fortune of the Crown through the three kingdoms, and never compounded with the rebels though strongly invited. And on the 25th of August was here slain, commanding as major-general under the Earl of Derby. To whom the grateful Erector, Alexander Rigby, Esq., was cornet. And when he was high sheriff of this county A.D. 1679, placed this high obligation on the whole family of the Tyldesleys.'

NOTES

[1] He was still alive in 1673 when he appealed for financial relief (Preston Quarter Session Rolls).

[2] *Perfect Diurnall*, No. 57, 26 August-2 September 1644.

[3] British Museum, *Harleian MS.* 1852, f. 297.

[4] H.M.C. *Portland*, Vol. I, p. 344.

P.D.

SIR HENRY VANE
(1589-1655)

HENRY VANE, up at Brasenose College, Oxford, in 1604 and knighted in 1611, married in 1612 a Kentish girl, Frances Darcy of Tollehurst Darcy. With her portion he bought a share in the subpoena office in Chancery, and with his own money a Court-carver's place and the cofferership to the Prince of Wales. He was thus well placed in the race for profitable Court appointments. The eldest son of Henry Vane of Hadlow, Kent, and Margaret, daughter of Roger Twysden, he sat in Parliament for Lostwithiel (1614), Carlisle (1621 and 1624-6), Retford (1628), Wilton (1640), and Kent (1654). Charles I sent him in 1629 to seek aid for the Elector Palatine from the United Provinces; and also in 1631, from Gustavus Adolphus, who said it was impossible at the price offered. Cottington, however, praised Vane for his 'wise and dexterous carriage of that greate business' which had 'saved His Majesty's money and his honour.'[1] By 1629 Vane was Comptroller of the Household and a Privy Councillor and rich enough to buy estates in Kent and Yorkshire as well as Barnard Castle, and Raby Castle where he entertained the King on his way to Scotland in 1639. In January 1640 the King created Wentworth Earl of Strafford and, at his request, made his son Viscount Raby, an honour which Vane had justifiably considered his. Next month Charles made him Secretary of State, a surprise appointment to everyone except the Queen and Hamilton, whose favourite he was, for he was a slow writer and unmethodical.

As Secretary in the newly elected House in April Vane so mishandled the King's offer of the abolition of Ship Money in return for subsidies that the demands of the King's opponents were doubled, and shortly afterwards Parliament was dissolved. On the day of its dissolution, at a Council meeting where the impending Scots War was discussed, Vane noted an offer by Strafford of his Irish army 'to reduce this kingdom'. Young Vane found this note among his father's papers and, sensing its significance, copied it. Pym copied Vane's transcription, and kept it for further use. His opportunity came during Strafford's trial which had begun on 22 March 1641. When Vane was called to give evidence in Westminster Hall as to what Strafford had actually said, he refused to explain what had been meant by 'this kingdom', although he must have known it was Scotland, and not England as Pym implied. But 'his malice to the earl of Strafford', wrote Clarendon, 'transported him to all imaginable thoughts of revenge, which is a guest that naturally disquiets and tortures those who entertain it'.[2] So far the prosecution had only Vane's memory and the uncertain memories of other Councillors to rely upon, and the impeachment looked like failing. Pym therefore had a Bill of Attainder proposed, and produced in the Commons as written evidence the copy he had made of Young Vane's note which the latter had prudently destroyed. Vane was horrified at what his son had done, and at this exposure of his own carelessness. But although there was still only one witness, and two were needed, the Bill passed the House nine days later with an overwhelming majority, and Strafford was beheaded on 12 May. In August Vane accompanied the King to Scotland, but on their return in November was replaced by Nicholas as Secretary of State, and joined the Parliamentarian leaders. In 1644 he became a member of the Committee of Both Kingdoms, and in Cromwell's first Parliament sat for Kent. His death, which occurred about May 1655, was said by the Royalists to be suicide in remorse for his part in Strafford's execution. His widow died eight years later, and was buried at Shipbourne, Kent. They had six sons and four daughters. Clarendon, who disliked and suspected him, said 'he was of very ordinary parts by nature, and he had not cultivated them at all by art; for he was illiterate. But being of a stirring and boisterous disposition, and very industrious and very bold, he still wrought (himself) into some employment.'[3] A modern commentator adds that he was not only a fool, but also a knave.

NOTES
[1] M. A. E. Green, *Lives of the Princesses of England*, Vol. V, pp. 488-504, and S. R. Gardiner, *History of England* (1603-42), Vol. VII, p. 206.
[2] Clarendon, Bk. VI, § 411.
[3] *Ibid.*

SIR HENRY VANE THE YOUNGER
(1613-1662)

HARRY VANE, dedicated to Puritanism from the age of 15 and for the rest of his life a seeker after truth, was the eldest son of Sir Henry Vane of Raby(q.v.), and Frances Darcy. From Westminster School he went up to Magdalen Hall, Oxford, in 1629 and then travelled abroad. In 1635 he emigrated to Massachusetts and was elected Governor; but his advocacy of unlimited religious liberty lost him his post and he returned to England after a mere year's tenure of office. In 1640 he was knighted, was M.P. for Hull in the Long Parliament, supporting the Root and Branch Bill, and married Frances Wray, daughter of Sir Christopher Wray of Barlings, Lincolnshire. Whilst searching among his father's papers this year for a family document, he found a Council minute, in Sir Henry's hand, of Strafford's offer of his Irish Army 'to reduce this kingdom', which he copied and showed to Pym who made a copy for himself. When the Bill of Attainder against Strafford was proposed in the House next year, Pym produced this copy as written damnatory evidence of Strafford's treachery, implying that by 'this kingdom' Strafford meant England. From 1642 Vane was Treasurer of the Navy, and during 1643 negotiated the Scottish Alliance, persuading the Scots to prefix the word 'League' to 'Covenant' and add 'according to the word of God', which lent elasticity to their rigid demands for enforcing Presbyterianism.

On Pym's death Vane succeeded him as leader of the House. He was sent to York in June 1644 to sound the generals in the leaguer there on the deposition of the King, a suggestion which they roundly rejected. Still fearing Presbyterian intolerance, he supported the 'Accommodation' of tender consciences, which was passed in September. He also seconded the motion for the Self-Denying Ordinance, furthering the formation of the New Model Army by appealing to the City for funds. To the King's offer in March 1646 of an alliance to expel the Scots Army he made no reply, but urged him next year to accede to the *Heads of the Proposals*. Pride's Purge he considered a violation of Parliament and, although a republican, he disapproved of the King's execution. He was chosen chairman of the committee for drawing up the constitution of a new Parliament, but his persistency in pushing his own views caused Cromwell to expel the Rump which he himself had wished to retain. This disagreement must have ended the correspondence between 'Brother Heron' (Vane) and 'Brother Fountain' (Cromwell) as they called each other, and Vane retired to Belleau in Lincolnshire, where he lived in seclusion. In 1656 he produced a tract entitled *A Healing Question Propounded*, proposing the calling of a convention to set up a free constitution, for which he was summoned before the Protector and imprisoned for three months.

Sitting for Whitchurch, Hampshire, in Richard Cromwell's first Parliament, Vane pressed for a definition of the Protector's authority before acknowledging Richard. In January 1660 he was expelled for taking the Army's part and relegated to his Durham estates. On the King's return, he was sent to the Scillies and excepted from the general amnesty. In October he was brought to the Tower and next year tried for treason and sentenced to death. Pepys watched his execution on 14 June 1662 and declared him 'the most resolved man that ever died in that manner.'[1] He was buried in Shipbourne church, survived by his wife who had borne him seven sons and seven daughters. Socially charming, he had 'a wonderful sagacity' for penetrating the designs of others while concealing his own, but was thought by all parties to be changeable. Perhaps he was nearer the truth than those who distrusted him. But the King, who had weighed him up, considered him 'too dangerous a man to live if he could honestly be put out of the way.'[2]

NOTES
[1] Pepys, *Diary*, 14 June 1662.
[2] Burnet, *History of his own Times*, ed. O Airy, Vol. I, p. 286.

SIR EDMUND VERNEY
(1590-1642)

'I HAVE EATEN his bread, and served him near thirty years, and will
not do so base a Thing as to forsake him ; and chuse rather to lose
my Life (which I am sure I shall do) to preserve and defend those
Things which are against my Conscience to preserve. For I will
deal freely with you, I have no Reverence for the Bishops, for whom
this general Quarrel subsists.' Thus did Sir Edmund reveal to
Hyde the agony of his mind at the outbreak of the Civil War. He
was the second son of Sir Edmund Verney of Penley, Hertfordshire, and Claydon, Buckinghamshire, and Mary Blakeney. After
graduating in 1604 from St Alban's Hall, the Protestant strong-
hold in Oxford, he went to observe the wars in the Low Countries
with Lord Goring, and the Courts of France and Italy with Lord
Herbert and Sir Henry Wotton. On his return in 1606 he entered
the Household of Prince Henry as Chief Sewer, and was knighted
in 1611. The death in 1612 of the Prince, who shared the same
religious feelings for simplicity in worship as himself, was one of the
great sorrows of his life. In 1613 he was appointed to the Household of Prince Charles, and married Margaret Denton, daughter
of Sir Thomas Denton of Hillesden, near Claydon. Ten years later
he was one of the gentlemen who went with the Prince and Buckingham to Spain in the hope of winning the hand of the Infanta.
Some of the Englishmen were shocked at the way in which
Catholicism was practised in Spain, and Sir Edmund had forcibly
to defend Washington, one of the Prince's pages, against a priest
who was trying to convert him as he lay on his death-bed.

In 1624 Verney was elected M.P. for Buckingham, in 1628
for Aylesbury, and for Chipping Wycombe in the Short and Long

Parliaments. In 1626 he was made Knight-Marshal of the King's Palace. Under his jurisdiction came the Marshalsea Court, and the prison where state prisoners not important enough to be lodged in the Tower were sent. He lost financially on the court fees, more on the Earl of Bedford's fen-drainage scheme, and over his patent for inspecting tobacco : money he lent to the King was not repaid. Still he remained an optimistic speculator. When summoned in 1639 to attend the King in the First Scots War, he was racked by sciatica, but more distressed by the folly of his master in trying to force episcopacy on the Scots. But he had the consolation of taking a message to the Scottish camp which, with his tactful handling, led to the Pacification of Berwick. In April 1641 his wife died suddenly, during Strafford's trial, and he could absent himself only to see her buried at Claydon. With the War came another shock when, though his other sons served the King, his eldest son, Ralph, joined the Parliamentarian side and the two were, unwillingly, divided. Sir Edmund received the Standard from the King at Nottingham and swore that whoever would wrest it from his hand 'would first wrest his soul from his body'. At Edgehill he fought amongst the King's Lifeguard of Foot where the battle raged most fiercely, and 'adventured with His Majesty's colours among the enemy so the souldiers might be engaged to follow him.'[1] Surrounded, he refused to surrender the Standard which he said was his and their sovereign's, while his life was his own. He put up a valiant fight, breaking 'the poynt of his standard at push of pike,'[2] and killing sixteen before being killed himself. It is said that his hand, still holding the Standard, had to be hacked off. It was identified only by the ring he was wearing, with a miniature of the King on it, but his body was never found. This ring is still preserved at Claydon. There is a monument to him in Claydon church. He left four sons and six daughters. Lloyd says of him that he was 'of the strictness and piety of a Puritan, of the charity of a Papist, of the civility of an Englishman.'[3]

NOTES

[1] Lloyd, p. 351.
[2] Letter of Sir Edward Sydenham to Ralph Verney quoted in Peter Verney *The Standard Bearer* (1963), p. 202.
[3] Lloyd, p. 352.

GENERAL SIR WILLIAM WALLER
(1598-1668)

THE SON OF Sir Thomas Waller, Lieutenant of Dover Castle, and Margaret Lennard of Knole House, Kent, he matriculated in 1612 from Magdalen Hall, Oxford, and subsequently went abroad, fighting, with Hopton, in the Queen of Bohemia's Lifeguard at Prague. In 1622 he was knighted, and married Jane, daughter of Sir Richard Reynell of Ford House, Wolborough, Devon. She died in 1633, after bearing two children, and five years later he married Lady Anne Finch, daughter of the Earl of Winchilsea. In November 1640 he became M.P. for Andover.

Joining the Parliamentarian side in the War, as an upholder of Parliamentary privilege and the liberties of the subject, Waller's first engagement was the seizure of Portsmouth. His capture in December 1642 of Winchester, Farnham Castle, Arundel Castle, and Chichester earned him the title of 'William the Conqueror'. But on 5 July 1643 he fought the Cornish army, under his old comrade-in-arms Hopton, in the indecisive Battle of Lansdown, and was badly beaten by him a week later (13 July) at Roundway Down, where he lost most of his army. He returned to London where a fresh army was raised for him to command. This caused a rupture with Essex, whose army was still unpaid. In November he laid siege to Basing House, but after two attempts to take it, his Londoners deserted. Next month, however, he defeated Crawford at Alton, and on 29 March 1644 beat Forth and Hopton at Cheriton and in May advanced on Oxford. But the King slipped out to the north on the night of 3 June and, pursued by Waller for twenty-five days, finally beat him soundly at Cropredy Bridge on 29 June. It was now that Waller, 'extremely plagued by the mutinies of the City Brigade,'[1] suggested the formation of a disciplined New Model Army. At Second Newbury he took part with Balfour, Skippon, and Cromwell in an outflanking movement to coincide with Manchester's frontal attack. But the Royalist Army escaped in the night.

The Self-Denying Ordinance of December 1644, and increasing desertions from his unpaid army, made Waller glad to resign his commission in April 1645. He was now a leader of the Presbyterian party in Parliament. When the Army was being disbanded in 1647 he was sent, with other Parliamentary Commissioners, to Saffron Walden to persuade the troops to volunteer for service in Ireland, but with little success. The Army now accused the Commissioners of opposing their just demands, and six of them, including Waller, of conspiring with the Scots to invade England. Parliament, determined to resist by force the Army's threatened march on London, put Waller and Massey on a reconstituted Committee of Safety. But it was too late, and Cromwell entered the City on 6 August. Ten days later Waller and five other Commissioners escaped to Calais, and thence to Holland. He returned to England in 1648, was arrested after Pride's Purge (6 December), and imprisoned without trial in Windsor Castle and then in Denbigh Castle. In 1652 he was released and in April married Anna Harcourt, daughter of Lord Paget and widow of Sir Simon, his second wife having died after bearing five children. He was again arrested in 1658 and examined by Cromwell, but freed although he had received a commission from Charles II. In 1660, with other excluded members, he was admitted to Monck's free Parliament and, as he entered, Prynne's 'long sword ranne between (his) shorte Legges, and threw him down, which caused laughter.'[2]

Waller died 19 September 1668 and was buried in a chapel in Tothill Street, Westminster. As a tactician, he was described by the intrepid Royalist Colonel Walter Slingsby as 'the best shifter and chooser of ground, when he was not Master of the field, that I ever saw.'[3] Others thought him 'colourless and somewhat lacking in resolution.' Perhaps what this 'brave little sparke'[4] lacked most was the money to pay his troops.

NOTES
[1] Waller to the Committee of Both Kingdoms, 2 July 1644: *C.S.P.D.* 1644, p. 301.
[2] John Aubrey, *Brief Lives*, ed. O. L. Dick (1960), p. 251.
[3] Hopton, *Bellum Civile*, p. 91.
[4] *The Knyvett Letters* (1620-44), ed. B. Schofield (1949), p. 146,

William Waller (signature)

ROBERT RICH, 2nd EARL OF WARWICK
(1587-1658)

ROBERT RICH, eldest son of Robert Rich, 1st Earl of Warwick, and Penelope Devereux, came to hate the Court life that his brother, Henry(q.v.), revelled in and went instead to plunder the Spaniards and plant colonies. After matriculating from Emmanuel College, Cambridge, and being created a K.B. (1603), he entered the Inner Temple (1604), was M.P. for Maldon (1610 and 1614), and succeeded to his father's title in 1619. Already a member of the Guinea Company for the plantation of the Somers Isles, or Bermudas, he now took a seat on the council of the New England Company. But he crossed swords with the Virginia Company when one of his ships poached Spanish prizes in their waters, and ensuing quarrels led the King to take over the Company in 1624 and set up a new council with Warwick as a member. Three years later Charles I granted Warwick a liberal privateering commission and he put to sea with eight ships. But he missed the Brazil Fleet and was himself nearly captured. With Saye, Brooke, Hampden, and Holland he now formed the Providence Company based on three islands whose settlers were to prey on Spanish ships in the Caribbean and lead godly lives in their homes. As President of the New England Company he was also much involved in the foundation of New Plymouth, Massachusetts, and Connecticut. Politically he aligned himself with the Puritan opposition to the King, supporting the Petition of Right (1628), refusing to pay forced loans or Ship Money and opposing Laud's ecclesiastical policy while not wishing to abolish the bishops. In 1641 he became a Privy Councillor, and next year Lord Lieutenant of Essex and Norfolk and Admiral of the Fleet, appointed by Northumberland who was sick.

On the outbreak of the Civil War Warwick secured the Fleet for Parliament, and in 1643 he replaced Northumberland as Lord High Admiral. His main task was to intercept supplies from the Continent or Ireland. But he helped in the defence of Hull and in the capture of Portsmouth, failed to relieve Exeter in September 1643 but did relieve Lyme when it was besieged by Prince Maurice in June 1644. The Queen, fleeing from Falmouth to France, eluded him, but he rescued his cousin Essex from Fowey when the latter abandoned his army. In October he issued his *Laws*

PLATE 89   Sir Henry Vane the Younger

PLATE 90   Sir Edmund Verney   *Sir Anthony van Dyck*

PLATE 91   General Sir William Waller   *Robert Walker*

PLATE 92   Robert Rich, 2nd Earl of Warwick, 1642   *Henry Stone*

PLATE 93   John Williams, Archbishop of York

PLATE 94 Colonel Sir Richard Willys, Bart. *William Dobson*

PLATE 96   Edward Somerset, 2nd Marquess of Worcester and titular Earl of
Glamorgan   *Engleheart after Sir Anthony van Dyck*

and Ordinances of the Sea for the better government of the Navy. When, two months later, the Self-Denying Ordinance forced him to retire he offered to serve in any capacity 'the cause of religion and liberty.' In pursuance of this he had already granted a charter to the Baptist Roger Williams, who had settled at a town which he named Providence, to found the Providence Plantation. In January 1647, with the Presbyterian peers Holland, Manchester, and Northumberland, he failed to persuade the King to accept Presbyterianism for three years ; and, with Waller and Massey at Saffron Walden, to persuade the Army to volunteer for service in Ireland. Next year (1648) the Navy revolted, but Warwick raised another Fleet and blockaded Prince Charles at Helvoetsluys. He disapproved of the abolition of the monarchy and the Lords, but supported the Protectorate and, in November 1657, his grandson Robert married Cromwell's youngest daughter, Frances. The young man died the following February and, replying to Cromwell's letter of condolence, Warwick wished the Protector 'long to continue an instrument of use, a pattern of virtue and a precedent of glory.'[1] Both men were to die within the next seven months, Warwick on 19 April and Cromwell on 3 September. Warwick was buried at Felsted, having married three times : Frances, daughter of Sir William Hatton; Susan, daughter of Sir Richard Rowe; and Eleanor, daughter of Sir Edward Wortley. He had four sons and four daughters. This 'jovial hypocrite' as Clarendon called him, could nevertheless climb the top yard as nimbly as any mariner, believed in liberty of conscience and fought for it, loved adventure and the sea, and knew how to lead men.

NOTES

1 William Godwin, *History of the Commonwealth of England*, Vol. IV (1828), p. 530.

COLONEL EDWARD WHALLEY
(d. 1675)

EDWARD WHALLEY, a cousin of Cromwell and a woollen draper, became a distinguished cavalry commander, a regicide, and in old age a legendary figure in New England. He was the second son of Richard Whalley of Kirkton and Screveton, Nottinghamshire, by his second wife, Frances, daughter of Sir Henry Cromwell of Hinchingbrooke. By 1643 he was a major of horse in Cromwell's Regiment, and in the Battle of Gainsborough carried himself 'with all the gallantry becoming of a gentleman and a Christian.'[1] At Marston Moor he was a Lieutenant-Colonel, and after the surrender of York a fortnight later, rode along with some of the Royalist officers 'discoursing of the fight'[2] and trying to persuade them to go home. In the New Model Army he commanded a half of Cromwell's old double regiment which he led at Naseby on the victorious right wing. In September 1645 he took part in the storming of Bristol. Next year he captured Banbury after an 11 weeks' siege, and then went on to besiege Worcester, which fell in July, though not until he, as a Presbyterian, had been superseded by Rainsborough, a Leveller. When the King was removed from Holdenby by Cornet Joyce, Sir Thomas Fairfax sent Whalley with his regiment to guard him, which he continued to do at Hampton Court. Here he fulfilled his duties so courteously, refusing Parliament's order to remove the episcopalian chaplains without further orders from his general, showing the King Cromwell's warning letter of a plot against him, and promising him protection, that when Charles escaped on 11 November he left behind him a letter of thanks for his civil usage. In May 1648, with Fairfax, Whalley defeated the Kentish Royalists in Maidstone after bitter street-fighting, and went on to join the Siege of Colchester. With Ireton and Rainsborough, he was appointed to witness the execution of Lucas and Lisle. He attended all the sittings of the King's 'trial' and signed the death warrant.

In the spring of 1649 the more extreme Levellers in Whalley's Regiment mutinied, but of the six ringleaders sentenced to death only one, Lockyer, was shot. Next year he was with Cromwell in Scotland and distinguished himself at Musselburgh in July and on 3 September at Dunbar where he was wounded, as well as having three horses shot under him. He fought at Worcester, Cromwell's 'crowning mercy', approved of his dismissal of the Rump and becoming Protector in 1653, and sat in his first two Parliaments as member for Nottinghamshire. In 1655 he was made Major-General of the Midlands district where he operated actively against ale-houses, Cavaliers, and scandalous ministers. Although opposed to Cromwell's assuming the royal title, he accepted a seat in the Lords in 1657. On Cromwell's death he supported Richard and would have fought for him had his regiment not refused.

Excepted from the Act of Indemnity at the Restoration, he escaped with his son-in-law, Major-General Goffe, to Cambridge, Massachusetts. Orders for their arrest, with a price on their heads, followed them, but they left Cambridge for New-Haven (new-born Harvard for embryonic Yale!) where, for the most of the next four years, they hid in a cave in the woods. The discovery of this by Indians forced them to move to Hadley where they lived for 11 or more years in the greatest secrecy, helped by trusted friends and receiving occasional letters from their wives in England. When the Indians attacked Hadley in 1675 'a grave elderly person'[3] of strange mien and dress, who suddenly appeared, led the inhabitants to victory and as suddenly disappeared. This was probably Goffe, for Whalley was very infirm and is thought to have died the same year. He had first married Judith Duffell of Rochester, by whom he had a son, John, and a daughter, Frances, who married Goffe. His second wife was Mary Middleton.

NOTES
[1] Carlyle, *Cromwell's Letters and Speeches*, ed. S. C. Lomas (1904), Letter XII, p. 143.
[2] Slingsby, p. 122.
[3] Thomas Hutchinson, *History of the Colony of Massachusetts Bay*, Vol. I (1760), pp. 213-19.

JOHN WILLIAMS, ARCHBISHOP OF YORK
(1582-1650)

THE SECOND SON of Edmund Williams of Conway, he was educated at Ruthin and St John's College, Cambridge, where he graduated B.A. in 1601, being made a Fellow in 1603. He became one of the Royal chaplains, high in favour with James I, and with Buckingham for whom he gained the hand of Lady Catherine Manners by persuading her to renounce her Catholicism. His reward was the Deanery of Westminster. In 1621, on Bacon's fall, he became Lord Keeper and the same year, to compensate him for the loss of future emoluments, was made Bishop of Lincoln. When Prince Charles went with Buckingham to Spain he warned both of them of the dangers of their journey and advised James, in order to secure the Prince's safe return, to sign articles of pardon and dispensation for Roman Catholics, but not to give immediate effect to them. On Charles I's accession he found himself unpopular with the new King, and with Buckingham who wanted money for the Cadiz expedition which Williams, who was against war with Spain, opposed. When therefore his probationary term of office as Lord Keeper expired, it was not renewed. There was a reconciliation with Buckingham but his murder in 1628 ended Williams's hopes of regaining Court favour. This same year he was charged with betraying secrets of the Privy Council, but before his trial, delayed for 9 years, he committed the more serious crime of suborning some of the witnesses.[1] In July 1637 the Star Chamber fined him £10,000 and sent him to the Tower; and the High Commission suspended him from all episcopal functions.

After being released in 1640, Williams's first act, as chairman of a committee to consider religious innovations, was to move the Communion Table in St Margaret's, Westminster, down to the middle of the church. Shortly before Strafford's trial, when Pym was advocating a bill to deprive the Bishops in the Lords of their vote, Williams assured them that in such cases of life and death they need neither speak nor vote. When the Bill of Attainder against Strafford had been passed, unlike other clerics whom the King consulted, Williams advised him to satisfy his public conscience, and save much bloodshed, rather than his private conscience, and save one man. In December 1641, in order to conciliate anti-episcopal opinion, Charles appointed him, as a known moderate, Archbishop of York. But when he and the Bishops were on their way to take their seats on the reassembly of Parliament they were mobbed by crowds shouting 'No Bishops, no Popish Lords!' Williams struck out with his fists, and had to be rescued.

A protest was signed by the eleven Bishops and handed by Williams to the King, asking him to declare Parliamenary business conducted in their absence null and void. Pym retaliated in the Commons by impeaching them all and sending them to the Tower. Next year (1642) Williams was released on bail on condition that he did not go to Yorkshire. But, forfeiting his bail, he joined the King at York and on 27 June was enthroned there. He was all but captured in Cawood Castle by young Hotham (who had sworn to cut off his head), but he escaped to Conway Castle and fortified himself there as Royalist commander in North Wales. However, in 1643 a Royalist colonel, Sir John Owen, seized the castle, and all the property which the Welsh had deposited there. Failing to get it restored, Williams finally came to terms with Mytton, the Parliamenarian commander, by which the latter would help him to recapture the castle and then restore the property to its owners.

This Mytton did, when the King was already a prisoner, so Williams considered himself no traitor. Thereafter he lived in peace till his death of a quinzy at Gloddaeth 25 March 1650. He was buried at Llandegai. Among his bequests were £2000 for building a library at St John's College, Cambridge, and the foundation of two fellowships and four sizarships there.

Eloquent, passionate, and worldly-wise, the words and deeds of this 'super-subtle Welshman' were often open to suspicion. But had he occupied the primacy instead of Laud his liberal views might have bridged the gulf between Anglican and Puritan, and so changed the course of English history.

NOTES
1 C. V. Wedgwood, *The King's Peace* (1955), p. 97.

COLONEL SIR RICHARD WILLYS, BART.
(1614-1690)

THE SON OF Richard Willys of Fen Ditton, near Cambridge, he was educated at St John's School, Hertford, Christ's College, Cambridge, and Gray's Inn. By 1637 he was serving in Holland and distinguished himself at the Siege of Breda. He served in the Scots Wars of 1639-40 and in 1642 was knighted at Shrewsbury. At Edgehill he fought as Major of Lord Grandison's Regiment of Horse, and in 1643 was appointed Sergeant-Major-General of Horse in Lord Capel's army in Shropshire and Cheshire. In January 1644 he was captured at Ellesmere and not exchanged until October. Early in 1645 he was made Governor of Newark and Colonel-General of the forces in Nottinghamshire, Lincolnshire, and Rutland. When King Charles came to Newark in October of this year Willys offended him by meeting him at the gates instead of riding out to meet him, as he did to Rupert arriving soon after to demand a court-martial to justify his surrender of Bristol. After the scene that followed between Rupert and the King, Willys was replaced as Governor by John Belasyse. Angered by this, he challenged Belasyse to a duel, which was prevented. When Rupert and his friends left Newark, and the King's service, Willys rode with them. He was pardoned by the King in April 1646 and created a baronet. Thereafter he went abroad and remained in exile until 1652.

Next year Willys returned to England and became one of the six members of the Sealed Knot. After the Gerard Plot of 1654 he, among others, was arrested on suspicion and, believing that Belasyse was responsible for this, again challenged him. After the ill-fated Royalist Risings of 1655, with other members of the Knot he was once more arrested and imprisoned in King's Lynn and the Knot temporarily broke up. In April 1656 Willys and Edward Villiers, another member, revived it, but in November Willys's movements between Fen Ditton and London aroused justifiable suspicion. Next year he entered into an understanding with Thurloe, Cromwell's Secretary, copying and passing on to him a letter he had received from Hyde instructing him to bestir himself as a Royalist invasion was imminent, for which some East Coast port would be needed. When Ormonde arrived in London in January 1658 to investigate the preparedness of the risings planned to precede this invasion, Willys was pressed by Thurloe to betray him. Carte says he did even better, telling Thurloe of Ormonde's whereabouts, but tipping off Ormonde in time for him to escape.[1] No wonder Ormonde found this hedger the most pessimistic of all the members of the Knot whom he consulted. Next year Willys was publicly accused of treason in an anonymous placard posted at the Exchange, and Morland, Thurloe's assistant, forwarded to Charles II as evidence of this certain letters alleged to have been written by him to Thurloe under the pseudonym of Barrett. It is now believed that Morland forged these letters, but at the time they were considered sufficient proof of Willys's guilt. Many of his friends refused to believe in his treachery, but others saw in it a cause of the Knot's persistent failure to support the various risings, especially in East Anglia which, since the admission to the Knot in 1657 of Lord Maynard of Essex and Sir Simon Fanshawe of Hertfordshire, had five members. Morland's motive may well have been to insure himself against a Restoration, while at the same time spreading doubt and confusion among the Royalists. Willys's are much harder to discern. He may have done it for money (which he needed), or because of depression due to ill-health and recurrent spells of imprisonment, or of hopelessness in the Royal cause and a wish to save his friends as well as himself, even perhaps from mental instability (his son died 'bereft of his wits' in 1701, and with him the baronetcy). The most that can be said for Thurloe's 'masterpiece of corruption',[2] as Willys has been called, is that the government knew most of the information he passed on.

At the Restoration Willys was mercifully ignored, and lived on in obscurity for the next 30 years in the peace of Fen Ditton, overlooking the river that winds through meadows towards the spires of Cambridge. When he died in 1690, enigmatic to the end, he was buried on 9 December, in the church alongside his home.

NOTES

[1] David Underwood, *op. cit.*, p. 217.

[2] *Ibid.*, p. 194.

P.S.W.D.

JOHN PAULET, 5th MARQUESS OF WINCHESTER
(1598-1675)

JOHN PAULET, third, but eldest surviving, son of William the 4th Marquess, and Lucy, daughter of Sir Thomas Cecil (afterwards Lord Burghley and Earl of Exeter), was to earn the name of 'the great loyalist'. Brought up as a Catholic, he kept terms, but never matriculated, at Exeter College, Oxford. In 1620 he was M.P. for St. Ives, Cornwall, and in 1624 took his seat in the Lords as Baron St. John of Basing. Captain of Netley Castle in 1626, he succeeded to the Marquessate in 1629, becoming Keeper of Pamber Forest, and for the next ten years lived in comparative seclusion paying off his father's debts. But in 1639 he wrote to Secretary Windebank offering his services in the King's Scottish expedition. When the Civil War broke out, although he wished to remain neutral, Basing House, which commanded the main road to the West via Salisbury, was fortified and became a resort for the Queen's Catholic friends in the South-West. The words 'Aimez Loyauté' were cut, or fused, in the glass of every pane. From July 1643 with the Marquess's 100 musketeers and horse, the household servants, and Rawdon's Regiment of 240, Basing withstood for the next three months a desultory blockade. Waller's attack on 7 November, though pressed home with vigour, was finally beaten off and his unpaid mutinous troops went home. In the spring of 1644 an attempt by Lord Edward Paulet, Winchester's youngest brother and one of the garrison, to betray Basing, was discovered and he was court-martialled but his life was spared. In July Basing was again besieged and held out till September when Gage, in one of the most remarkable exploits of the War, made a forced night march from Oxford and drove the besiegers off. Leaving 100 Whitecoats behind him, he went on to take Basingstoke and sent back supplies of food, arms, and ammunition. The siege was resumed, but in November the news that the King was advancing from Marlborough and that Gage was again approaching, broke it up. In August 1645 Dalbier renewed the siege with 800 horse and foot and was joined by Cromwell in October, with about 6000 men and a siege train, determined to destroy this 'nest of Romanists'. When his summons was rejected, and the guns had breached the walls, the storming parties went in. Among the 100 slain was a girl trying to protect her clergyman father, and among the 300 prisoners was Inigo Jones. While the troops were pillaging, the house went up in flames. The Marquess, spared by Colonel Hammond, who was then his prisoner, but tackled by Hugh Peters on the hopelessness of the Royal cause, replied 'If the King had no more ground but Basing House I would adventure as I did . . . Basing House is called Loyalty'.[1] Winchester was committed to the Tower, charged with high treason, and his estates were sequestrated. Next year his wife joined him there on an allowance of £15 for herself and her children provided they were brought up as Protestants. In September he was allowed to drink the waters at Epsom for six months, and in October the Lords asked Cromwell to release him on grounds of ill health. But, although it was decided not to proceed against him, he was neither released nor allowed to compound for his estates. Not till the Restoration was the sale of his lands discontinued. He then retired to an estate at Englefield, Berkshire, acquired through his second wife, Lady Honora de Burgh, daughter of the 4th Earl of Clanricarde and 1st Earl of St. Albans (who bore him three daughters), and lived there for the rest of his life in privacy, occupied with agriculture and literary work which included the translation of books from the French. He died there 5 March 1675 and was buried in the church. His first wife was Jane, daughter of the 1st Viscount Savage, and her son succeeded to the title. His third wife, Isabella Howard, daughter of William, 1st Viscount Stafford, who survived him, erected a marble monument to him in Englefield church with an epitaph by Dryden to this 'loyal servant' who

> 'Rests here, rewarded by an heavenly Prince
> For what his earthly could not recompense.
>
> Few subjects could a King like thine deserve,
> And fewer, such a King could so well serve.'

NOTES
[1] S. R. Gardiner, *op. cit.*, Vol. II, p. 347.

EDWARD SOMERSET,
2nd MARQUESS OF WORCESTER, and titular
EARL OF GLAMORGAN
(1601-1667)

EDWARD SOMERSET, inventor of the 'water-commanding machine' for irrigation (one man in one minute raising four buckets of water to a height of four feet) and sundry pumps and hydraulic lifts for Raglan Castle, where he was born, was the eldest son of Henry, 1st Marquess of Worcester and Anne, daughter of John, Lord Russell. He was bred a Roman Catholic. When war broke out in 1642, although he had no military experience, but great wealth and influence, he was appointed Lt-General in South Wales and raised six regiments for the King, to whom in this year alone he advanced more than £100,000. On 24 March 1643 his untrained Welsh levies, the 'mushroom army', was surprised and routed at Highnam by Waller, who took 1600 prisoners.

In the early spring of 1644 the King sent Somerset on a secret mission to Ireland to organize an Irish invasion of England with an army of 10,000, and another invasion from the Spanish Netherlands to be financed by the Pope and Catholic Princes. He had recently married as his second wife Margaret, daughter of Henry O'Brien, 5th Earl of Thomond. There were other inducements in addition to this Irish connexion. He was to become Baron Beaufort of Caldecote and Earl of Glamorgan, Generalissimo of all forces, and Admiral of the Fleet at sea, a K.G., and Duke of Somerset, and his son would marry Princess Elizabeth, the King's second daughter. He sailed for Ireland in March 1645, but was shipwrecked and did not reach Dublin till July where Ormonde, the Protestant Lord Lieutenant, ignorant of his secret commission, received him hospitably. From Dublin he went to meet the priestly

Assembly at Kilkenny, where the secret Glamorgan Treaty was signed which abolished all penal laws against the Catholics and handed back all their churches seized since 1641. These terms were extended by the Papal Nuncio, Rinuccini, who arrived in November, to include a promise that the King would never again appoint a Protestant Lord Lieutenant. Glamorgan then returned to Dublin to obtain Ormonde's agreement. But Ormonde had already learned of the treaty, and arrested him on arrival for having forged his commission. In January 1646 the King felt himself bound to denounce his emissary. But he also wrote to Ormonde asking him to deal leniently with Glamorgan, and also to Glamorgan creating him Duke of Somerset. Glamorgan was released, and returned to Kilkenny to find Rinuccini insisting on even more concessions before producing the army of invasion. The loyalists among the Confederate Irish lords, however, had assembled 3000 troops, ready by February to embark at Wexford for the relief of Chester. Before they could sail Chester had fallen. When Ormonde submitted to the English Parliament in September 1646, Rinuccini planned for Glamorgan to succeed him, and next year made him commander of the the Munster army. But neither move prospered and, in March 1648, Glamorgan left for France where he remained in exile till 1652. Returning to England, he was committed to the Tower, but Cromwell disallowed proceedings against him. He was freed in 1654 and at the Restoration returned to his laboratory, publishing, in 1663, his *Century of Inventions*, dedicated to Charles II, an account of those which he had perfected. He died 3 March 1667 and was buried in Raglan parish church. By his first wife, Elizabeth, daughter of Sir William Dormer, he had one son (later 1st Duke of Beaufort) and two daughters ; by his second, one daughter who died in infancy.

'His chivalrous devotion to Charles's person', wrote S. R. Gardiner, 'was blended in his mind with no less chivalrous devotion to his church.'[1] It was this that led him into the maze of Irish religious politics which bewilders all who enter, and he was fortunate at the end of his life to return to his first, more constant, love of hydrodynamics.

NOTES
[1] S. R. Gardiner, *op. cit.*, Vol. II, (p. 109.